DESIGN LIFE NOW
NATIONAL DESIGN TRIENNIAL 2006

BARBARA BLOEMINK
BROOKE HODGE
ELLEN LUPTON
MATILDA MCQUAID

D0565600

Smithsonian
Cooper-Hewitt, National Design Museum
NEW YORK

CONTENTS

008   FOREWORD
Paul Warwick Thompson, Director
Cooper-Hewitt, National Design Museum

010   INTELLIGENT DESIGN
Barbara Bloemink, Curatorial Director
Cooper-Hewitt, National Design Museum

018   CRAFT AND COMMUNITY IN DESIGN
Brooke Hodge, Curator of Architecture and Design
The Museum of Contemporary Art, Los Angeles

024   DESIGN AND SOCIAL LIFE
Ellen Lupton, Curator of Contemporary Design
Cooper-Hewitt, National Design Museum

034   TRANSFORMING DESIGN
Matilda McQuaid, Deputy Curatorial Director
Cooper-Hewitt, National Design Museum

040   DESIGNER PROFILES

215   INDEX

216   ACKNOWLEDGMENTS

217   BIOGRAPHIES

FOREWORD
PAUL WARWICK THOMPSON

The 2006 *National Design Triennial*—Cooper-Hewitt's third in the series—is its largest to date, spanning three floors of the Museum with aeronautics and military design, architecture, fashion, furniture, graphics, Web, multimedia, landscape architecture, and more. This three-year survey presents a nation at a crossroads—and one where design has increasingly become recognized as a powerful catalyst for change: as the social cement that can rebuild communities in the Mississippi delta, or the spur that brings competitive edge to business.

The two previous *Triennials* presented projects created for American markets by designers residing and working in America. This year, the curators have included work by architects based or working overseas, such as Rem Koolhaas working in Seattle and New York–based architect Toshiko Mori designing in Beijing. To describe design as a global activity has long been recognized as a truism; but the 2006 *Triennial* further attests to the artificiality of defining American design without noting the impact of cross-border commissions on both client and designer.

The Board of Trustees and I wish to thank Cooper-Hewitt's *Triennial* curators, Barbara Bloemink, Ellen Lupton, and Matilda McQuaid, and Brooke Hodge of The Museum of Contemporary Art, Los Angeles, for their skill, flair, and perspicacity in organizing this stunningly varied survey of contemporary American design.

Design Life Now would not have been possible without the generosity of Target as our lead sponsor, and we thank the entire Target team for their embrace and promotion of the exhibition. Cooper-Hewitt Trustee Michael Francis showed terrific enthusiasm for the exhibition at its earliest days of planning, and we are grateful for his confidence and support. We also extend our sincere thanks to Cooper-Hewitt Trustee Agnes Bourne for her continued support of the *Triennial* series since its start in 2000; Agnes was instrumental in the shaping of the series and continues to advocate its importance from west to east coasts. Maharam is a longtime supporter of Cooper-Hewitt exhibitions, and we thank Michael Maharam and everyone at the firm for their wonderful support of the *Triennial*. This unique publication is made possible in part by the Andrew W. Mellon Foundation.

I extend my sincere appreciation to Jeremy Strick, Director, and Paul Schimmel, Chief Curator, at The Museum of Contemporary Art, Los Angeles, who very graciously permitted Brooke Hodge to serve as a curator of our *Triennial*. And special thanks to COMA, a graphic-design firm based in Brooklyn, New York, and Amsterdam, the Netherlands, whose work was selected for display within the *Triennial* and who were also commissioned by Cooper-Hewitt to design this book and accompanying font. My thanks also to Tsang Seymour Design for their work on the exhibition graphics and related materials, and to Matter Practice, who designed the exhibition installation both in 2003 and again in 2006.

Finally, thanks to the following at Cooper-Hewitt: Susan Brown; Alicia Arroyo; and Elizabeth Chase and Wava Carpenter, formerly of the Museum, who provided much-needed support to the curators; Chul R. Kim, Head of Publications, who with this book has launched Cooper-Hewitt's first self-publishing venture in nearly three decades; Jill Bloomer, Head of Image Rights and Reproduction, and Annie Chambers, who edited the more than 400 images contained in the book; Jocelyn Groom, Head of Exhibitions, who supervised the exhibition and the installation work of Mick O'Shea, Mathew Weaver, and crew; Registrar Steven Langehough and his team; Caroline Payson, Director of Education, and her staff for producing a terrific series of programs to complement the exhibition; Jennifer Northrop, Director of Communications and Marketing, and her staff, who produced the exhibition's graphic, Web, and press materials; and Caroline Baumann, Deputy Director, and her entire Development team, who ensured the exhibition was properly supported.

INTELLIGENT DESIGN

BARBARA J. BLOEMINK

"A designer is an emerging synthesis of artist, inventor, mechanic, objective economist, and *evolutionary strategist*."[1]
—R. Buckminster Fuller

What is the essence of "life?" And is this a relevant question for an essay on design? As many of the designers in *Design Life Now* demonstrate, the natural world—its appearance, materials, processes, and laws—has returned as a dominant subject in contemporary design. In the three years since the last *National Design Triennial* in 2003, traditional oppositions—real versus virtual, natural versus artificial, human versus computer—have increasingly fallen away in significance. Many designers in a wide range of disciplines are exploring how biological inspiration and the laws of physics can be used to design and explore the nature of life. For example, in forums such as the 2004 annual meeting of the Industrial Design Society of America, the discussion was expanded from designing "things that people can use" to "using living things to design."[2] Similarly, at a 2004 conference exploring the boundaries between art and design, the artist John Chamberlain was asked, "Who are the best designers today?" His answer, "genetic engineers,"[3] led the four other panelists to nod their heads in agreement.

In one of graphic designer Rick Valicenti's (1) recent projects, which he titled *Intelligent Design*, he used aluminum cans of Coke Zero and Pepsi One to ironically represent a digital translation of the Bible's Book of Genesis, with each can representing the digits "zero" or "one." The highly controversial term "intelligent design" (which is redundant, as all design necessarily implies intelligence), whether it posits divine intervention or nature as the initiating "designer," refers to the manner by which life is thought to have begun. Until recently, we lacked the capabilities, information, tools, and materials for designers to consider what constitutes "life." However, we are on the brink of an engineering revolution, known as "synthetic biology," that will transform our ability to not only emulate, but also manipulate and redesign aspects of the biological world. Scientists are unlocking the secrets of deoxyribonucleic acid (DNA), and beginning to control and program living cells. Full-scale cloning of small animals using DNA to recreate new DNA has become a familiar occurrence, despite the moral questions it raises. Meanwhile, many designers' works reference nature, emulating the look of living organisms and displaying functional traits often used to define "life," including mutation and evolution; the ability to autonomously respond and adapt to one's environment; autopoesis,[4] or generational self-reproduction; motion; and intelligence in some form.[5]

Since the earliest efforts of human creativity, objects have copied

1 Rick Valicenti/Thirst. *Intelligent Design: Creating an Evolved Red vs. Blue State of Mind*, 2005. **CONCEPTUAL DESIGNER** Rick Valicenti. **GRAPHIC DESIGNERS** Rick Valicenti and John Pobojewski. **PHOTOGRAPHY AND DIGITAL IMAGING** Gina Vieceli Garza. **JAVA SCRIPT FOR PAGE COMPOSITION** Robb Irrgang. Fox Starwhite Flash, 100#T. **PUBLISHER** Rick Valicenti, Thirst
2 Clear Blue Hawaii. *Napali* kayak, 2003. **DESIGNER** Murray Broom. Military grade urethane/PVC and carbon Kevlar®. **PHOTO** Clear Blue Hawaii
3 Nike, Inc. Nike FREE 5.0, 2004. **DESIGNER** Tobie Hatfield. Nylon, synthetic microfiber, rubber. **PHOTO** Nike, Inc.
4 Joseph Ayers. First-generation Biomimetic Underwater Ambulatory Robot (Robolobster), 2005. **SPONSOR** Office of Naval Research. **PHOTO** John F. Williams

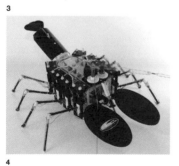

1

2

3

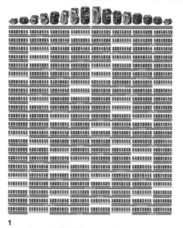

4

and imitated the appearance of living things. This continues today in the work of designers such as Hitoshi Ujiie, who utilizes digital printing to reproduce ephemeral images of leaves and cross-sections of vegetables on his translucent textiles; Jason Miller, whose table legs sprout realistic "mushrooms" along their lengths; and David Wiseman, whose delicate leaf, flower, and vine trellises wind across interior ceilings and down adjacent walls. The works of all three designers bring natural forms into the domestic environment, soften the interiors' angularity, and visually break down the division between interior architecture and the natural world outside. In a similar spirit, Clear Blue Hawaii's (2) kayak, with its transparent, pliant body, creates for users closer visual and physical proximity to the life teeming below the water's surface.

The discipline of landscape design has achieved maturity, and designers such as Field Operations are integrating architecture, ecology, and infrastructure in postindustrial landscapes: reclaiming landfills, preserving natural reserves, and softening urban grids with tracts of green. Others including Ken Smith and Andy Cao use recycled glass pebbles, hand-sewn materials, and artificial flowers in place of natural vegetation. These new landscapes replicate nature, but without the complexities of continual maintenance and sustenance natural landscapes require.

For billions of years, nature has evolved strategies for solving myriad problems and challenges. The earliest humans learned to survive by observing and imitating the actions of their fellow creatures. Over the last few centuries, however, we have largely abandoned nature as a guide, preferring technology that has enabled us to ignore the natural world. During the past three years, violent earthquakes, tsunamis, and hurricanes have proved that nature cannot be discounted, and remains an indomitable force in our lives. Moreover, technology is not proving to be the promised panacea. In this post-digital era, we are often turning back to the natural world for possible solutions.

Biomimicry, a term often used in conjunction with design, represents a form of reverse engineering, with designers studying and copying the appearances and forms of natural organisms in order to reproduce various processes and functions.[6] The Nike Free Shoe (3), for example, resulted when a group of Nike designers spent time exploring the physiognomy of the human foot and sketching and studying the natural movements of animals. Joseph Ayers's Robolobster (4) is a robotic crustacean whose form consciously mirrors that of its living counterpart. The lobster's biological structure enables it to "hang" in place despite strong water currents, and its sensitive antennae allow it to "smell"

INTELLIGENT DESIGN

changes in the water. Ayers is adapting his aquatic robot to recognize changes in seawater caused by bacteria and alien substances and to locate underwater mines.

Looking to nature for solutions to specific problems does not work unless there is sufficient technological and engineering knowledge to support it. Early attempts at flight by constructing wings that "flapped" like birds were unsuccessful, as were endeavors to attach undulating "tails" to the end of submarines. Although the submersibles *Deep Flight* and *Wet Flight* resemble large sea mammals, Graham Hawkes (5) maintains that his designs did not originate through biomimicry, but instead represented a successful convergence of technology, math, biology, engineering, and physics. These principles combine to enable his submersibles to "fly" through the water like great sea creatures, emulating the graceful gliding motion of rays; and allow humans to reach great depths. In this case, nature and technology have both created highly similar forms for highly similar functions.

Autonomous motion is one of the key criteria we use to identify something as being "alive." Dr. Robert Full, professor and Head of the Polypedal Lab at the University of California, Berkeley, has conducted numerous experiments on motion across a full continuum of creatures, from the smallest invertebrate to full-sized, complex vertebrates. As part of his research, he identified a specific forward-to-sideways ratio of movement shared by all living organisms. A few years ago, Full was consulted to assist in determining the authenticity of characters' movements in Pixar Films' animated film *A Bug's Life*. By studying the movements of cockroaches, Full discovered that when roaches scurry extremely rapidly, they become bipedal—rising to an erect position and running on two legs. This information contributed to the realistic movement of the animated insects in the final film.

The quest for authenticity is a central tenet of design at Pixar. Teams of designers, artists, animators, and computer scientists initially begin with an idea of what they want to portray, and then conduct extensive research on how to achieve it. According to director Brad Bird, their success has less to do with simulating physical reality than with capturing and reflecting how our minds "perceive" reality.[7] The latter usually manifests itself through the portrayal of motion. When Pixar artists and designers animate images so that they perfectly reproduce reality, they often find that the results appear lifeless. For the animated film *Finding Nemo*, for instance, they faithfully reproduced the appearance of water; however, it didn't visually "read" as real until they began working to design how water "feels." The feature film *Ratatouille*, forthcoming in 2007, tells the story of a talented rat who lives in an elegant Parisian

5 Graham Hawkes. *Deep Flight I* winged submersible, 1997. **MANUFACTURER** Hawkes Ocean Technologies. **FOUNDING SPONSOR** Autodesk, Inc. **PRODUCT SPONSORS** Ansys, Inc., Electronics Workbench, Hewlett Packard. **PHOTO** Hawkes Ocean Technologies
6 Pixar Films. Gusteau's Kitchen lighting study, from *Ratatouille*, 2006. Digital painting over computer model. **ARTIST** Dominique Louis

5

6

restaurant run by an eccentric chef. In order to capture the movements of the animal, including the intricate motion of its fur, within the film's settings, the designers studied live rats in their studio. They also worked in a chef's kitchen (6) and toured the Paris sewer system to ensure the authenticity of the final animated scenes.

Natural organisms continually evolve and adapt according to their environment, rejecting what does not work. While it does not claim to resemble "life," the phenomenon of Apple's iPod portable digital music player displays a kinship with nature's characteristics of rapid mutation and change. The iPod has proved to be sustainable and self-organizing along adaptive, rather than mechanical, models. For example, it only "functions" when customized by individual users; it can continually "grow" as users upload music to it; and its designs are evolutionary—from the basic iPod to the Mini, Shuffle, Nano, and Video iPod, which have all appeared on the market within the last five years. Since its introduction to the marketplace, the iPod's form and functionality have evolved so quickly that it has been the subject of a *Saturday Night Live* comedic skit in which Apple CEO Steve Jobs introduces a new iPod model every second. The "iPodding" movement has led numerous outside designers including Scott Wilson to create imaginative products to enhance the iPod experience, ranging from podcasting to accessories which transform the iPod into a complete music system.

DNA is the basis of everything that constitutes life. Although we have not yet learned how to create DNA, we have learned how to program software to mirror its generative and self-reproducing capabilities. Life reproduces itself through the splitting and rejoining of DNA's four proteins and the newly aligned forms retain various proportional characteristics of their originating molecules. The slight mutations that occur during this process enable life to change and evolve. Similarly, in creating his flatware, Greg Lynn programs basic traits, characteristics, and structures into a "beta" software program,[8] which then accelerates the process of mutation, creating virtually endless and unique variations that remain visibly part of the same family. Computers are rigid by nature, and are not traditionally considered "creative" from a design perspective. Joshua Davis, however, designs "generative machines" by writing custom algorithms (in open-source software such as Java) which randomly select elements from Davis's image bank of natural and artificial forms, and morph and mix them into countless, unique, single-image variations of colors, shapes, and forms.

A number of years ago, the futurist Alvin Toffler predicted that "we are about to become *the designers of evolution*."[9] Will Wright's new interactive game *Spore*, in development and due to be released in the next year, represents a paradigm shift in gaming technology. The user begins the game with the most elementary single-cell organism. *Spore* then gives the user the "divine" capacity to create and manipulate the manner in which this life form mutates and evolves into a more complex being. Users add physical attributes that can be rapidly assimilated and that the organism autonomously "learns" to use. For example, if the user gives his or her creature three legs, it quickly discovers how to use these limbs to move, explore, and adapt to its environment. The user may continually add features and functions, including increasing intelligence, to the creatures, adjusting their physiognomy and capabilities through multiple generations and mutations. Each life form faces increasingly complex challenges—building shelter, foraging for food—which further its evolution; and eventually, it mates, reproduces, forms families, tribes, cities, civilizations—all designed and tracked by the user. Once they have the ability and means to explore outer space, the creatures begin colonizing other planets and galaxies, where they encounter and interact with living beings designed by other players.

Although humans are not yet capable of creating a life form from scratch, we are now able to create and design life from life by cloning animals. The questions cloning engenders may well be among the most important moral issues of our time. Meanwhile, a number of designers are currently experimenting with giving human attributes to robots. A 2004 report by the United Nations predicted that the robot market would expand sevenfold by 2007. Among the most significant recent shifts have been the migration of robotics from the military, industrial, and scientific sectors to the home, and the increased availability of affordable robots— from toys and companions to domestic assistants. These are not the stiff, menacing alien robots of science-fiction films such as *Forbidden Planet* and *The Day the Earth Stood Still*. Instead, they are benign and display ambient intelligence (the seamless integration of computer technology and interfaces that take on specific human characteristics), allowing them to respond intelligently and move autonomously. Some designers are working closely with technicians to endow these robots with a "personality," which can result in the formation of an emotional bond between robot and user.

There is nothing anthropomorphic in the Frisbee-like shapes of iRobot's Roomba and Scooba (7). Their actions, however, closely resemble those of an animal foraging for food. Using search algorithms, the Roomba seeks out dirt on floors. When its path takes it close to an area of potential "danger," such as the edge of a stair or a wall, it changes direction, remembering where it has already been. Similarly, Scooba goes out in search of stains and grime, cleaning and drying a dirty spot

7 iRobot. Roomba® Scheduler Vacuuming Robot, 2002. PHOTO iRobot Corp.
8 Wowwee Ltd. Roboreptile entertainment robot, 2005. Plastic. PHOTO © 2005
  Wowwee Ltd.
9 Mars Exploration Rovers 1 and 2 with predecessor *Sojourner* Rover, 2003.
  PHOTO: NASA's Jet Propulsion Laboratory

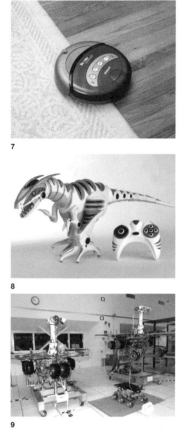

7

8

9

before moving on to the next one. Just as an ant "remembers" to always return to its nest, the Roomba and Scooba return "home" to their power source when their work is completed or their power is running low. Enough owners have attributed moods and personalities to their flat domestic companions that the company has developed its advertising campaign around the phrase "I ♥ robots."[10]

Wowwee's Robosapien is a robotic toy that looks like an advanced version of a traditional robot, with arms and legs, fully articulated joints, and a movable head. Designed by Mark Tilden, Robosapien's artificial intelligence software, paired with its mechanics, allows it to perform over one hundred preprogrammed functions, including picking up objects, dancing, moving forward and backward, seeing and maneuvering around obstacles, and hearing and answering questions. The companions Roboraptor (8) and Robopet also perform numerous functions and can be programmed to display various moods through their interactions. By making their toys both affordable and open-source, Wowwee encourages hackers to customize and personalize their programming to suit their own needs—much as Natalie Jeremijenko adapts and customizes her robotic feral dogs to ferret out pollution in the environment.

The most advanced robots in terms of adaptation to environment and outside stimuli are NASA's Jet Propulsion Lab's Mars rovers, *Spirit* and *Opportunity* (9). Beyond displaying unusual durability—they were expected to last three months and are still functioning years later—both operate almost autonomously and display advanced intelligence and decision-making abilities. When instructed to go to a certain area and retrieve soil samples or temperature readings, for example, the rovers independently decide which are the best routes to take to the site. They see and avoid obstacles, self-correct, and, like insects, their six legs operate independently to step over rocks and rough terrain. Scientists even use anthropomorphic language when describing the rovers: a recent article referred to them as "baby boomers, as they are in their 50s and 60s in human years, who are experiencing some of the maladies associated with human aging. . . . [The rovers] 'keep on keeping on' despite having to drag squeaky wheels, losing full range of motion in stiff arms, and needing to reboot the old computer brains every now and then to cure memory problems."[11]

Robots are progressively taking on many traits and functions previously thought to be exclusively "human." Although we do not as yet know whether they will ever be capable of imaginative thinking or self-consciousness, they have already surpassed us in intelligence, as defined by storing and quickly accessing enormous amounts of infor-

INTELLIGENT DESIGN

mation. As the design and capabilities of robotics and artificial intelligence continue to evolve, so does the question of how *human* we want our robots to be, in both appearance and personality.

Although clearly an animated avatar projected on a translucent screen, The Institute for Creative Technology's Sergeant Blackwell is nonetheless disconcerting in his ability to visually track movement and answer visitors' random questions. Blackwell's artificial intelligence allows him to recognize words in sentences and match these with appropriate responses. Even when faced with an open-ended, repeated question, such as "What time is it?" Blackwell provides logical answers from "What do you think I am, a clock?" to "You are asking me the wrong question; you should be asking me . . ." Through the technology developed by ICT, the latest avatars can also be programmed to respond aggressively, enthusiastically, or skeptically, displaying different emotional states.

David Hanson's research indicates that the time when convincingly sociable robots demonstrate aspects of both human intelligence and demeanor is not far away. Combining innovations in art, science, and technology, Hanson's robots mimic human behavior, expressions, and appearance to an unprecedented degree. His work contradicts what some roboticists term the "uncanny valley," after the 1970s experiments by Dr. Masahiro Mori, who stated that the more robots are given the realistic appearance of humans, the more they repulse us. Mori and others have long maintained that humans prefer that our avatars maintain a mechanical, nonhuman appearance.[12] Countering this belief, Hanson has designed highly realistic, responsive, skin-like Frubber™ to cover the technology operating his robots. By virtue of the Frubber, Hanson's robots, such as Albert Einstein (10), are able to achieve extremely subtle, authentically human facial expressions and gestures. The illusion of living animation is quickly mitigated as the back of the figure's head is cut away, revealing its technical infrastructure and its attachment to a mechanical "body." Meanwhile, Einstein's AI "brain" has been programmed to recognize tens of thousands of words and answer visitors' unscripted questions and forms credible replies.

The choice of Philip K. Dick[13] as the subject of Hanson's first life-size, Frubber-covered robotic head was a compelling one. In his essays, short stories, and novels, Dick explored the nature of life, and through his characters, whether human or replicants, repeatedly questioned reality, what it means to be human in a digital world, and the value of real versus artificial life. One of his best-known works was the 1968 novel *Do Androids Dream of Electric Sheep?*, adapted into the 1982 cult film *Blade Runner.* The novel, like many of Dick's works, deals with the progressive blending of the human and the artificial.

10

The book is set in a post-apocalyptic world, where most animals have died, and entire species have become extinct. Live animals are precious status symbols, humans are less valued than animals, and replicant androids—visually indistinguishable from humans—are deemed to be valueless. Eight rogue androids have killed their human masters on Mars and illegally returned to Earth. Bounty hunter Rick Deckard, charged with hunting down and killing the androids, grows increasingly uneasy with the blurred lines between the sentient androids and humans. As the plot progresses, the humans act inhumanely, while the replicants display many human characteristics. Eventually, Deckard questions his own humanity, as the androids question their artificiality: Who are the real humans, and why?

The continuing trend in various areas of design is to emulate, reproduce, and replicate nature and its functions. The day when many topics of science fiction are no longer fiction, but real areas of science and design, may not be so far away.

1 Italics are the author's, not Fuller's.

2 Quotations attributed to Professor Lee Silver, professor of molecular biology and public affairs at Princeton; McKee, Bradford, "In this Ring, a Designer Slugfest," in the *New York Times*, online at www.nytimes.com/2004/11/04/garden/04club.html?ei=5070&EN+7a.

3 In a symposium on art and design in conjunction with the exhibition *Design ≠ Art*, organized by Cooper-Hewitt, National Design Museum in 2004.

4 Term coined by Dr. Humberto R. Maturana and Dr. Francisco J. Varela, *The Tree of Knowledge* (Boston & London: Shambhala, 1992), pp. 47–49.

5 These are not the only attributes used to differentiate living from nonliving things; others include containing DNA, the need to consume energy, and having a life span from creation to death.

6 In 1997, Janine Benyus coined the term "biomimicry" to define how scientists are "learning from and then emulating life's genius." See Janine Benyus, *Biomimicry: Innovation Inspired by Nature* (1997).

7 Brad Bird is the director of *Ratatouille*, scheduled to open in June 2007, and was the director, writer, and voice of the character Edna in the 2005 animated film *The Incredibles*.

8 An early stage of the software, while it is still available for testing and customization.

9 Alvin Toffler, *The Third Wave*, Bantam, 1980. Italics are the author's, not Fuller's.

10 Marriott, Michel, "The Shape of Robots to Come," in the *New York Times*, March 16, 2006, p. C7.

11 "Baby Boomers on Mars," Engineering Team Chief Jake Matijevic, http://marsrover.nasa.gov/spotlight/20060320.html, March 20, 2006.

12 Masahiro Mori, "Bukimi No Tani" (English title: *The Uncanny Valley*), in *Energy*, 1970.

13 In early 2003, Hanson's Philip K. Dick head was mistakenly left in the overhead compartment of an airplane and never found. While unfortunate, this ending would no doubt have pleased the science-fiction writer.

CRAFT AND COMMUNITY IN DESIGN

BROOKE HODGE

Craft has always been an important part of any design enterprise. Whether the end product of that enterprise is a high-tech, manufactured object such as an iPod (1) or a scarf created through the relatively low-tech act of knitting together yarn with a pair of needles, craft enters and shapes design at many levels and at different stages in the process of making. In recent years, perhaps as an antidote to the proliferation of high-tech, high-design objects on the market, handcraft has experienced a remarkable resurgence in popularity. One does not take the place of the other, but each offers satisfaction and beauty in its own way. The owner of an iPod experiences pleasure listening to songs on a playlist that has been thoughtfully and painstakingly gathered from a panoply of sources, just as the recipient of a scarf lovingly knitted by a friend who has gone to the trouble to choose the perfect yarn in the perfect colors treasures it and appreciates the effort that has gone into it. Craft is no longer the poor stepsister of design. The two coexist peacefully and are ineffably intertwined in contemporary culture. The knitter may listen to an iPod while knitting. A runner may carry his iPod in a hand-knitted pouch. Rather than sitting at opposite ends of a spectrum, as they did at the beginning of the twentieth century, when machine-made products were considered far superior and more sophisticated than handmade goods, in the twenty-first century, both craft and design are thriving and inspiring each other.

For this *Triennial*, the curatorial team selected products, objects, installations, landscapes, buildings, and books (to name just a few of the many types of works we considered), all of which provide through design important observations about the way we live now. Today's consumer or artist or fashion designer is equally at home with the handmade and the high-tech, with the unique and the mass-produced. We were struck by the prevalence and presence of craft, both sophisticated and homespun, across the diverse range of work we surveyed.

Knitwear designer Tom Scott uses his knowledge of the history and techniques of knitting to shape intricate patterns and complex geometries for the scarves and sweaters he designs. While Scott uses a knitting machine to produce the pieces, the touch of his hand is still very much in evidence, since he first sketches his patterns and then programs the machine, still a relatively low-tech piece of equipment. The clothes Ralph Rucci designs could not be classified as "couture" without the painstaking handwork that goes into their construction and embellishment. Haute-couture garments earn that appellation because each garment is custom-made and often features hand-stitched hems and seams and the finest embroidery and beading in the fashion industry. The construction of many of Rucci's gowns and dresses is so involved that sometimes

1 Apple Computer, Inc. iPod advertising campaign, 2005. DESIGNER Apple and
TBWA\Chiat\Day. Courtesy of Apple Computer, Inc.
2 Thom Browne. Grey/green beaded lace suit with grosgrain tipping, fall/winter
2006. PHOTO Matt Flynn
3 Judy Geib. The Thing, 2003–04. Boulder opal, 18- and 24-karat gold, fine silver,
enamel. PHOTO Dirk Vandenberk

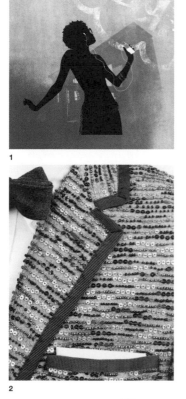

1

2

3

close to one hundred individual pattern pieces are needed to construct
a single garment. Thom Browne is another contemporary designer
who incorporates detailed handwork into his garments. Browne originally started his menswear business by designing custom-tailored, or
bespoke, suits. Although he now focuses primarily on ready-to-wear
pieces, his attention to craft and to individual touches has not wavered.
Luxurious fabrics and unexpected details such as grosgrain ribbon
trim on a lapel (2) or working buttonholes on the sleeve of a jacket set
his work apart from the mainstream. In fashion design, craft can be
combined with mass-production techniques to make garments more
special. Because of the time and expense involved in adding hand-exe-
cuted touches to a garment, very few designers are able to incorporate
them into their work. Browne and Rucci have distinguished themselves
in the field by creating highly refined, exquisitely crafted clothes that
reveal the signature hand of the designer.

Jewelry designer Judy Geib works alone at a worktable strewn with
gems, wires, and sheets of precious metals. Like an artisan in an atelier
from earlier times, she studies her array of raw material and lets the
shapes, colors, and textures suggest compositions and combinations.
Geib makes each piece by hand, and as a result, each one is unique (3).
She is not drawn to highly polished and perfect stones or settings; rather,
she revels in the slight imperfections and rough quality of some of the
stones and metals she uses, creating opulent pieces which, because of
their obvious handcrafted nature, possess a rustic charm. The Ladd
Brothers also work in an independent, highly individual manner. Like
Geib, they design and fabricate everything themselves, from the pieces
of jewelry and dioramas created with small beads to the quirky pre-
sentation boxes and handmade books they use to promote and display
their work.

Design has many faces. When we think of "design objects," many
of us think of things that are sleek, smooth, sensual, and perfect. Yet
design can also be rustic and rough around the edges and still be pleas-
ing to the eye and to the touch. The desire to create or to own something unique and personal is influenced by the urge to balance the cool
sameness of many contemporary machine-made, mass-produced
goods. Like many designers who work alone in a craft-based practice,
David Wiseman's work is not driven by the demands of the market or
the vicissitudes of popular taste. Wiseman also works independently,
and his design practice encompasses unique objects and commissioned
sculptural pieces or installations. Craft enters his practice in the nature
of his work and in his role as contemporary artisan—he is at once
designer, fabricator, and executor. Wiseman's process is organic: much

CRAFT AND COMMUNITY IN DESIGN

of it occurs in his head. He says that sketching slows him down. In his garage studio, he casts plaster branches and fires porcelain blossoms. Then he spends hours, even months, on a ladder, like a Renaissance sculptor or a turn-of-the-century plasterer, applying and reapplying the intricate network of branches to the ceiling of a dining room (4), and, for the *Triennial*, to the entry foyer of a gallery at Cooper-Hewitt. Soon these surfaces are abloom with branches and blossoms and sometimes even small birds, the ceiling transformed into a rich, rococo canopy. Because all of his work is handcrafted, Wiseman's output is small and his progress is steady. Sometimes his hand cannot keep up with his vision for a project, and he seeks out manufacturing processes like laser-cutting to assist him. Like Wiseman, many of the designers featured in this year's *Triennial* possess a work ethic and a personal style that almost dictate that they work independently to preserve the singularity of their creations. Their love of craft is most at home and most productive in the atelier-like environments they have created for themselves.

As Ellen Lupton points out in her essay, design is a social activity. Like other social activities, both design and craft generate communities and networks. Our curatorial team noted a resurgence in the idea of community as a critical element of contemporary design practice. They can be formed by networks of users—witness the iPod generation—or by groups of doers, from knitters and sewers to architects and designers. The collective approach seems to have taken on greater strength and appeal, perhaps because we feel increasingly isolated in today's globalized, fragmented society. It may be supremely efficient and easy to communicate by telephone, Blackberry, or instant messaging. We can do this anywhere—on the go from an airport, a train, a car, or without ever leaving home. We can conduct business almost anywhere, too, thanks to the preponderance of wireless networks. Even Starbucks, a company that built its business on the to-go cup of coffee, has now become a place to linger, a sort of gathering spot. Freelancers gather in the neighborhood café to work on their laptop computers while enjoying a latte. They soon become regulars and trade texts and writing tips. The isolation of working independently is replaced by temporarily joining a loose assembly of individuals engaged in similar endeavors. The very technologies and devices that can create a feeling of isolation by making it possible to communicate without the necessity of live social interaction can also make new types of collaboration or community possible. Designers can share files, thoughts, and expertise online across thousands of miles, tapping into design potential that might have been out
of their reach without advanced communications technology. It is not uncommon these days to have a rich working relationship with someone

4 David Wiseman. Cherry Blossom Canopy installation, 2005. **COMMISSIONED BY** Rodman Primack, interior designer, for clients Anne Crawford and Dudley De Zonia. Porcelain, plaster, fiberglass, steel. **PHOTO** David Wiseman
5 Lazor Office. FlatPak House, view of main façade, Minneapolis, MN, 2004. **DESIGNER** Charlie Lazor. **PHOTO** Joel Koyama
6 Konyk. up! house 1500 prototype, main view, 2003–05. **ARCHITECT** Craig Konyk. **RENDERING** David Fano

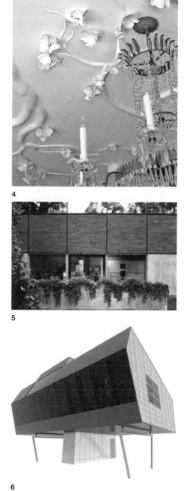

4

5

6

without ever seeing him or her in person. While these advances signify great potential for design practice, a craving for old-fashioned social interaction of the face-to-face kind is responsible for the renewed interest in the simple pleasures of working with one's hands at sewing bees, crafting sessions, and knitting circles as well as for the growth of other types of community made possible by design and craft.

Community, like craft, comes in many shapes and sizes and pops up in unlikely places. It can be short-lived, coalescing to serve a specific purpose, or enduring. The prefab-housing movement has established a vast network, with roots in towns and cities across the country and around the world. The tremendous surge of interest in prefabricated homes in recent years is nothing short of phenomenal, as real-estate prices become so steep that they are out of reach of the majority of first-time home buyers. Its success is due to the growth of the Internet and the accompanying accessibility to an almost unlimited array of prefab solutions.

I recently attended a conference, sponsored by *Dwell* magazine, dedicated to prefabricated housing. I was astonished by the overwhelming response: developers, architects, clients, and contractors came from all over to listen to lectures and presentations about specific models and new developments; other professionals, like writers and curators, with an interest in prefab were also present, a newly spawned community united by its belief in the future of this type of housing. Prefab housing appeals to first-time homeowners and empty-nesters alike because it is affordable and adaptable to almost any site, whether urban, surburban, or rural. Many architects have recognized and tapped into the potential of prefab for the same reasons. Charlie Lazor, of Lazor Office, initially developed the FlatPak House (5) as a housing solution for his own family. He has since transformed FlatPak from a unique design into a full-fledged business, offering it as a system that can be customized by individual buyers. Craig Konyk has likewise translated his up! house concept (6) into a product that can be marketed to a vast community of potential clients. Eventually, dwellers in an up! house or a FlatPak will form a community because they have been attracted to the same design and can share their tales—both the triumphs and the trials—of living in a prefab house. The prefab movement promises to grow in leaps and bounds as more of these homes are built and occupied.

Magazines like *Readymade* and *Make* engender communities—at both ends of the craft/tech spectrum—of Do-It-Yourselfers with more time than money on their hands. Martha Stewart, perhaps the preeminent proselytizer of the DIY ethic, has embraced both high design and craft, and is largely responsible for encouraging people to do it themselves as long as they do it well. *Readymade* (7) is quirkier and more eccentric than *Martha Stewart Living*, and the DIY projects in its pages are less about beauty and polished refinement than they are about ingenuity and economy. Howtoons, the online do-it-yourself site for children, provides an arsenal of activities perfect for a snow day or a Saturday afternoon.

The design process can also be the catalyst for doers and thinkers to come together, just as a finished product, park, or building provides a gathering place for a group of users. For each of its landscape architecture projects, Field Operations creates a networked assembly of creative collaborators. Architects and landscape architects have always benefited from those that come together to get a job done—contractors, plant specialists, engineers, painters, and others. Recently, however, these designers have formed communities at the design stage, each member bringing to the table his or her particular vision or expertise, and all of them working together to shape the design of a building or a park. For Teardrop Park, Michael Van Valkenburgh formed one made up of artists Ann Hamilton and Michael Mercil, civic officials from the Battery Park City Authority, and his studio associates.

The Seattle Central Library would not be the innovative and beautiful building it is without the convergence of graphic designers, artists, furniture and textile designers, and, of course, the architects at OMA's offices in Rotterdam and New York and at LMN on the ground in Seattle. The city librarian, Deborah Jacobs, was a key member of this collaboration, and her vision for the library and the role it could play in greater Seattle had a major impact on design decisions. The building has been a critical social hub since its doors first opened to the public (8). That designers of large-scale, highly complex projects have come to welcome, and even promote, the formation of ensembles from the beginning of a project marks a radical shift in the way design is practiced in the realm of architecture. There has always been a team of people standing behind the designer, but in the past, it was the designer alone who received the recognition. Today, more and more creative practitioners are emphasizing the role of the team in the design process.

Many of today's designers occupy critical roles in different organizations or endeavors simultaneously. Scott Wilson must be a master juggler, or at the least an amazing multitasker, since he participates in many creative efforts at once. As former global creative director for Nike Explore, he was a member of a large corporate design family. As the principal of his own practice, Mod, he creates a virtual community of designers linked by their contributions to a particular project, and with his recently

7 *ReadyMade* magazine. *ReadyMade: How to Make {Almost} Anything* book cover, 2005. **DESIGNERS** Eric Heiman, Akiko Ito, Elizabeth Fitzgibbons. **ILLUSTRATOR** Kate Francis. **AUTHORS** Shoshana Berger and Grace Hawthorne. **PUBLISHER** Clarkson Potter/Random House. **PHOTO** Jeffery Cross
8 Office for Metropolitan Architecture (OMA). Seattle Library Mixing Chamber, Seattle Central Library, Seattle, WA, 2004. **PHOTO** Philippe Ruault
9 Scott Wilson. iBelieve replacement cap and lanyard for iPod, 2005. **MANUFACTURER** Scott Wilson, China. ABS, nylon, metal. **RENDERING** Scott Wilson

7

8

9

launched OOBA brand, he interacts with design-conscious, first-time parents as both consumer and designer. His recognition of the powerful role of community today is evident in his tongue-in-cheek iBelieve (9), which makes a crucifix out of an iPod and, with a wink and a nod, acknowledges the obsessive devotion of iPod's global following.

Several of the young designers featured in the *Triennial* have created unique relationships based on their own special interests and needs. Greg Lynn has developed a network of manufacturers and technology providers to support his pursuit of design using the most advanced digital methods available. In all of her work, J. Meejin Yoon seeks to engage the world around her through her interactive environmental installations. Her desire for visitor involvement motivates what she designs as well as plays an indispensable role in how the project will work and what it will look like when it is activated. Tobias Wong has created a very different kind of community for himself—one that is not based on the objects he creates or the people he works with to develop his designs. He has resisted the idea of working in a studio of his own, developing instead a mobile atelier situation for himself by counting on the goodwill of various showrooms and retail spaces around Manhattan to let him temporarily set up shop on their premises. He conducts meetings, draws inspiration, and works on his design concepts in these spaces, which allows him to participate in an association of individuals and businesses involved in design-related activities.

Both the rise in popularity of craft and the emergence of new types of collaboration have opened up design in a remarkable way. Uniqueness is appealing to both designers and consumers as an indication of individual taste and identity, and also a necessary counterbalance to the ubiquity of many contemporary design items. Like craft, communities have the potential to make design more accessible than we ever could have imagined. Whether we participate as a user or a maker, the idea that we, as individuals, can have some sense of ownership and understanding of both process and product ensures that design will become an even more indispensable part of our lives in the twenty-first century.

DESIGN AND SOCIAL LIFE

ELLEN LUPTON

Sitting on my desk is a monograph about the Dutch designer Hella Jongerius. The book was designed by COMA, a design partnership based in New York City and Amsterdam. In place of the digital renderings and photos of finished goods that dominate most design books, this volume presents objects as part of social life: Products appear in a workshop or studio, often in multiples, in spaces inhabited by people. The cover photograph, shot in an immaculate factory workroom, shows seven red and white vases cradled in the arms of seven men who, presumably, helped birth them (1).

The book you are looking at now also was designed by COMA. It resulted from a social process that transpired among curators, writers, designers, editors, manufacturers, and booksellers—a process that now includes you, the reader. Perhaps you bought or borrowed a copy of the book, or you have picked it up in a store, or maybe you are viewing a digital version on the pages of Amazon or another online seller.

Across the room from me, my eleven-year-old son Jay and his friend Tony are playing Will Wright's game *The Sims* (2), which models the workings of an ordinary household. As players decide how people in their artificial family unit will spend their time and money, the software spins out a life, generated automatically according to simple rules that yield unpredictable results. Some households hum with joy and prosperity, adding rooms and attracting friends; others go bankrupt or catch on fire.

Jay and Tony have built a pair of unemployed Sims who have purchased a huge television set for every space in the house, even the bathroom. These characters are headed for disaster. The boys squeal with delight when a social-service worker arrives to take their baby Sim into custody. "We neglected it!" they exclaim happily as the infant is carried off. The TVs remain, but not for long.

These two artifacts—a sophisticated art book and a hugely popular video game—mark different positions along the spectrum of design practice today. One is a low-tech, high-minded publication aimed at design-world insiders; the other is a high-tech, mass-market product belonging to one of the world's most successful series of electronic games.[1] Both items exist without conflict in my house, sharing space with thousands of printed books and dozens of digital games. Drawing them together is a common interest in observing social systems, from how goods are produced to what patterns govern human behavior. These two works of design illustrate the social life of contemporary design and point to broader cultural movements that are shaping—and shaped by—design practice.

Design has always been a social activity, arising in response to a problem, opportunity, or circumstance in the world. Whereas we might think of an artist as a loner confronting a self-defined challenge, designers rarely work in solitude. The sociability of design is, indeed, what attracts

1 COMA (Cornelia Blatter and Marcel Hermans). *Hella Jongerius* book, 2003. **AUTHOR** Louise Schouwenberg. **PUBLISHER** Phaidon Press. **PHOTOGRAPHER** Joke Robaard with Maarten Theuwkens

2 Will Wright. *The Sims 2: Wright Wedding*, screen capture from electronic game, 2005. **GAME DESIGN** Will Wright, Electronic Arts. **PUBLISHER** Electronic Arts

3 Deborah Adler. Target ClearRxSM prescription system, 2004. A comparative study: generic container, Adler prototype, and ClearRx container. **SYSTEM AND GRAPHIC DESIGNER** Deborah Adler. **INDUSTRIAL DESIGNER** Klaus Rosburg/Sonic Design Solutions. **BOTTLE/CLOSURE** Berry Plastics Corp. **LABEL** Rx Label Corporation. **RUBBER COLOR-CODED RING** Minnesota Rubber. **CLIENT** Target. Polyethylene terephthalate, paper. **PHOTO** Matthew Klein

1

2

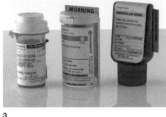

3

many creative people to this diverse field of practice. To make their projects happen, designers collaborate with clients, fabricators, suppliers, retailers, editors, illustrators, art directors, ad agencies, schools, community boards, end users, and more. The ClearRx project by Deborah Adler and Target Corporation began with a single design student's observation that standard pharmaceutical packaging was failing people in her life. Her project grew to include the efforts of other graphic and industrial designers as well as a major corporation with the power to bring her idea to market (3).

Design has connected with the living fabric of human use in new, once unimaginable ways, and this has been especially true over the past decade. Designers are creating not only finished images and objects, but also tools that people put to work, spaces that people bring to life, and forums that buzz with the exchange of ideas. Designers no longer view the public only as a "consumer" to be persuaded or as a "user" to be studied and analyzed, but also as a community of intelligent individuals equipped to engage objects and information through customization, reverse engineering, do-it-yourself production, and two-way feedback. "Push media"—which thrusts itself unbidden in the face of viewers—must compete with user-driven "pull media," a fact that is changing the face of advertising. Design has also helped build new associations, drawing individuals together around a common interest or a shared piece of software.

The burgeoning of the blogosphere is a key event in design's recent social transformation. Blogs (short for "Web logs") give voice to everything from the political views of prominent activists to the personal musings of anonymous teenagers. Blogging software makes it easy for authors to post information and for readers to join and follow threaded conversations. Although the medium dates back to the early 1990s, blogging blasted into public view during the presidential election of 2004, when unaffiliated writers from both the left and right trailed the candidates' campaigns on their own blog sites, speaking in independent voices unfettered by journalism's customary civility.[2] "Netroots" emerged as a new breed of political activist who uses the Web (especially blogs) as a means to actively participate in politics— locally, nationally, and globally.[3]

Numerous blogs have bubbled up from inside the design community as well, including Speak Up and Typographica (founded 2002) and DesignObserver (founded 2003). Each of these blogs has helped build a new, participatory design discourse. Armin Vit, creator of Speak Up, describes his site as a "community shaped by its authors, readers, and random contributors." Blogs have triggered a journalistic paradigm shift: the editor is now charged with setting forth an inviting social space. A blog is not just a publication; it's a party. Twenty-five years ago, the future of design criticism was assumed to lie in books, magazines, academic journals, and museum catalogues like this one: expensive, slow-moving media to which only a few writers could expect to contribute. Now, an inclusive body of design writing is being produced every day—more than nearly anyone has time to read (4).

Design authorship, a theme explored in the 2003 *National Design Triennial*, remains a strong impulse within the design community, but for many designers, collaboration is becoming more important than the individual signature.[4] Designers are using their own social networks to build partnerships whose value exceeds the sum of individual efforts. Designer and illustrator Nicholas Blechman published a book-length edition of his independent zine *Nozone* in 2004, launching a collective visual assault on the deadening effects wrought by "empire" on the world's ecology, economy, and culture. Blechman's project pulled together the efforts of dozens of illustrators, designers, cartoonists, and writers. As in a rally or a march, the book's impact derived from the combined efforts of the group, not from a single voice (5).

Blechman, an art director at the *New York Times*, is one of many designers producing independent projects while also working for pay in the profession. Rick Valicenti, a graphic designer in the Chicago area, has been combining experimental design with a successful commercial practice for over twenty-five years. Through his company Thirst, Valicenti has constantly experimented with new ways to collaborate with designers inside and outside his own business. Recently, he formed a new partnership with two designers in Los Angeles, Louise Sandhaus and Lorraine Wild. Working under the moniker Wild LuV, the threesome is able to take on bigger projects than they would individually. J. Meejin Yoon operates under two different company names: MY Studio, for her independent artistic work, and HY Architecture (with Eric Höwler), for collaborative building projects.

This move to collaborate is taking place across the disciplines of design. In architecture, many younger practitioners have formed partnerships that allow them to attract prominent commissions and make a bigger impact on the field than if they were working alone or for an established firm. Studios such as Open Office, FACE, Freecell, Lewis Tsurumaki Lewis, and ShoP are pursuing a hands-on workshop model that allows architects to test and prototype details in their studios rather than working in a purely digital mode.[5] Rejecting traditional corporate hierarchies, these designers are tapping the energy that comes from working side-by-side with creative peers, often sharing tools and overhead costs with other young businesses.

4 SpeakUp. SpeakUp T-shirt, 2003. **DESIGNER** Marian Bantjes. **PRINTED BY**
  Shirts Our Business. **COMMISSIONED BY** UnderConsideration. Silkscreen on
  cotton. **PHOTO** UnderConsideration
5 Nicholas Blechman. *Empire: Nozone IX* book, 2004. **PUBLISHER** Princeton
  Architectural Press
6 Ransmeier & Floyd. D.I.Y.M. (Do-It-Yourself-Modern) lamp shade, 2005.
  Polypropylene. **DESIGNER** Gwendolyn Floyd. **MANUFACTURER** Droog Design.
  PHOTO Ransmeier & Floyd
7 Jason Miller. *Can of Play-Doh*, 2004. Play-Doh. **PHOTO** Jason Miller

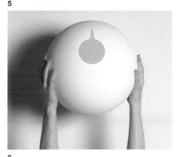

The impulses to make a blog, publish a zine, or prototype a wall structure by hand reflect another revolution in contemporary culture: the exploding interest in DIY processes. The 2003 *Triennial* documented the allure of craft and making things in contemporary design.[6] This fascination continues, as witnessed in the obsessively produced jewelry of Steven and William Ladd and the hand-wrought decorative wall sculptures of David Wiseman. Bringing such desires home to consumers, various new products invite people to customize their living spaces. Blik's removable vinyl wall graphics are an instant, reversible alternative to paint and wallpaper, while the pre-fabricated housing projects of Craig Konyk and Charlie Lazor are exploring the house as a flexible, customizable kit of parts. Ron Gilad's Vase Maker is a ceramic holder that doesn't become functional until the user places it over a piece of glassware or other container. Ransmeier & Floyd's DIYM (Do-It-Yourself-Modern) lampshade is designed to easily slip on and off any hanging light bulb, providing an instant retrofit for utilitarian fixtures (6).

Just as professional designers want to become authors, publishers, builders, and fabricators, members of the so-called "general public" want to try their own hands at designing spaces, making furniture, building Web sites, editing video, modifying software, and so on. Arts and crafts have become a big business. Crafts warehouse stores provide consumers with a bewildering array of supplies and equipment for everything from decorative painting to scrapbooking, a growing hobby that has spawned its own vast consumer subculture.[7] The international Church of Craft, founded in 2000, is an urban, noncommercial off-shoot of the mass-market craft explosion.[8] The furniture and objects of Jason Miller quietly nod to the new craft populism, employing such humble materials as Play-Doh, Popsicle sticks, and colored glue (7).

Design technologies—and information about how to use them—have become widely available. Especially among people who have grown up with Internet access, the urge to make and share media is second nature. Just as the professions of law and medicine were transformed in the Internet age by public access to information, design has become more open to participation. The self-taught multimedia designer Jakob Trollbäck, founder of Trollbäck & Company, was a disk jockey and nightclub owner in Stockholm, Sweden, before moving to New York City to begin a career in graphic design—a field Trollbäck refers to as "visual deejaying." He learned his trade by doing it, working in the legendary offices of R/Greenberg Associates.

At the core of DIY is self-education. *Readymade* magazine, founded in 2001, shows readers how to produce domestic items—from coffee tables to garden furniture—out of recycled or repurposed materials. Howtoons, founded in 2005, brings DIY technology to children through a Web site and other publications that show how to make rocket launchers, marshmallow shooters, hovercrafts, and other devices out of ordinary household stuff. *Make* is a "mook," a book/magazine hybrid, launched in 2005. Aimed at tech-savvy geeks from all walks of life, *Make* celebrates the right of citizens to "tweak, hack, and bend" the technologies they encounter at home and work by showing readers how to build their own gadgets and get under the hood of products (8).

A pioneer of this reverse-engineering vanguard is Natalie Jeremijenko, whose work examines the ecological impact of high-tech manufacturing and the interface between nature and technology. Her Feral Robotic Dog project (an experiment in "do-it-yourself toy mechanics") invites high-school students to rebuild and reprogram commercially made mechanical dogs so that they seek out toxins in public parks and landscapes. Jeremijenko is an artist, scientist, designer, and engineer. "I choose a label based on convenience," she explains. In some cases, it is easier to get approval for an "art" project (because scientists require clearance for work involving human or animal subjects), while other pieces move more smoothly under the aegis of science (getting a green light for research can be faster than for public art). All her activities are framed under the name of her research lab, xdesign, an entity that has moved with her as she has joined the faculties of Stanford, Yale, and the University of California, San Diego, where she currently teaches (9). Like the readers and producers of *Make*, *Readymade*, and Howtoons, Jeremijenko approaches design as an open network rather than a closed discipline.

In a similar vein, members of the open-source software movement view operating systems and other programs as public property to be tested and refined by a broad community. Wikipedia, founded in 2001, is a vast online encyclopedia to which anyone can contribute.[9] Creative Commons, founded the same year, is developing new standards of intellectual property that protect authors while encouraging the spread of ideas; the phrase "some rights reserved" has become the hip way to license content on the Internet.[10] Like DIY, these social movements reflect the opening up of knowledge for public use and public authorship—the construction of an "information commons."[11]

DIY relies on access to tools and materials on the one hand, and access to information about how to use them on the other. Computer languages reflect a highly ordered mode of DIY. A program is a set of instructions: loops, subroutines, *if/then/else* statements, and so on. Saul Griffith, creator of Howtoons, argues that all forms of physical making are, at bottom, "programmable." A recipe is a unique string of generic "subroutines"

8 *Make* magazine. *Make: Premiere Issue* cover, 2005. **CREATIVE DIRECTOR**
   David Albertson. **ART DIRECTOR** Kirk von Rohr. **PHOTOGRAPHER** Emily Nathan.
   ILLUSTRATOR Kirk von Rohr. **EDITOR AND PUBLISHER** Dale Dougherty.
   EDITOR IN CHIEF Mark Frauenfelder. **MANAGING EDITOR** Shawn Connally
9 Natalie Jeremijenko/X Design Lab. Robotic dog. **PHOTO** Emily Nathan
10 Processing. *Substrate*, 2003. **DESIGNER** Jared Tarbell. **PROCESSING DESIGNED BY**
   Benjamin Fry and Casey Reas. Digital drawing generated with Processing code
   and interface

8

9

10

(sautéing, frying, chopping) applied to particular ingredients (chicken, fish, onions).[12] Digital designer Golan Levin argues, "If writing is a medium of thought, then software is an agent of will," a set of actions performed on the physical world.[13] The popular interest in arts and crafts (expressed by *Readymade*) and the parallel play with digital tools and programming (voiced in *Make*) stem from a common instinct: to produce things via transparent forms of mental and physical knowledge: *knit one, purl two; for i data, perform x function*.

Most commercial software is packaged inside an interface that hides its command language from users. Benjamin Fry and Casey Reas are the creators of Processing, an open-source programming language made for students, artists, designers, architects, researchers, and hobbyists. Processing is at once a tool, a social space, and an educational resource being creatively deployed by people all around the world.[14] Processing builds on the work of John Maeda, Fry and Reas's teacher at the MIT Media Lab, who pioneered the use of computer languages to open up public understanding of how things work in the digital age[15] (10).

The impulse to expand our knowledge of digital tools drives designers using commercial software as well. Joshua Davis is called the "guru" of Flash, the widely used application for Web design and animation. Flash is an accessible commercial product that nearly anyone, from kids to professional designers, can learn to implement to some degree.[16] Davis, however, like other high-functioning Flash designers, has mastered this standard-issue software from the inside out, using the program's custom-scripting language to construct complex interfaces and interactive digital environments. Not interested in keeping his working methods a secret, Davis writes books about Flash coding and conducts frequent seminars and workshops.[17]

"Remix culture,"[18] which emerged in the 1980s and 1990s, has today become a matter of fact. The sampling of everything from audio loops to computer code—once employed by artists as an overt strategy—has merged with normal practice. Looking at a rising generation of digital producers, media critic Lev Manovich argues that borrowing and sharing have simply become second nature. In place of postmodernism's view of "appropriation" as a critical act, designers like Joshua Davis, Casey Reas, and Ben Fry are forging a new modernism that values production over appropriation and engages the structural possibilities of software rather than the universe of cultural quotation.[19]

From the user's perspective, interactivity is the social promise of the World Wide Web. Unlike a book or a conventional TV program, online media can anticipate our desires over time and assemble content on the fly in response to our queries. The rise of Google (marked by the com-

DESIGN AND SOCIAL LIFE

pany's IPO, filed in April 2004) is a fundamental event in design's social evolution. Google's "sponsored links" are generic text ads with no flashing graphics, no brand images, and no clever copy. They just may be the most influential typographic form of the current era.

Sponsored links have provided the advertising business with a new—and, to some ad agencies, scary—model of accountability: a fee is paid to the search engine only when a link is clicked.[20] Life in "Google World" requires advertisers to devise new ways to reach consumers, including marketing campaigns that append commercial messages to an interesting piece of Web content—the goal is to inspire people to pass the link on to their friends, affirming the coolness of the brand through word-of-mouth transmission. Design-driven multimedia companies such as PSYOP in New York City and Planet Propaganda in Madison, Wisconsin, create quirky, artistic Web spots that become entertainment in their own right. Whereas some traditional advertising slams viewers with information they cannot avoid, spots like these succeed by attracting notoriety and then traveling through social channels.

Meanwhile, "vlogging," or video blogging, allows amateur producers to circulate their own digital clips. Some sites tack a commercial message onto these homegrown movies, providing a financial reward to videos that attract downloads—viral marketing goes DIY.[21] Podcasting represents a similar revolution in audio media.[22] Soon after bloggers began publishing audio commentary on their sites, Apple integrated podcast subscriptions into its iTunes software service, creating what CEO Steve Jobs called "TiVo for radio."[23] Mainstream media quickly followed up on this DIY phenomenon, giving listeners access to audio content anytime, anywhere. Podcasting stems from an iconic work of industrial design whose importance lies as much in its link to social movements as in the sleek functionality of the thing itself.

There is an anti-utopian side to user-driven design. As advertising goes underground, we may worry about how it penetrates our personal lives. We used to watch TV; soon it will be watching us. A Web site that knows our preferences might be tempted to share them with others, assaulting us with unwanted offers. We may welcome an interface that anticipates our purchase patterns, or a car that knows our exact location—yet find it uncanny, too.

Stage designer Marsha Ginsberg has made surveillance a dramatic element in her design for George Bizet's *Carmen*, set in a suite of low-rent offices in present-day Brooklyn. Don Jose is cast as a security guard, and throughout the play he sits at his desk viewing Carmen—a woman he hardly knows—via video monitors. The monitors allow the audience to see into hidden parts of the set while participating in Don Jose's voy-

11

12

euristic obsessions (11). The human use of interior spaces is the subject of Ginsberg's work. Whereas architects typically construct new environments, she investigates the "mess" of living, revealed through peeling wallpaper, chipped paint, and worn furniture.

Electroland, a design partnership based in Los Angeles, creates environments that use tracking devices and lighting effects to respond to the movements of visitors. These systems openly engage participants in interactive experiences with buildings, but they also subtly suggest that technologies placed in public spaces may be following our movements in less visible ways. Electroland's projects render surveillance transparent (12).

Designers create interiors that support different kinds of human activity. Retail environments promote shopping, libraries inspire study, and pedestrian bridges and walkways (a specialty for Electroland) encourage people to move along toward their destination. The renowned furniture company Herman Miller, Inc., has created furniture systems that facilitate office work for over three-quarters of a century. The company is now developing the New Office Landscape, a series of furniture components that aim to stimulate creativity by providing places for spontaneous face-to-face social interaction. Hovering between furniture and architecture, the pieces create semi-enclosed areas that are less formal and static than a conference room and more private and inviting than the area around the watercooler.

The *National Design Triennial* is the result of joint social labor—albeit wholly unaided by collaboration-inducing furnishings. Launched in 2000, the *Triennial* has always been organized by a team of curators, drawn from Cooper-Hewitt, National Design Museum's own staff and from leaders in the design community. For this latest installment of the *Triennial*, the curators' work process emphasized group consensus over the individual curatorial voice. And, for the first time ever, we invited the public to bring ideas to the attention of the *Triennial* team. For nearly a year, we operated a blog-style Web site which collected nominations. These suggestions, regularly reviewed by the curators, exposed us to dozens of new names; those that made it into the exhibition's final cut include Electroland, Nicholas Blechman, ShoP, and Marsha Ginsberg. Although the *Triennial* remains a curated exhibition—not a juried competition—it has evolved into a more open, collaborative process.

Design builds, and participates in, society. Every designer is a citizen, and every citizen is, to some degree, a designer. The broad-based cultural and technological phenomena shaping the design professions in the new century are molding the consciousness of us all. These social transformations include the spread of blogging and two-way communication on the Internet, the accessibility of DIY design and technology, the growth of the open-source movement, and the push to protect and populate an information commons. The changes discussed here are, by and large, cause for optimism. We are living in a time of unprecedented public awareness of design. In the United States and around the world, people have more access than ever before not only to well-designed products but also to the tools and thought processes that designers use every day. Such citizens are well equipped to face the future.

1 On the rise of *The Sims* and its innovative modeling of social life, see Steven Johnson, *Emergence: The Con nected Lives of Ants, Brains, Cities, and Software* (New York: Simon & Schuster, 2001).

2 Matthew Klam, "Fear and Laptops on the Campaign Trail," *New York Times Sunday Magazine* (September 26, 2004). Blog readership increased 58% in 2004; report published by the Pew Internet and American Life Project, 2005. http://www.pewinternet.org/PPF/r?144/report_display.asp (December 27, 2005).

3 Jerome Armstrong and Markos Moulitsas Zuniga, *Crashing the Gate: Netroots, Grassroots, and the Rise of People-Powered Politics* (White River Junction, Vermont: Chelsea Green Publishing Company, 2006).

4 Ellen Lupton, "The Producers," *Inside Design Now: National Design Triennial* (New York: Cooper-Hewitt, National Design Museum and Princeton Architectural Press, 2003), 22–7.

5 William Menking, "Back to the Future," *The Architect's Newspaper*, Vol 3, Issue 01_01.19.2005, page 8.

6 Susan Yelavich, "The New Iconoclasts," *Inside Design Now: National Design Triennial* (New York: Cooper-Hewitt, National Design Museum and Princeton Architectural Press, 2003), 32–7. The trend continues, as witnessed in *Metropolis* Magazine's May 2005 cover story, "Handmade Modern."

7 Michaels Stores became a publicly held company in 1984, with sixteen stores located primarily in Texas. The company expanded rapidly during the 1990s (with 500 stores by 1995). There were 804 Michaels Stores operating in 2004. The company launched a new chain called ReCollections, devoted entirely to scrapbooking, in 2004. http://www.michaels.com/art/online/static?page=corp_aboutus (December 27, 2005). On scrapbooking, see Ginia Bellafante, "Trafficking in Memories (for Fun and Profit)" (*The New York Times*, Thursday, January 27, 2005), F1+.

8 The mission of the Church of Craft is to promote "any and all acts of creation as a means to live life best." http://www.churchofcraft.org/ (December 27, 2005).

9 http://en.wikipedia.org/wiki/History_of_Wikipedia (December 24, 2005).

10 http://creativecommons.org/ (December 23, 2005). On the "copy left" movement, see Lawrence Lessig, *Free Culture: How Big Media Uses Technology and the Law to Lock Down Culture and Control Creativity* (New York: Penguin, 2004).

11 http://www.info-commons.org/ (December 26, 2005).

12 http://www.instructables.com/about/ (January 10, 2006).

13 Golan Levin, "Is the Computer a Tool?" in John Maeda, *Creative Code* (London: Thames & Hudson, 2004), p. 140.

14 Processing can be downloaded for free at http://www.processing.org/ (December 26, 2005).

15 John Maeda, *Design by Numbers* (Cambridge: MIT Press, 2001).

16 Flash was created by Macromedia, acquired by Adobe Systems in 2005. http://www.adobe.com/aboutadobe/main.html (December 26, 2005).

17 Joshua Davis, *Flash to the Core: An Interactive Sketchbook* (Indianapolis: New Riders, 2003).

18 My colleague Barbara Bloemink has for the past two years been researching and gathering materials for an exhibition entitled *Remix Culture*, which examines the remix phenomenon in a variety of media, including product design, architecture, and music.

19 On "remix culture" after postmodernism, see Lev Manovich, "Generation Flash," 2002, http://www.manovich.net/ (January 30, 2006). Cooper-Hewitt's 1996 exhibition *Mixing Messages* asserted that "mixing" is an underlying condition of graphic design practice. See Ellen Lupton, *Mixing Messages: Graphic Design in Contemporary Culture* (New York: Cooper-Hewitt, National Design Museum and Princeton Architectural Press, 1996).

20 See "Crowned at Last," *The Economist*, March 31, 2005; and John Markoff and Natives, "Web Search Sites Add Up to Big Dollars," *The New York Times*, Friday, February 4, 2005, C1, C5.

21 Rich Hoxsey, "Will Blogging Kill the Video Star?" *Print* (January/February 2006): 98–9.

22 Steve Friess, "Podcasting Goldrush Is On," *Wirednews.com*, September 28, 2005, http://wirednews.com/news/digiwood/0,1412,68950,00.html (January 4, 2006).

23 Shayne Bowman and Chris Willis, "The Future is Here, But Do News Media Companies See It?" *Nieman Reports*, Volume 59, Number 4 (Winter 2005): 6–10. http://www.nieman.harvard.edu/reports/05-4NRwinter/Bowman&Willis-NRw05.pdf(February 11, 2005).

TRANSFORMING DESIGN

MATILDA MCQUAID

"Any sufficiently advanced technology is indistinguishable from magic."
—Arthur C. Clarke

In the 1960s and 1970s, science-fiction writer and discoverer Arthur C. Clarke proposed three "laws" of prediction: The first two sought to convey that nothing is impossible, and that shooting for the impossible was the only way to attain the limits of the possible.[1] The third law, featured in the above quote, related the awe, excitement, and even astonishment that innovative objects can provoke. As examples of design, they are simply "magical" because of how they change shape, function, or alter surface and surrounding space. They are transformative, defy practical analysis, and, in the end, revolutionize our lives.

The work of the eighty-seven designers in this exhibition and catalogue exemplifies eighty-seven different design approaches. Each has changed not only the nature of an object, but also a segment of our sensory world—whether it is how we acquire, listen, and, ultimately, look at music and video, as with Apple's ubiquitous iPod; or how we are affected by Tobias Wong's rose corsage, which is in fact a sinister bullet-resistant brooch. More than a token of friendship, the bloom becomes a metaphor for our time: protecting your heart and love in times of conflict.

It is difficult to imagine a more transforming moment than two years ago, when viewers saw for the first time images of the Martian surface (1). In our collective consciousness, "Martian" no longer meant "little green men," but a real planetary surface with beautiful sand dunes and a blue sunset. Our knowledge of Mars would have been limited without the research performed by the rovers *Spirit* and *Opportunity* (2), which have now spent two years on the red planet transmitting images and data not only to scientists but to children, teachers, and the entire world as well. Mars was a global discovery that gave viewers the opportunity to share in an extraordinary adventure.

Space will continue to provide this kind of experience as new technology evolves, especially in the field of robotics. While the rovers have certainly changed our visual perception of the universe, they also represent decisive changes in how we work, too. The *Lemur IIa*, for example, one of the National Aeronautics and Space Administration (NASA)'s Jet Propulsion Laboratory's newest rovers, is currently being tested for its ability to be a mechanical "Leatherman" (3). Scientists and engineers hope that the *Lemur* will eventually be able to construct small structures in space, reducing the risk factors for human explorers as they venture beyond Earth's atmosphere.

Machines like the *Lemur* are invented and controlled by humans, yet their incredible precision and adeptness at certain types of tasks can

1 NASA's Jet Propulsion Laboratory. *Spirit* beholds bumpy boulder, Mars, Taken by Mars Exploration Rover *Spirit*, 2006. **PANORAMIC PHOTO.** Courtesy of NASA/ JPL-Caltech/ Cornell/ NMMNH
2 NASA's Jet Propulsion Laboratory. Artist's concept of Mars Exploration Rover. Digital rendering. Courtesy of NASA's Jet Propulsion Laboratory
3 NASA's Jet Propulsion Laboratory. *Limbed Excursion Mechanical Utility Rover* (*LEMUR*) *IIa*, 2004–present. **DESIGN TEAM** Brett Kennedy, Hrand Aghazarian, Mike Garrett, Lee Magnone, Avi Okon. Aluminum, Nylon, Graphite, Nomex composites. **PHOTO** NASA's Jet Propulsion Laboratory
4 SHoP. Camera Obscura, Mitchell Park Phase 2, Greenport, NY, 2005. **ARCHITECTS** SHoP Architects, P.C.: Christopher R. Sharples, William W. Sharples, Coren D. Sharples, Kimberly J. Holden, Gregg A. Pasquarelli. **PROJECT TEAM** Mark Ours, Reese Campbell, Jason Anderson, Keith Kaseman, Basil Lee. **PHOTO** Seong Kwon
5 Hitoshi Ujiie. *Virtual Fruit* printed textile, 2003. **DESIGNER** Hitoshi Ujiie and Ceri Isaac, ION Design. Equipment lent by Mimaki Industry, Dystar, ErgoSoft. Digital inkjet printing with acid dye on silk. **PHOTO** Matt Flynn

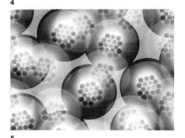

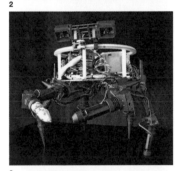

make them notably more efficient than their human counterparts. SHoP, an architectural firm in New York, has been investigating these advantages in terms of building: how is it possible to make construction more efficient and cost-effective at every level, from designing to manufacturing? The Camera Obscura (4), located in the village of Greenport, Long Island, is designed entirely as a three-dimensional computer model, with machines cutting building components by laser using digital files extracted directly from the model. Crucial information is etched into the components for ease of fabrication, which avoids the need for middlemen and for converting drawings into a different program in order to be compatible with the manufacturer or architect. Instead, SHoP's approach allows direct transmission of construction documents to the manufacturer. Greater efficiency, a reduction in the margin of error, and a more streamlined building process are just some of the benefits that architects like SHoP have found by working in this manner.

Working with computers and special software programs has also revolutionized conventional textile-making techniques, as seen in the work of textile designers Lia Cook and Hitoshi Ujiie. Each uses digital technology, but in a very different way. Cook combines photographic media and computer-aided technologies with the Jacquard loom to create pixellated portraits that play with scale, surface pattern, and textile structure. Ujiie focuses on the limitless possibilities of working with digital inkjet printing. Unlike conventional rotary screen printing, which allows only a limited number of colors—usually fewer than a dozen— digital inkjet printing achieves a full range of effects, including infinitesimal tonal gradation and no repeats (5).

Ideas of transformation can also occur within larger structures, and this has been the main focus of inventor and engineer Chuck Hoberman. He bases his practice on the fundamental idea that a designed object can change shape and form like natural organism. While the alteration of size and shape is ubiquitous in the natural world, it is rare among manmade objects. According to Hoberman, what is required is "a new design theory, a conceptual framework that draws on mathematics, mechanics, and structural engineering to integrate change as a basis for design." Over the years, his work has oscillated between small- and large-scale projects, with work in one scale sometimes leading to production in another scale. Through his years as a toy manufacturer, when his collection of innovative expanding and contracting toys included the famous Hoberman Sphere, he has been "obsessed with the idea of making objects disappear . . . not as a magic trick but where the object could self-transform—change itself by itself."[2]

TRANSFORMING DESIGN

The idea of looking at nature or using natural forms as inspiration for design is present in objects like Nike's Free 5.0 shoes, where designers created a shoe that is based on the notion of barefoot running—there is less structure and restriction, so the foot remains in control. The foot becomes stronger, relying more on itself and less on a constrictive, and sometimes overly supportive, shoe.

While architects and product designers confront the resistance of physical materials, graphic designers manipulate multiple, diaphanous layers of image and text. Trollbäck & Company's online animation "Evolution in Golf" for Nike builds a butterfly out of a pair of gold shoes. Mounted like specimens in a natural history display, the shoes come to life and fly away, suggesting the evolution of a fixed, old archetype into something light, new, and magical. Taking a darker view of transformation, Chip Kidd's jacket design for *Dry*, a memoir about alcoholism by Augusten Burroughs, appears to melt away into the surrounding white space.

Comfort for the human body is first and foremost the inspiration for Niels Diffrient's Liberty chair, along with everything he has designed over the past fifty years (6). Diffrient has spent half a century studying and documenting how the body reacts to certain activities, and then prescribing furniture guidelines for design professionals. Far from promoting a particular styling for a chair, he has tailored a seating structure, rather than a machine, which takes its cues from the complexities of the human form in a variety of poses.

There is an important experiential component in design. Its benefits and successes are determined by how one interacts with, manipulates, or ultimately uses something like a chair. For example, it would be impossible to make a satisfactory judgment about the comfort of a chair without sitting in it; its aesthetic appeal is only part of the story. Design relies upon participation, whether it is simply holding a knife or interacting with the surrounding environment. Abhinand Lath's line of materials for SensiTile requires the viewer's involvement in order for the dynamic surface qualities of this product to be seen (7). Like mirrors set in a foundation of concrete, Terrazzo, for example, produces an animated surface when one passes a hand in front of it. It seems to flash on and off, scattering light and shadows across the concrete face. Decoration is no longer applied to surfaces to make them dynamic; instead, materials are integrated within the substrate to make them active. Panelite has a similar quality, although the surface itself is not animated in the same way as Sensitile. The lightweight honeycomb core panel is a clever and colorful alternative to a sheetrock wall. The fiberglass or polyester resin sheets that cover the core can be custom-colored, and the entire panel is structural. By providing a range of both functional and appealing visual effects, Panelite has expanded the role of a partition wall.

6 Niels Diffrient. Study for Liberty ergonomic task chair, 2004. **PHOTO** Humanscale
7 Abhinand Lath. Scintilla, 2005. **MANUFACTURER** SensiTile Systems. Cast PMMA acrylic. **PHOTO** SensiTile Systems
8 Toshiko Mori Architect. The Newspaper Café, Jindong New District Architecture Park, Jinhua City, China, 2004–06. **DESIGNER** Toshiko Mori. **PROJECT TEAM** Jolie Kerns, Sonya Lee. **CLIENT** Jindong New Distrct Constructing. **RENDERING** Toshiko Mori Architect
9 Moorhead & Moorhead. *Metropolis* magazine booth, ICFF, New York, NY, 2005. **DESIGNERS** Robert Moorhead and Granger Moorhead. Polypropylene and wood. **PHOTO AND RENDERINGS** Moorhead & Moorhead

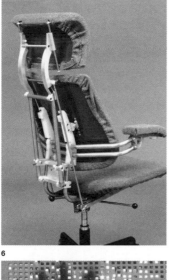

6

7

8

9

The perforated surface of Michael Meredith's aluminum Shed has the potential to be an incongruous object in the pastoral landscape of upstate New York. Yet Meredith makes the structure virtually disappear by closely grouping the perforated holes so that one sees through them to the forest behind. By altering the surface, Meredith has maintained a balance between nature and the manmade.

The ephemeral character of news is an unlikely source for transforming the façade of a building, but in the Cargo Wall by Moorhead & Moorhead and Toshiko Mori's Newspaper Café, they have used news—design magazines or current events—as the element that activates and gives meaning to each façade (8, 9). Colorful magazine covers in uniform pockets and the pictures and characters in the featured Chinese newspapers animate the structures. Randomness plays a role in the design, but not in the same manner as conventional city newsstands. The containers and unit proportions remain the same; only the printed word and image change, revealing how the smallest item can alter a space.

Similarly, anyone who has lived in a city where space is a premium understands the need for multi-use or collapsible furniture, such as Christopher Douglas's Knock-down, Drag-out series. The dining table, chairs, benches, and coffee table can be easily disassembled, slid under the bed, or moved, quickly transforming a furnished apartment into a bare studio.

Light is intangible yet mutable, and its evanescence can affect the spatial quality of a room or a building or even an aircraft. It becomes an essential factor in human comfort. The new airbus interior by Boeing is a composite single body (as opposed to being made from multiple parts), which not only makes the aircraft more fuel-efficient, thereby allowing for more passengers, but is also structurally capable of incorporating larger windows. Imagine a picture window at 30,000 feet. On an even a larger scale, architect and engineer Santiago Calatrava talks about light from a structural perspective. He has described his transportation hub for the World Trade Center as being supported by columns of light—evoking both the ghost of the Twin Towers destroyed on September 11, 2001, and the light brought into the terminal through a glass roof which illuminates the levels below. James Carpenter, designer and sculptor of glass and light, always refers to light as another architectural medium. He creates light-filled interiors in marginal, often cavernous spaces, where harnessing natural light from remote locations is often circuitous (10). Alison Berger uses glass and light in a fashion similar to Carpenter, but on a more intimate scale. Trained as a glass blower, Berger designs and fabricates containers for light—like capturing fireflies in a jar. The subtlety and fragility of the light combined with the simplicity and refinement of the container create a quiet ambience.

The physicality of light can also radically affect an individual's mood and sensory perceptions. The soft, cascading lights made by textile designer Suzanne Tick are woven with fiberoptics. Pinpoints of light emanate from the tiny hair-like filaments, producing a mysterious but delicate centerpiece. Hervé Descottes/L'Observatoire International and Leni Schwendinger's Light Projects reflect, reduce, and otherwise manipulate light so that there often is no intermediary, such as glass or fiber. They create new environments not through anything tangible, but rather their carefully controlled and ingenious methods of coloring the air around us.

Architects are experts at altering and transforming spaces. This is in part their mission: to listen to the needs of the program and client and conceive a solution within an existing context. Landscape architect Ken Smith is possibly the ultimate magician, converting dumpsters into huge planters or a blank wall into a vertical field of daisies. Whether in an urban or rural setting, he radically changes the context with something as little as an artificial flower. Bernard Tschumi Architects' headquarters and watch factory for Vacheron creates a dramatic contrast to its relatively rural surroundings. It appears like an object in the landscape when compared with his athletic center at the University of Cincinnati, which nestles between the stadium and an indoor arena, the heart of the campus. Inversely, Predock Frane takes the context of Venice and the phenomenon of Acqua Alta (high water), which sieges the city up to one hundred times a year, and puts it in a room-size installation.

Design is magical, yet it is not sleight of hand. In each object we handle or in each environment we enter, time, labor, thinking, and manufacturing have brought form and function to an assortment of raw materials. As consumers, we only see the end product, and rarely do we have the opportunity to discover either the creative or technical process by which these products came to be. It is this leap from idea to object, raw to finished, that can seem like magic, but in reality, it is a combination of experience, education, insight, knowledge, and, not least, creativity.

1 The laws were proposed by Arthur C. Clarke in the essay "Hazards of Prophecy: The Failure of Imagination", in *Profiles of the Future* (1962 and revised edition of 1973). The first two laws are: 1. When a distinguished but elderly scientist states that something is possible, he is almost certainly right. When he states that something is impossible, he is very probably wrong. 2. The only way of discovering the limits of the possible is to venture a little way past them into the impossible.

2 John Seabrook, "Child's Play: What Makes a Toy Fun?" *The New Yorker*, December 15, 2003, p. 58.

10 James Carpenter Design Associates. Solar Light Pipe, Washington, D.C., 2000–01. **DESIGNERS** James Carpenter and Davidson Norris, Carpenter Norris Consulting, Inc. **PROJECT ARCHITECTS** Studios Architect. **STRUCTURAL** David Kufferman, PE. Lighting: Matthew Tantari/ Ann Kale Associates. **PHOTO** Paul Warchol

10

ACCONCI STUDIO
VITO ACCONCI
BROOKLYN, NEW YORK

1

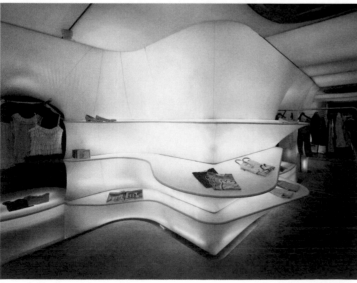

2

Born in the Bronx in 1940, Vito Hannibal Acconci spent two decades as a literalist concrete poet, photo-conceptualist, performer, videographer, filmmaker, and installation artist. During the 1980s, his sculptural work displayed overt references to architecture and design, exploring issues of public and private spaces and viewer interaction.

Using many of the same tools and interests of his earlier years, he founded Acconci Studio in 1988 "for theoretical design and building." Acconci rejects the modernist idea of the autonomous artist, and has wholly embraced a team approach in his recent work. Untrained in architecture, he sees the discipline in terms of activity, behavior, and performance. Over the last few years, Acconci Studio has created works that reveal an affinity for "stretching, braiding, knotting, twisting, warping, and morphing." Its work involves modeling architecture like clay so that surface and structure are united, and space is malleable and flexible—both physically and socially.

In 2003, Acconci Studio was hired to design a performance space, cafì, and children's playground on the River Mur in Graz, Austria, as part of the European Capital of Cultures Festival. The result, an extraordinary pod-shaped "island" that traverses the river, made of interlaced steel mesh, glass, asphalt, rubber, and light, has become a visual symbol of the city. The island is a dome that morphs into a bowl that morphs into a dome. When the bowl is not used as a theater, it becomes a plaza where people can sit and interact. The playground doubles as the backdrop of the stage and as a ceiling for the cafì. The entrance canopy twists down into lounge seats, the curved tables are movable, and the rubber edge of the terrace twists down to make bar counters.

The same year, Acconci Studio was commissioned to design the United Bamboo store in Tokyo, Japan. Using its signature "push-pull" method of design, the studio replaced the nonstructural walls of the old building with bulging glass alcoves in which clothes appear to hang from the shrubbery outside. The exterior was re-clothed with a stainless-steel mesh and glass façade on which images of clothed people in the store are projected out to the street. Inside, translucent PVC sheeting is literally pulled down from the ceiling and walls to make shelves and counters so that the entire store seems to be one surface. Fluorescent lighting behind the PVC diffuses light throughout the store and illuminates the clothing from behind.

By creating and merging various stylistic and functional categories the studio makes work which straddles sculpture, furniture, public art, design, and architecture. Acconci Studio epitomizes a design methodology and strategy that Acconci believes will lead to more and more "spin-offs"—houses and buildings on the one hand and clothing, products, packaging on the other—in the future.

1 Roof Like Liquid Flung Over the Plaza, Center for the Performing Arts,
  Memphis, TN, 2003. Stainless steel, mirrored and perforated, fluorescent light.
  PHOTO Chip Pankey
2 United Bamboo Store. Daikanyama, Tokyo, Japan, 2002 03. **PHOTO** United
  Bamboo
3 Mur Island, Graz, Austria, 2001–03. **PHOTO** Harry Schiffer

DEBORAH ADLER FOR TARGET CLEARRX^{SM}

NEW YORK, NEW YORK

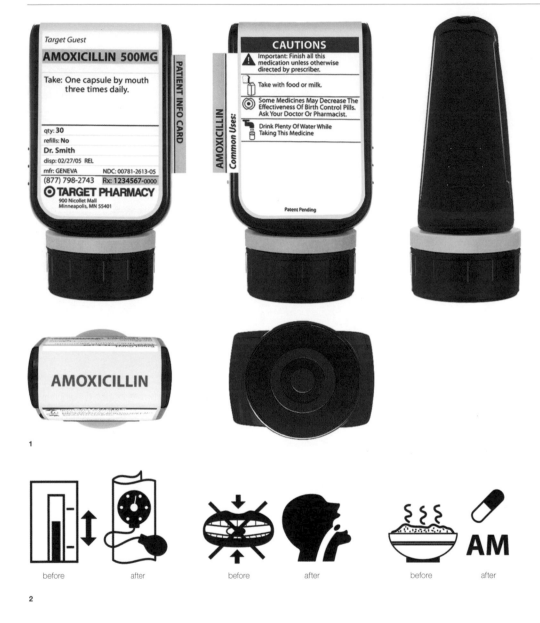

1

2

From conception to prototype to nationally available product, the Target ClearRx^{SM} prescription system exemplifies design's potential to change people's lives. The idea originated with Deborah Adler, an MFA student in graphic design at the School of Visual Arts in New York City. After her grandmother inadvertently took the wrong medication, Adler began reevaluating the standard prescription pill bottle. Her simple yet groundbreaking design caught the attention of Target, known for its philosophy, "Design for All."

Adler initially focused on the graphics applied to standard pharmacy bottles. Observing that the cylindrical shape hindered the display of information, she developed a D-shaped container. Her design incorporated a logical hierarchy of information, with the most important information at the top, color-coding for each family member, and a slot to hold extra information about the medication.

Target paired Adler with industrial designer Klaus Rosburg, who developed the bottle's shape. The final design incorporates a child-resistant cap to meet federal regulations and a cap-down orientation to permit a single label to cover more of the bottle's surface and to allow the name of the medicine to be visible from the top and the sides. Adler, who now works in the office of Milton Glaser, also teamed up with the legendary graphic designer to create new warning icons that are more intuitive.

Launched in Target pharmacies nationwide in 2005, the ClearRx Prescription System includes pill and liquid containers, a measuring syringe, a completely overhauled labeling system, and an integrated patient information card.

1 Target ClearRx℠ prescription system, 2004. **SYSTEM AND GRAPHIC DESIGNER**
Deborah Adler. **INDUSTRIAL DESIGNER** Klaus Rosburg/Sonic Design Solutions.
BOTTLE/CLOSURE Berry Plastics Corp. **LABEL** Rx Label Corporation. **RUBBER
COLOR-CODED RING** Minnesota Rubber. **CLIENT** Target. Polyethylene terephthalate,
paper. **PHOTO** Target
2 Target ClearRx℠ prescription system, 2004. Before and after warning icons.
DESIGNER Milton Glaser, Inc.
3 Target ClearRx℠ prescription system, 2004. Prototype with slide-out information
card, 2002. Plexiglas, Plexiglas tubing, styrene dollhouse materials, laser printed
paper. **PHOTO** Matthew Klein
4 Target ClearRx℠ prescription system, 2004. A comparative study: generic
container, prototype, and ClearRx container. **PHOTO** Matthew Klein

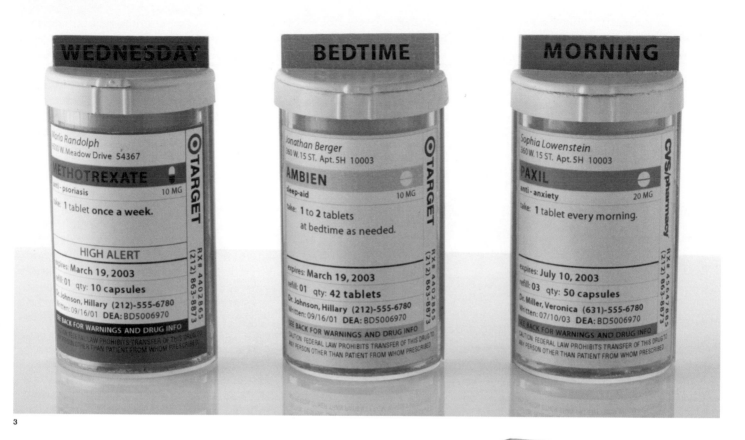

3

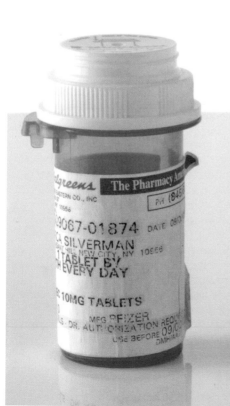
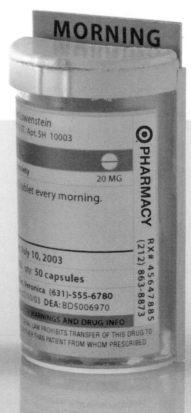
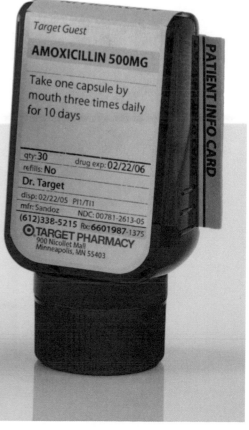

4

APPLE COMPUTER
CUPERTINO, CALIFORNIA

1

2

There is no question that Apple's iPod has transformed our entire relationship to music in the twenty-first century. We can download it. We can share it. Now we can even watch music videos, television shows, and movies on our iPods, or listen to "podcasts" of our favorite radio programs. The simple device has created a community united by the thin white cables emanating from its members' ears.

First released by Apple in 2001, the original translucent white iPod was an object that everyone wanted to own, as much for how it looked as for what it could do. Streamlined, simple, and pure, the iPod looked good next to a beautifully designed sound system or atop a mid-century modern sideboard. But it has only been during the last three years that the device's extraordinary potential has been recognized and its range of options and functions significantly expanded.

The integration by Apple of all things "i" is a stroke of marketing genius and an indication of just how visionary the company is. In rapid succession, Apple has released new iterations of the iPod, each unique in its own way. The iPod Mini, which came in a range of pastel colors, was the smallest digital music player on the market and sold more units than any other iPod. In 2004, Apple introduced the Shuffle, a much more compact, less expensive iPod, no bigger than a pack of gum, which shuffles songs randomly every time it is turned on and was the first iPod to work with either a Mac or a PC. Then came the Nano, perhaps the most elegant of all the iPods, super-thin but capable of everything the full-sized model does. In October 2005, Apple introduced the iPod Video, transforming not only the way consumers watch moving images but also how television and motion picture companies do business.

iPod has now come to signify a revolutionary family of products born under the sign of Apple. Equally impressive is what some are calling "the iPod ecosystem"[1]: the torrent of accessories designed by a variety of companies in response to the iPod. These add-ons alone are a $1 billion business. Perhaps we already live in an iPod universe?

1 Damon Darlin, "The iPod Ecosystem," *The New York Times*, February 3, 2006.

1 iPod Advertising Campaign, 2005. **DESIGNER** Apple and TBWA\Chiat\Day.
Courtesy of Apple Computer, Inc.
2 iPod minis in a variety of colors, 2004. Anodized aluminum and polycarbonate
ABS. **PHOTO** Apple Computer, Inc.
3 Third-generation iPod, 2003. Polycarbonate and stainless steel. **PHOTO** Apple
Computer, Inc.
4 iPod photo, 2004. Polycarbonate and stainless steel. **PHOTO** Apple Computer, Inc.
5 iPod nano, 2005. Polycarbonate and stainless steel. **PHOTO** Apple Computer, Inc.
6 iPod shuffle, 2005. Polycarbonate. **PHOTO** Apple Computer, Inc.

3

4

5

6

ARCHITECTURE FOR HUMANITY

SAUSALITO, CALIFORNIA

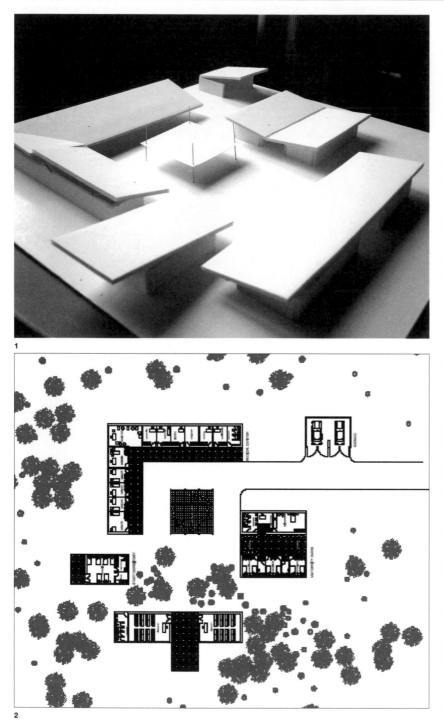

1

2

Architecture for Humanity demonstrates that design can actively change and improve lives. In 1999, Cameron Sinclair, who trained as an architect in London before coming to the United States, and freelance journalist Kate Stohr founded AFH as a charitable organization to promote architectural and design solutions to global, social, and humanitarian crises. With the idea that innovative, sustainable, and collaborative design can make a difference where resources and expertise are scarce, AFH launched an international architectural competition directed at solving the housing problem facing returning refugees in Kosovo, Serbia. The following AFH competition, for a mobile AIDS medical unit in Africa, also received a great deal of international attention and participation.

Over the last seven years, AFH, which is entirely open-source and works with 2,200 volunteers in forty countries, has worked on projects in over twenty different countries, often in response to natural disasters. These include building a combination girls' soccer field and AIDS treatment center in Syyathemba, Zulu, South Africa; and an immediate response to the destruction and flooding in New Orleans after Hurricane Katrina. In December 2004, a series of earthquakes in Northern Sumatra resulted in tsunamis leaving 200,000 dead in twelve countries. AFH worked with the Web site worldchanging.com to raise $100,000 in twelve days, and used its worldwide network of volunteers to organize the construction of emergency shelters, community centers, and schools in Tamil Nadu, India, and Pottuvil and Kirinda, Sri Lanka.

Sinclair has increasingly taken on the role of advocate for humanitarian-directed design. He has consulted with government bodies and relief organizations on a number of subjects, including mine clearance in the Balkans, earthquake-resistant construction techniques in Turkey and Iran, and refugee housing on the borders of Afghanistan.

AFH is completing the construction of a joint school and AIDS information and treatment center in Ipuli, Tanzania. The project, initiated by Nobel Prize nominee Neema Mgana, is designed by former competition finalists Nicholas Gililand and Gaston Tolila of Paris, France. Part of a larger complex, the building, due to be completed by June 2007, will stand as a testament to what a few people, a vision, a need, and a small amount of money can accomplish.

1 Mother and Child Medical Center, Massing Model, Ipuli, Tanzania, 2006
DESIGN TEAM gilliland.tolila architecture (Gaston Tolila and Nicholas Gilliland)
SPONSOR Africa Regional Youth Initiative, Architecture for Humanity
2 Mother and Child Medical Center, Plan, Ipuli, Tanzania, 2006 **DESIGN TEAM**
gilliland.tolila architecture (Gaston Tolila and Nicholas Gilliland) **SPONSOR**
Africa Regional Youth Initiative, Architecture for Humanity
3 Collage. Courtesy of AFH

3

JOSEPH AYERS

NORTHEASTERN UNIVERSITY
NAHANT, MASSACHUSETTS

1

2

Robolobster, an underwater robot crustacean with eight plastic legs, fiberoptic antennae, and an industrial-strength plastic shell, is remarkably similar to a living lobster in both its form and the manner in which it behaves. Invented by Dr. Joseph Ayers, a marine biologist and neuroscientist at the Marine Science Center at Northeastern University, it was developed in collaboration with Massa Products Corporation, an innovator in electro-acoustic products.

The Robolobster's groundbreaking new design is an example of biomimicry, an emerging science that develops solutions to human problems through the imitation of biological organisms and processes. Lobsters have the ability to adapt and maneuver in almost every type of environment, and Ayers and his team have adopted the lobster's strategies for their robots.

Between 1999 and 2002, with the support of the Office of Naval Research and the Defense Advanced Research Projects Agency, Ayers created the first two generations of robotic lobsters, with the goal of understanding how a lobster's nervous system controls its movements in the water in response to the variable conditions of its environment. The success of the project has led to a third-generation Robolobster that will be autonomous and controlled by an electronic nervous system. The intent is to design a robot capable of conducting mine countermeasures, collecting marine-science data, and patrolling for underwater pollution.

A lobster's body shape, weight, and buoyancy are optimal for walking underwater. Their natural inclination to prey on sea life near the coast theoretically translates to an artificial lobster being able to trawl for mines in harbors and along coastlines. According to the Office of Naval Research, it is particularly difficult to search for mines in these shallow waters due to crashing waves and currents which cause low visibility. In the future, Robolobsters will be fitted with sonar for detecting mines acoustically, chemical sensors to detect trace amounts of explosive material leaking from the mines, and optical sensors that visually detect mines. In each of these cases, the robot will detect the mines autonomously, without human direction, potentially saving thousands of lives.

1 First- and Second-generation Biomimetic Underwater Ambulatory Robot
(Robolobster), 2005. **SPONSOR** Office of Naval Research. **PHOTO** John F. Williams
2 First-generation Biomimetic Underwater Ambulatory Robot (Robolobster), 2005.
SPONSOR Office of Naval Research. **PHOTO** John F. Williams
3 Second-generation Biomimetic Underwater Ambulatory Robot (Robolobster),
2005. **SPONSOR** Office of Naval Research. **PHOTO** John F. Williams

3

ALISON BERGER GLASSWORKS
WEST HOLLYWOOD, CALIFORNIA

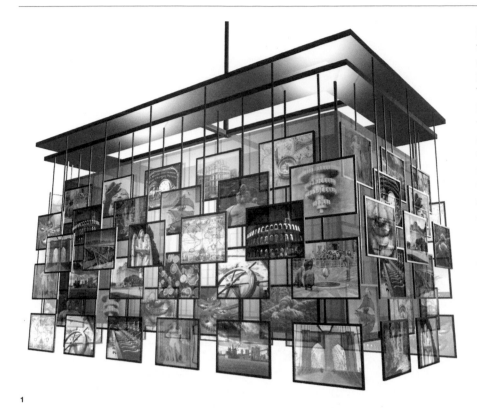

1

2

Her medium is light, her material is glass: that is how glass designer Alison Berger describes her craft. Introduced to glass blowing as a curious teenager in Dallas, Texas, Berger took a circuitous route to her chosen profession. She received a fine-arts degree at the Rhode Island School of Design, attended architecture school at Columbia University, then worked with a number of architects, including Frank O. Gehry and Associates, until 1995, when she began to devote herself full-time to glass design.

Berger's glassworks are like center-pieces in a room devoid of decoration, except for the light that the pieces attract and ultimately refract. Glass Slide Chandelier resists being categorized as decorative. The turn-of-the-twentieth-century glass slides that comprise the chandelier depict portraits as well as industrial, agricultural, and architectural scenes—a light box which lures us with imagery from the past while providing a timeless and contemporary structure.

Berger's inspirations for both her lighting and glass vessels range from bell jars and apothecary shapes to scientific beakers and glass jars in which she used to capture fireflies as a child. A kindred spirit of Bauhaus designer Wilhelm Wagenfeld, she finds beauty in the bulb and in the subtlety of light, as exemplified by her hand-blown crystal pendants, in which bulb, shade, and light appear as one.

Berger is guided by memory—not only of personal experience but also of centuries-old glassblowing techniques that are now virtually extinct. Bubbles and other imperfections intrinsic to glass are neither romanticized nor hidden in Berger's works, but rather honestly reflect the nature of the material.

About forty percent of Berger's work is on commission, some of it from actors who have seen her work on stage sets for films and music videos like *Practical Magic* (1998, Warner Brothers), *Tank Girl* (1995, MGM), and Madonna's *Bedtime Stories* (1995). Her passionate, almost spiritual attachment to her medium has earned her an enthusiastic following. For those who own one of her works, Berger's message is clear: "The pieces are at home waiting for you; they act as a quiet beacon."

1 Glass Slide Chandelier, 2005. Bronze frames and found photographic glass slides.
   PHOTO Josh White. **RENDERING** Amanda Hunter
2 Vessels, 2003–present. Cast and hand-blown lead crystal. **PHOTO** Josh White
3 Crystal Sphere Chandelier, 2003 04. Open bronze frame hand-blown lead crystal
   pendants. **PHOTO** Josh White
4 Pendant 2004 lamp, 2004. Hand-blown lead crystal. **PHOTO** Josh White
5 Word Pendant lamp, 2004. Etched hand-blown lead crystal. **PHOTO** Josh White
6 Pendant 2005 lamp, 2005. Hand-blown lead crystal. **PHOTO** Josh White

3

4   5   6

NICHOLAS BLECHMAN

NOZONE MAGAZINE
NEW YORK, NEW YORK

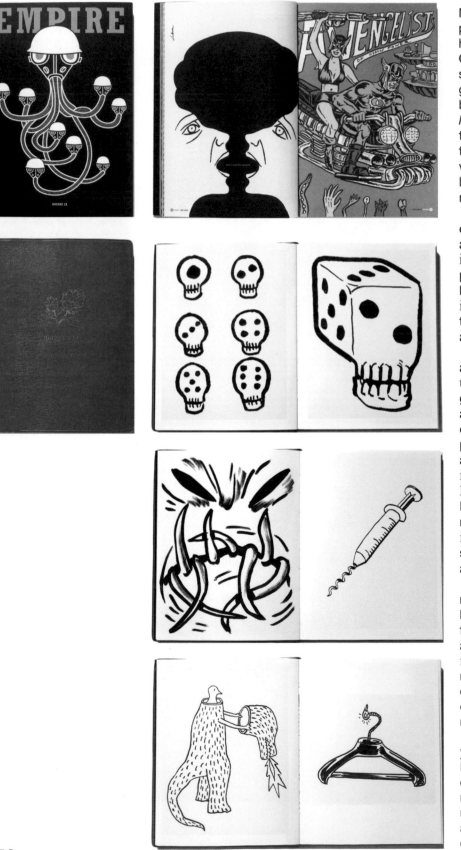

1

2

Nicholas Blechman founded the independent 'zine *Nozone* in 1990, during his senior year as a liberal-arts major at Oberlin College in Ohio. Blechman, the son of illustrator R. O. Blechman, had grown up knowing some of the world's best illustrators and cartoonists. *Nozone*, published as a zero-profit venture on a tiny budget, attracted attention with its eccentric format, skeptical view of contemporary politics, and A-list contributors, including Gary Baseman, Joost Swarte, and Chip Kidd.

When Blechman became art director of the *New York Times* Op-Ed page at age thirty, *Nozone* fell dormant while its founder kept pace with the newspaper's relentless schedule. Blechman left the *Times* in 2000 to focus on his independent design work, returning to the paper four years later to become art director of the Week in Review.

In 2004, *Nozone* came back to life as a book, *Empire: Nozone 9*, which used illustration, comics, writing, and graphics to proclaim collective dissent against the corporate/military control of the world's ecology, economy, and politics. Blechman defines "empire" as the diffused power of global capitalism, motored by such forces as the International Monetary Fund, the World Bank, and the United States government: "Billions drink its sodas, listen to its music, breathe its air, drive its cars, smoke its tobacco . . . pay its debts, and benefit or suffer from its policies."

For Blechman, design is a collaborative enterprise. To co-author the book *100% Evil*, Blechman and his friend Christoph Niemann each created a series of disturbing yet funny images depicting war, greed, and the needless destruction of self and others. The two sides meet at the center of the book in a devastating battle of mutual annihilation.

Building on his roots as a do-it-yourself designer and publisher, Blechman is authoring original publications while conceiving and commissioning art for one of the world's most influential newspapers. He is a leading voice using design as an editorial medium that gives opinions a complex and memorable visual form.

1 *Empire: Nozone IX* book, 2004. **PUBLISHER** Princeton Architectural Press
2 *100% Evil* book, 2005. **ILLUSTRATORS AND DESIGNERS** Nicholas Blechman and
Christoph Niemann. **PUBLISHER** Princeton Architectural Press

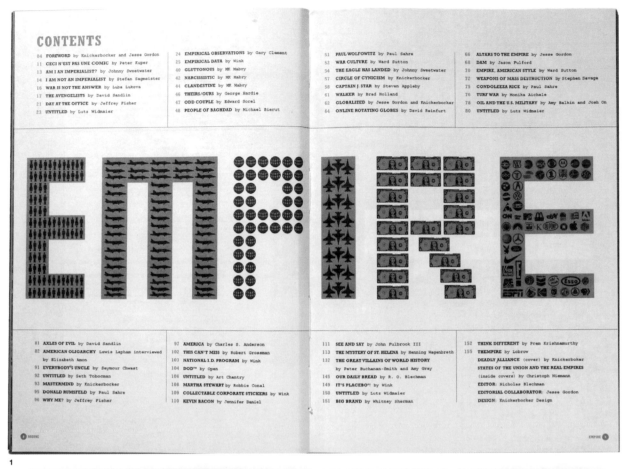

CONTENTS

04 FOREWORD by Knickerbocker and Jesse Gordon
11 CECI N'EST PAS UNE COMIC by Peter Kuper
13 AM I AN IMPERIALIST? by Johnny Sweetwater
14 I AM NOT AN IMPERIALIST by Stefan Sagmeister
16 WAR IS NOT THE ANSWER by Luba Lukova
17 THE AVENGELISTS by David Sandlin
21 DAY AT THE OFFICE by Jeffrey Fisher
23 UNTITLED by Lutz Widmaier

24 EMPIRICAL OBSERVATIONS by Gary Clement
25 EMPIRICAL DATA by Wink
40 GLUTTONOUS by MK Mabry
42 NARCISSISTIC by MK Mabry
44 CLANDESTINE by MK Mabry
46 THEIRS/OURS by George Hardie
47 ODD COUPLE by Edward Sorel
48 PEOPLE OF BAGHDAD by Michael Bierut

51 PAUL WOLFOWITZ by Paul Sahre
52 WAR CULTURE by Ward Sutton
54 THE EAGLE HAS LANDED by Johnny Sweetwater
57 CIRCLE OF CYNICISM by Knickerbocker
58 CAPTAIN J. STAR by Steven Appleby
61 WALKER by Brad Holland
62 GLOBALIZED by Jesse Gordon and Knickerbocker
64 ONLINE ROTATING GLOBES by David Reinfurt

66 ALTARS TO THE EMPIRE by Jesse Gordon
68 DAM by Jason Fulford
70 EMPIRE, AMERICAN STYLE by Ward Sutton
72 WEAPONS OF MASS DESTRUCTION by Stephen Savage
75 CONDOLEEZA RICE by Paul Sahre
76 TURF WAR by Monika Aichele
78 OIL AND THE U.S. MILITARY by Amy Balkin and Josh On
80 UNTITLED by Lutz Widmaier

81 AXLES OF EVIL by David Sandlin
82 AMERICAN OLIGARCHY Lewis Lapham interviewed
    by Elizabeth Amon
91 EVERYBODY'S UNCLE by Seymour Chwast
92 UNTITLED by Seth Tobocman
93 MASTERMIND by Knickerbocker
95 DONALD RUMSFELD by Paul Sahre
96 WHY ME? by Jeffrey Fisher

97 AMERICA by Charles S. Anderson
102 THIS CAN'T MISS by Robert Grossman
103 NATIONAL I.D. PROGRAM by Wink
104 DOD™ by Open
106 UNTITLED by Art Chantry
108 MARTHA STEWART by Robbie Conal
109 COLLECTABLE CORPORATE STICKERS by Wink
110 KEVIN BACON by Jennifer Daniel

111 SEE AND SAY by John Fulbrook III
113 THE MYSTERY OF ST. HELENA by Henning Wagenbreth
137 THE GREAT VILLAINS OF WORLD HISTORY
    by Peter Buchanan-Smith and Amy Gray
145 OUR DAILY BREAD by R. O. Blechman
149 IT'S PLACEBO! by Wink
150 UNTITLED by Lutz Widmaier
151 BIG BRAND by Whitney Sherman

152 THINK DIFFERENT by Prem Krishnamurthy
155 THEMPIRE by Lobrow
DEADLY ALLIANCE (cover) by Knickerbocker
STATES OF THE UNION AND THE REAL EMPIRES
    (inside covers) by Christoph Niemann
EDITOR: Nicholas Blechman
EDITORIAL COLLABORATOR: Jesse Gordon
DESIGN: Knickerbocker Design

1

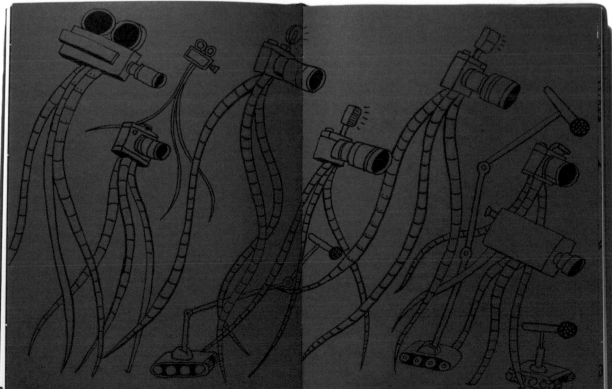

2

BLIK, LLC
SCOTT FLORA AND JERINNE NEILS
VENICE, CALIFORNIA

With blik's pre-cut, simple, and widely varied forms and shapes, the walls in our homes can be changed according to each of our whims, moods, ages, hobbies, interests, or aesthetics. Embodying both the current trend toward individual customization and the increasingly transient nature of our lives, blik offers an innovative alternate to traditional wallpaper and painted walls for the "commitment-phobic": designs come in over fifty variations, including dots, circles, birds, flowers, clouds, aliens, ellipses, paisleys, words, and numbers. Additional designs are released annually.

blik's shapes and forms are made from computer-generated images that are transferred onto thin, removable PVC stickers. Users can choose to install the designs in any configuration: using a single design repeated over the wall's surface, decorating only a small part of the wall, or mixing different designs in any combination or arrangement. The designs can also be placed against flat surfaces such as walls, ceilings, furniture, and floors. The decals can be peeled off and leave no residue.

The company, founded by food editor Jerinne Neils and architect Scott Flora, was originally Web-based only. Neils and Flora were inspired by the cubed, site-specific wall drawings of conceptual artist Sol LeWitt from the 1960s. However, blik's imagery ranges from minimalist simplicity to highly decorative motifs that can be combined or stand alone to create unique wall "murals." Their initial use of decals as individualized wallpaper has also been applied to functional objects such as furniture and glasses. In addition, Neils and Flora created a temporary outdoor installation, *Big Red Wall*, consisting of a 100-foot-long wall "graffiti'd" with blik designs, in Silverlake, California.

1 Custom blik Karel Wall Graphics, 2005. **DESIGNERS** Scott Flora and Jerinne Neils (principals), Chris Fava. PVC graphic film on drywall. **PHOTO** Jeremy Williams
2 The Big Red Wall Project, 2005. **DESIGNERS** Scott Flora and Jerinne Neils (principals), Chris Fava. **CLIENT** Barbara Bestor Architecture. PVC graphic film on masonite. **PHOTO** Jeremy Williams

THE BOEING COMPANY
CHICAGO, ILLINOIS

Boeing's 787 *Dreamliner* is reinventing air travel. The only major new American passenger airplane to be built in ten years, its composite structure and wing components, interior cabin and flight deck, and advanced computing systems are new milestones for industrial design and manufacture. The *Dreamliner* is a mid-size, wide-body jet whose design radically departs from traditional commercially produced vehicles. A super-efficient airplane—the 787 uses twenty percent less fuel than similarly sized aircraft—it dramatically lowers operating and maintenance costs and sets unprecedented standards for environmental protection.

A key element of the *Dreamliner*'s design is its incorporation of new technologies in airplane construction and composition. The bulk of the airplane's wings and fuselage is made of a single piece of carbon-plastic-fiber composite, rather than aluminum plates, which results in greater resistance to fatigue, less corrosion, and significant weight reduction. The 787's engines, being developed by General Electric and Rolls-Royce, contribute as much as eight percent of the increased efficiency, representing a nearly two-generation jump in technology. The engines are also significantly quieter, emphasizing the airplane's environmentally friendly features.

For passengers, this new "plastic" material and single-piece construction will result in a wider interior, aisles, and seats and far larger windows. Other innovative features of the interior include larger overhead storage bins; room-like cabins rather than the traditional single long tube; a ceiling lit by light-emitting diodes which flight attendants control to mimic daylight or evening skies; electronically dimmable windows; increased air filtration and humidity; more comfortable cabin pressure; and total connectivity, including in-flight Internet access.

787 *Dreamliner*, business class, 2004. **DESIGNERS** Boeing and Teague Associates.
Fiberglass with LED lighting. **PHOTO** The Boeing Company

THOM BROWNE
NEW YORK, NEW YORK

Thom Browne believes the suit makes the man—only not just any suit and not just any man. The menswear he designs is inspired by a cool, early 1960s vision of suave sophistication. The uniforms of airline pilots, photographs of his father, J. C. Penney catalogs, and debonair movie icons like Sean Connery's James Bond and Steve McQueen in *The Thomas Crown Affair* all make an appearance in a visual repertoire rooted in a truly American sensibility.

"Men should dress like bureaucrats or airline pilots. I love uniforms! They make everything so effortless and easy," he says. Thom Browne has taken the uniform of the late 1950s and early 1960s—the suit—and made it sexy again, updating it in a way that is at once quirky and refined.

When Browne could not find suits to wear, he designed his own and had them made by a tailor. He opened his own business in 2001, offering custom-made clothes only. In 2004, he entered the ready-to-wear market while maintaining his bespoke, or made-to-order, business. What sets Browne's suits, sweaters, shirts, and coats apart from the rest of men's fashion is their concern with quality, fit, and detail rather than the latest trend. His suits have unexpected proportions. Jackets are chopped. The fit is lean. Trousers have high waistbands and the leg is cropped. Browne wears his own pants cropped just above the ankle, revealing a stretch of bare leg above his sturdy shoes. However, rather than dictating the same style to all his clients, he believes in an individual look personalized by the wearer. He likes to play with fabrics both high and low, especially in the unexpected details that wait to be discovered: a dinner jacket of white cotton canvas lined with white football-jersey mesh; a sportcoat made of terrycloth. And that most traditional of men's suiting fabrics, pinstripe, is paired with red, white, and blue grosgrain ribbon trim.

1 Grey wool flannel Chesterfield, light gray cotton corduroy suit with shorts,
  cashmere cap and mittens, fall/winter 2006. Wool, cotton, cashmere, Velcro.
  PHOTO Dan Lecca
2 Grey/green beaded lace suit with grosgrain tipping, fall/winter 2006. **PHOTO** Matt
  Flynn
3 Wool parquet suit and Chesterfield coat with matching tie and white cotton oxford
  cloth shirt, spring 2006. **PHOTO** Matt Flynn
4 Navy nylon football-jersey mesh suit over a base of cotton pique, white cotton
  oxford cloth shirt and a navy necktie, spring 2006. **PHOTO** Matt Flynn

2

3

4

SANTIAGO CALATRAVA

ZURICH, SWITZERLAND; VALENCIA, SPAIN; AND NEW YORK, NEW YORK

1

Santiago Calatrava is a bridge builder. Both an architect and engineer, he links disciplines as well as riverbanks using the tools of his professions, along with science, art, and music, to create some of the most expressive structures of our time.

Calatrava has completed more than thirty bridges internationally; his Sundial Bridge at Turtle Bay in Redding, California, is his first in the United States. The cable-stayed structure links the north and south sections of an exploration park, and features a towering 217-foot steel pylon with a glass and granite deck which hovers above the Sacramento River. The bridge's translucency lends a feeling of lightness; more important, it serves an ecological purpose by not casting a shadow on the spawning salmon pond below.

Trained initially as an architect in Spain, Calatrava obtained a doctorate from the ETH (Federal Institute of Technology) in Zurich, Switzerland. He won his first competition for a railway station in Zurich, which became a significant urban insertion, linking a neighborhood to a town square as well as providing a full-service train station. Calatrava has also accomplished this, but on a much larger scale, in his design for the World Trade Center Transportation Hub in Lower Manhattan. Conceived as a soaring, free-standing structure of glass and steel with a vast network of underground connections to subway and New Jersey Transit Path lines and adjacent buildings, the terminal is a gathering place. On mild, sunny days as well as on September 11th each year, the roof will part mechanically to a maximum opening of approximately forty feet, bringing both light and sky into the building. For this reason, Calatrava speaks of light as a structural element, and states that the building is supported by "columns of light."

Like his monumental bridges, Calatrava's towers at 80 South Street in New York City and Fordham Spire in Chicago are both sculptural and virile in their structural expression. They offer a bolder new skyline for each of these cities known for their skyscrapers and, like all of Calatrava's structures, perform as an aerialist—effortlessly stretching, waving, twisting, and cantilevering their forms in midair.

1 World Trade Center Transportation Hub, New York, NY, 2003–09. **PROJECT TEAM** Downtown Design Partnership, a joint venture of DMJM + HARRIS and STV Group, Inc., in association with Santiago Calatrava, S.A. **CLIENT** The Port Authority of New York and New Jersey. Glass, steel, concrete, stone. Renderings courtesy of the Port Authority of New York and New Jersey
2 Fordham Spire, Chicago, IL, 2005–present. **CLIENT** The Fordham Company. **RENDERING** Santiago Calatrava, S.A.
3 Sundial Bridge at Turtle Bay, Redding, CA, 2004. Steel structure with galvanized steel cables; non-skid glass panels with granite accents (deck). **PHOTO** Alan Karchmer

2

3

CAO | PERROT STUDIO

ANDY CAO AND XAVIER PERROT
NEW YORK, NEW YORK; LOS ANGELES, CALIFORNIA; AND PARIS, FRANCE

1

2

3

4

5

A quiet ephemerality characterizes the work of Cao | Perrot Studio. Creating work that lies between installation and landscape architecture, the duo of Andy Cao and Xavier Perrot uses natural and artificial materials to design environments that transport us beyond the everyday.

For *Cocoons*, a temporary art installation commissioned by the City of Emeryville in Northern California and sited on a rocky point opposite the Golden Gate Bridge, Cao | Perrot designed three spinning cocoons that resemble a cross between gigantic tops and moored air balloons. Five miles of colored monofilament were wrapped around laser-cut stainless-steel armatures fabricated by architect William Massie.

Lullaby Garden, an installation commissioned for the Cornerstone Festival of Gardens in Sonoma, California, in 2003, perhaps best captures the essence of the studio's work. Tranquil and delicate, the garden must be experienced, ideally while barefoot, in order to appreciate the subtleties of its design. Inspired by the unique reflective quality of the monofilament they had used for *Cocoons*, Cao and Perrot commissioned sixty Vietnamese artisans to hand-knit carpets of colored nylon line in shades of faded gold and orange. Two hundred carpets were sewn together on-site at Cornerstone and draped over a sculpted landform foundation. The entire garden area was wrapped with strands of clear monofilament that formed a translucent wall, concealing or revealing the garden depending on the time of day. Visitors were invited to take off their shoes and walk the stylized, curvaceous landscape inspired by the nineteenth-century woodblock prints of the Japanese artist Hokusai Katsushika. Strains of a Vietnamese lullaby completed the otherworldly experience.

In 2005, Cao and Perrot were invited to design an installation at the Medici Fountain in Paris's Luxembourg Gardens for the Fíte du Mimosa. Cao likened the path of brilliant yellow winter-blooming mimosa floating on the water to a dreamy and metaphorical lover's lane.

1 *Cocoons* installation, Emeryville, CA, 2003. **DESIGNERS** Andy Cao and Xavier Perrot. **PHOTO** Stephen Jerrom

2 Fontaine Médicis, Fête du Mimosa, Luxembourg Gardens, Paris, 2004, **DESIGNERS** Andy Cao and Xavier Perrot. **PHOTO** Stephen Jerrom

3 Vietnamese artisans knitting Lullaby Garden carpet, 2004. **PHOTO** Stephen Jerrom

4 *Lullaby Garden*, Cornerstone Festival of Gardens, Sonoma County, CA, June 2004. **DESIGNERS** Andy Cao and Xavier Perrot. **SOUND** Huong Thanh and Nguyen Le. Commissioned by Chris Hougie. **SPONSOR** House & Garden, Jean Simpson, Glass Garden Inc. 200 hand-knitted nylon carpets, coconut shells, coconut wood, oversized zipper, monofilament. **PHOTO** Stephen Jerrom

5 *Le Jardin des Hesperides*, Metis International Garden Festival, Québec, Canada, 2006. **DESIGNERS** Andy Cao and Xavier Perrot. **PHOTO** Louise Tanguay

JAMES CARPENTER DESIGN ASSOCIATES
NEW YORK, NEW YORK

1

2

For James Carpenter, working with glass means designing with light. Reflection, refraction, luminosity, and transparency are the natural phenomena of light that he explores through the medium of glass, ultimately shaping the surrounding architectural space. Carpenter's mission has been to make light visible, and he draws from architecture, engineering, materials science, landscape architecture, and sculpture to accomplish his goals.

When James Carpenter Design Associates (JCDA) worked with HOK to develop the winning entry in a 2005 design competition for the redevelopment of the new Pennsylvania Station on the site of the James A. Farley Post Office, across the street from the existing Penn Station in New York City, it harnessed and redirected natural light from the outside, transforming a dark interior into a light-filled, animated atrium. In reestablishing a central train hall, it created a glass grid roof comprised of vaulted shells which illuminate the concourse hall below. The lattice columns that support the roof redirect sunlight down to the track platforms. The original Penn Station relied on an abundance of light and air, and JCDA's design embraced the same concept in an entirely new way.

Light and glass are fundamental to the Skidmore, Owings & Merrill design of Seven World Trade Center, for which JCDA designed the podium's interactive skin and cable net entry and collaborated with Jenny Holzer on the lobby wall. Pedestrians are an interactive part of the base volume, as a camera-recognition system is able to track them and signal the LED bars to follow their path. The LEDs between the two prismatic wire layers of the podium's skin also allow for the programming of a blue volume of light to visually lock the podium and tower. From the podium to the curtain wall, the light appears to be projecting from the building itself.

JCDA employs LEDs in a special installation for the *Triennial, Landscape/Light Threshold*, and reinterprets the conceptual idea of the window as a light and information threshold. Similar to *Reflection Passage, Landscape/Light Threshold* uses LED circuit boards and live video feed from a camera located in the Museum garden to explore and redefine the relationship between the interior room and the garden landscape. This work abstracts and isolates defining qualities of light and information as glass transforms light pixels into diffused images that traverse the glass surface.

1 *Reflection Passage*, Museum of Jewish Heritage, New York, NY, 2006. **PHOTO** Andreas Keller
2 Moynihan Station redevelopment, New York, NY, 2005. **ARCHITECTS** HOK. **STRUCTURAL** Severud Associates, Schlaich Bergermann and Partners. **PHOTO** Jock Pottle/ESTO
3 Seven World Trade Center, Building Skin-Podium Light Wall, New York, NY, 2006. **ARCHITECTS** Skidmore, Owings & Merrill; MEP: Jaros Baum & Bolles. **STRUCTURAL** Cantor Seinuk Group, Schlaich Bergermann und Partner, SOM Engineering Chicago. **LIGHTING** Cline Bettridge Bernstein. **CONTRACTOR** Tishman Construction. **PHOTO** James Carpenter Design Associates

3

CLEAR BLUE HAWAII
HONOLULU, HAWAII

Clear Blue Hawaii's *Napali* kayak, the only transparent, foldable kayak in the world, enables users to skim the ocean's surface like sea mammals. Designed in 2003 by New Zealander Murray Broom, it was voted one of the top twenty-five products by *Fortune* and one of the coolest inventions by *Time* magazine.

The *Napali* is a superb example of the integration of aesthetics and function. The complete transparency of the body allows the single user unprecedented intimacy with a normally concealed world. Instead of sliding through the water oblivious to what lies beneath, the kayaker coexists in two visible ecological systems at once.

The idea evolved out of a shallow-water military surveillance project in May 2000. Made of military-grade, transparent urethane casing with a Kevlar$^\mu$ frame, the *Napali* is corrosion-resistant, lightweight, and durable, and its narrow hull enables greater speed and less drag. The whole kayak weighs only twenty-six pounds, and, when folded, is small enough to fit into a backpack. The *Napali* is designed to be used by intermediate and experienced kayakers.

Clear Blue Hawaii, based in Honolulu, represents several designers of water-sports equipment. In 2004, it diversified into travel bags and gear, including the Blue Sun Solarpac, which features a six-watt removable solar panel and can charge a cell phone in two hours. The company's research and development team continues to develop prototypes of innovative adventure and sports gear.

Napali kayak, 2003. **DESIGNER** Murray Broom. Military grade urethane/PVC and carbon Kevlar®. **PHOTO** Clear Blue Hawaii

PRESTON SCOTT COHEN
CAMBRIDGE, MASSACHUSETTS

Preston Scott Cohen's architecture is shaped by complex geometries. Since establishing his practice in 1989, Cohen has designed projects ranging in scale from modest domestic and commercial interiors to cultural institutions. Never satisfied with easy solutions, Cohen revels in difficult sites, programmatic constraints, and complex spatial configurations. The virtuosity of his approach is evident in recent projects such as the Goodman House (2001–04), the Tel Aviv Museum of Art (2003–09), and the Robbins Elementary School (2005–08), each of which embodies his elaborate investigations into geometry's potential to reshape architectural form.

When Cohen adopted computer-aided design in the early 1990s, his work moved from "inventions"—intricate hand-drawn geometric projections that remarkably foreshadowed computer models—to projects with multiple layers which aim to solve concrete problems posed by construction. The process has expanded his repertoire. Although every project has used familiar architectural forms, Cohen distorts and mutates them with oblique projections, creating designs that challenge our perceptions about the nature of order in architecture.

The Goodman House, in Dutchess County, New York, one of Cohen's first major projects, is a rewrapped nineteenth-century Dutch barn inspired by a torus, or donut, shape. In 2003, Cohen won an international competition for the Tel Aviv Museum of Art. The ambitious addition, due to be completed in 2009, includes an extraordinary spiraling atrium composed of multiple hyperbolic parabolas, which pulls light three stories below the ground. The "lightfall" represents Cohen's simultaneous fusion of baroque and modern spaces. The unexpected combination of discrete geometries resolves the relationship between dynamic spaces and flexible rectangular galleries.

1 Tel Aviv Museum of Art, Tel Aviv, Israel, 2003–09. **DESIGN TEAM** Scott Cohen, Amit Nemlich, Tobias Nolte, Steve Chistensen, Guy Nahum, Cameron Wu, Andrew Saunders, Janny Baek. **MODEL MAKERS** Jonathan Lott, Isamu Kanda. **RENDERINGS** Chris Hoxie, Agito Design Studios

2 Robbins Elementary School, Trenton, NJ, 2005–09. **DESIGN TEAM** Scott Cohen, STV Inc., David Ziskind, Andre Abrantes, James Forren, Jered Serwer, Greg Spaw. **MODEL** Matt Trimble. **RENDERINGS** Andrew Bacon

COMA

CORNELIA BLATTER AND MARCEL HERMANS
BROOKLYN, NEW YORK, AND AMSTERDAM, THE NETHERLANDS

1

The book you are looking at and the font it is set in are designed by Cornelia Blatter and Marcel Hermans, the founders of COMA, designers of some of the new millennium's most memorable and inventive publications. These designers think like architects and film-makers as well as graphic designers, bringing a sense of time and a concern for program to the printed page.

Frame magazine, published in the Netherlands, documents the international world of interior architecture and design. COMA designed *Frame* from 2003 through 2005, and the magazine's design changed from issue to issue, a move that defied standard publishing practice to adapt the strategy of a good architect: to treat each space as a new problem demanding a customized solution. In *Frame* 34, on the subject of uncertainty, text appeared on opaque slabs of color floating over images. *Frame* 39 commented on its own status as a printed medium—the crop marks offsetting the photographs refer to trim lines used in the printing process.

Across the issues of *Frame*, funky display fonts mingle with structured layouts, reflecting COMA's enjoyment of American pop culture alongside Northern Europe's more rational design ethos. Blatter, who is Swiss, studied fine art in Zurich and at Yale University School of Art. The Dutch-born Hermans trained in the Netherlands and met Blatter while teaching in Stuttgart, Germany. The team now operates in both Amsterdam and New York.

Many designers today are practicing across national borders, including the Dutch product designer Hella Jongerius, the subject of a monograph designed by COMA. Responding to the mix of craft and industrial processes seen in Jongerius's work, COMA's book design aimed to feel open and unfinished. In place of polished product shots, the photography presented living portraits of Jongerius's objects in the factory, in the workshop, and at home, often in multiples.

Like DJs, graphic designers remix a body of content into a new work. Blatter and Hermans's design for *Rhythm Science*, an exploration of DJ culture by Paul Miller, a.k.a. DJ Spooky, approached the book as a temporal medium, reflecting Blatter's background in video and installation art. The team has applied this thinking to exhibition design as well, exploring time, space, and image in three dimensions, as seen in a project about the visionary architect/engineer John M. Johansen.

1 *John M. Johansen, Visionary Architect*, exhibition design and panoramic multimedia installation, Stroom, The Hague, the Netherlands 2003. **DESIGNERS** Cornelia Blatter and Marcel Hermans. **CURATORS** Lily van Ginneken and Jan Wijle. **PROGRAMMING OF PANORAMA** Ruppert Bohle. **EXHIBITION FURNITURE AND FIXTURES** Tejo Remy, René Veenhuizen, and Chris Kabel. **PHOTO** Michael Moran
2 *Frame* magazine covers, 2003–05. **DESIGNERS** Cornelia Blatter and Marcel Hermans. **EDITOR IN CHIEF** Robert Thiemann. **MANAGING EDITOR** Billy Nolan. **PUBLISHER** Frame Publishers
3 *Rhythm Science* book, 2004. **DESIGNERS** Cornelia Blatter and Marcel Hermans. **AUTHOR** Paul Miller. **PUBLISHER** MIT Press

4 *Hella Jongerius* book, 2003. **DESIGNERS** Cornelia Blatter and Marcel Hermans. **AUTHOR** Louise Schouwenberg. **PUBLISHER** Phaidon Press. **PHOTOGRAPHER** Joke Robaard with Maarten Theuwkens

2

3

4

LIA COOK
BERKELEY, CALIFORNIA

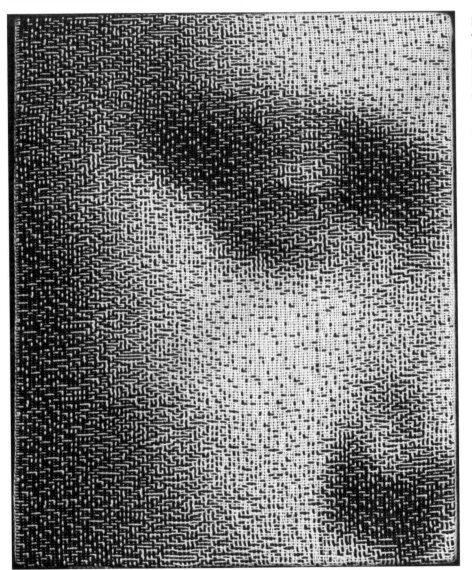

1

2

Lia Cook uses the structural language of weaving to make her images not merely physical, but also visceral. Enigmatic portraits and fragmentary details of hands and faces are woven in large scale to intensify the intimacy of a fleeting moment or expression. Examined closely, the evocative images dissolve into abstraction, revealing their complex structure and surface texture.

Cook's creative process combines photographic media and computer-aided technologies with her mastery of hand- and machine-powered Jacquard looms. Her recent black-and-white work is based on scanned photographs. These images themselves are manipulated on the computer; digital technology enables her to play with scale, detail, and focus. The visual information is translated through a CAD (computer-aided design) program into weaving instructions for a digital Jacquard head on a hand loom in her studio. *Face Maps: Halfseen* could be considered a sketch for the larger work; a black warp and white weft interact to create a loosely woven interpretation of the photograph. *Binary Traces: Kay* is woven in double-cloth, each pixel expressing the interlacing of either a black warp and weft or a white warp and weft. Computer-coded and hand-woven, the images are constructed rather than applied: the points of color that form the images and the crossing of threads that create the textiles are the same. Surface, structure, and imagery merge. Furthermore, the interaction between the binary coding and the physicality of the weaving leaves a distinctive surface pattern or trace, which Cook examines by zooming in on four square centimeters of the portrait, enlarging and re-weaving that detail, which in turn expresses the same labyrinthine surface pattern.

Cook's work stimulates conscious and unconscious pleasures by expressing advanced digital concepts in the sensual medium of cloth. In addition to the emotional freight of the image, the cloth itself is imbued with notions of comfort and kinetic memories of tactile experiences. Combining technical rigor and skilled handcraft, Cook brings an unusual richness to both textiles and images.

1 *Face Maps: Halfseen*, 2005. Woven cotton. **PHOTO** Lia Cook
2 *Digit Maps: Four Centimeters*, 2005. Woven cotton. **PHOTO** Lia Cook
3 *Binary Traces: Kay*, 2005. Woven cotton. **PHOTO** Lia Cook

3

ZERO MARIA CORNEJO
NEW YORK, NEW YORK

Maria Cornejo's specialty is softly minimal women's clothing. She finds inspiration in the world around her—the manmade and the natural as well as from her own keen observations of people "wearing the wrong clothes." Her remedy for this is her individual, well-made, wearable designs that flatter just about anyone, even though she claims she likes to "dress brainy women."

Her interest in architecture and nature is evident in both the forms and the construction of her garments. She uses volume and circular shapes as her starting points, manipulating them with unexpected results, such as a skirt that has the shape of a tulip or a coat which, through drape and seaming, envelops the body like a cocoon or shell. Her recent collections have featured a series of garments—both tops and bottoms—with gathered hems that create a gently puffed silhouette. While her clothes can be characterized as spare, minimal, and modern, they are never stiff or austere.

One can imagine Cornejo spending long hours playing with fabrics to discover how they will behave when stretched, ruched, or folded. From the nonchalant way her pieces caress and compliment a woman's curves, it is not immediately evident that she has carefully studied how they will fall when draped on a body. In fact, many of her garments are cut and draped from a single piece of fabric. Using a muted palette that occasionally erupts into bursts of vivid color, Cornejo also likes to combine unlikely fabrics and forms. She often makes soft forms from crisp fabrics like seersucker, and delights in the way folding the fabric across the surface of a dress will create layers that seem more natural than calculated.

1 Bubble corset, spring 2004. Plissé ultrasuede and watermark silk. **PHOTO** Monica Feudi
2 Plissé band dress and parka, fall 2004. Wool and silk. **PHOTO** Mark Borthwick
3 Allegra dress, spring 2006. Cotton voile jersey with silk slip. **PHOTO** Monica Feudi

2

3

JOSHUA DAVIS

MINEOLA, NEW YORK

1

The work of Joshua Davis reveals the power of tools—and the importance of understanding them—for designers in today's world. Davis explores the technical and aesthetic limits of the software programs Flash and Illustrator, industry standards in the design of images and interfaces. Davis writes his own code, in Flash ActionScript, to produce surprising interactions with users and to generate unique visual compositions according to rule-based, randomized processes.

Flash and Illustrator both produce vector-based graphics, which consist of relationships among points and lines (rather than pixels), and thus can be reproduced at any scale. (In contrast, a digital photograph breaks down when excessively enlarged.) In addition to working commercially for clients ranging from Nokia to the musical group Red Hot Chili Peppers, Davis exploits the scalability of vector art in his ongoing experimental project *Once Upon a Forest*, a series of "art-making machines" that allow users—including Davis himself—to generate one-of-a-kind images. Davis writes custom algorithms that randomly select elements from a database of hand-drawn imagery, then automatically transform, compose, and connect them. According to Davis, "The end result is never static. I'll program the 'brushes,' the 'paints,' the 'strokes,' the 'rules,' and the 'boundaries.' However, it is the software that creates the compositions—the programs draw themselves. I am in a constant state of surprise and discovery, because the program may compile compositions that I would never have thought to execute, and would take hours to create manually."

Davis's process yields magical landscapes where organic and geometric components swirl together across surfaces packed with complexity, taking the form of screen-based graphics, digital prints, or customized wallpaper. Disaster looms over some of these candy-colored dream worlds: a massive storm bubbles above *0282 - Coast of Kanagawa*, while the shard-like city in *021 - Honey Hive* is dwarfed beneath ominous clouds of smoke or dust. These images pulse with danger and possibility, depicting an artificial world whose destiny has slipped beyond the designer's control.

1 021 - Honey Hive, program-generated vector graphic, 2005.
http://www.once-upon-a-forest.com
2 016 – Maxalot, program-generated vector graphic, 2004.
http://www.once-upon-a-forest.com

HERVÉ DESCOTTES/L'OBSER-VATOIRE INTERNATIONAL

NEW YORK, NEW YORK

1

2

Whether it is subtly lighting the spatial sequences of Frank Gehry's Disney Concert Hall or underscoring the poetic lines of a Steven Holl building, L'Observatoire International has earned a reputation as being among the most creative, imaginative, and inventive lighting design companies in the world. As founder and principal Hervé Descottes remarks, "We move...towards a different wavelength, something you can't always perceive visually, but somehow sense."[1]

Descottes understands that lighting can create an atmosphere that leaves a lasting impression on our visual memory. It can provoke and affect our sensations of identity, belonging, and balance. The moods provoked by light can also have political and social ramifications. Descottes observes, "You can feel very violated by certain types of light; others make you feel secure, like being in a cocoon....The best result is when you don't understand the lighting of a space, but you feel very good about it—almost as if you see it with your eyes closed, like tuning a vibration."

With his international team of lighting designers, architects, interior designers, engineers, and artists, Descottes "organizes space" for myriad projects, whether areas of a landscape, building exteriors or interiors, historic faêades, or architectural details. Since 2003, L'Observatoire International has created lighting for more than nineteen highly significant international projects in cities such as Beijing and Shanghai, China; Paris and Lille, France; Targu-Jiu, Romania; Gstaad, Switzerland; Ontario, Canada; Tokyo, Japan; and, in the United States, Las Vegas, Houston, and New York. Rather than replicate aspects of the cultural heritage of the cities in which it works, L'Observatoire offers an unexpected, innovative vision that integrates with the specific needs and characteristics of the project. After spending time looking at one of their projects, "We see what we always see, but in a completely different way."[2]

1 *Ultimate Lighting Design* (New York: teNeues Publishing Company, 2006), pp. 12–13.
2 Ibid.

1 Interior, Gare de Lille, Lille, France, 2003. **INTERIOR DESIGNER** Agence Patrick Jouin. **LIGHTING** Hervé Descottes/L'Observatoire International. **COMMISSIONED BY** Lille2004. **PHOTO** Jean-Pierre Duplan/LightMotiv

2 Exterior, Gare de Lille, Lille, France, 2003. **INTERIOR DESIGNER** Agence Patrick Jouin. **LIGHTING** Hervé Descottes/L'Observatoire International. **COMMISSIONED BY** Lille2004. **PHOTO** Mario Pignata Monti

3 Walt Disney Concert Hall, Los Angeles, CA, 2003. **ARCHITECT** Frank O. Gehry & Associates. **LIGHTING** Hervé Descottes/L'Observatoire International. **COMMISSIONED BY** Los Angeles Philharmonic Association. **PHOTO** Roland Halbe

3

NIELS DIFFRIENT
RIDGEFIELD, CONNECTICUT

1

How do you design a chair that is a "verifiable performer, visually compelling," and a product in which anyone of any size can be comfortable? Niels Diffrient has accomplished his lifelong goal with the Liberty chair. Since his years as an associate and partner at Henry Dreyfuss Associates, beginning in 1955, Diffrient has been an engineer for the human body—studying and documenting how it responds and adapts to particular activities, from reading and typing to stretching and relaxing. The data he collected while at Dreyfuss were used for the pivotal series *Humanscale* (three volumes: 1,2,3; 4,5,6; and 7,8,9), published in 1974 and 1981, archetypal manuals for anyone interested or involved in the design profession. Containing specific guidelines for furniture—the chair was featured in the first issue—*Humanscale* carefully documented and dissected the variable functions and requirements of furniture design.

The Liberty chair, designed for Humanscale, a leading manufacturer of ergonomic products, is in many ways a culmination of this research. The revolutionary counter-balance system automatically senses the weight of the sitter and adjusts the recline tension accordingly. No controls are necessary, and there are no distracting and inessential levers and knobs that require an instruction manual to operate.

Diffrient had initially avoided designing a mesh chair due to the inherent difficulties in forming the compound curvatures needed for good back support; most mesh chairs need auxiliary lumbar devices to provide the missing support. Diffrient rectified this by assembling three textile panels on a contoured support frame—the same way textiles are cut to fit the body in clothing. Since a non-stretch textile is used, contours do not deform under load, and displace appropriately to accommodate users of various sizes. Working closely with Diffrient, Elizabeth Whelan created a variety of high-performance mesh designs to answer the required specifications of translucency, breathability, and a uniquely attractive appearance.

Many architects and designers have taken up the challenge to design the perfect task or work chair, and although they may have visual appeal, most of the resulting chairs are only somewhat comfortable, and complicated to use. But comfort is Diffrient's first priority, with aesthetics an integral consideration at every step. As he explains, "My work since 1981 has been an attempt to identify and solve real problems with refinement and elegance. I have chosen furniture, seating in particular, for this effort because it has a history of design and refinement on which to build, and it is in widespread use, yet not of great technical complexity so that the entire design can be within my control."

1 Liberty ergonomic task chair, 2004. **DESIGNER** Niels Diffrient. **TEXTILE DESIGNER**
Elizabeth Whelan Design. **PRODUCTION DEVELOPMENT** Tom Latone. **COMPUTER**
DEVELOPMENT Mark McKenna. **MANUFACTURER** Humanscale Corporation.
Dic-cast aluminum and injection molded plastic; various textile mesh designs
of polyester, nylon, urethane, metallic-plated yarn; various coordinated textiles,
leather (seat upholstery). **PHOTO** Humanscale
2 Studies for Liberty chair. **DESIGNER** Niels Diffrient. **PHOTOS** Niels Diffrient and
Sally Anderson Bruce

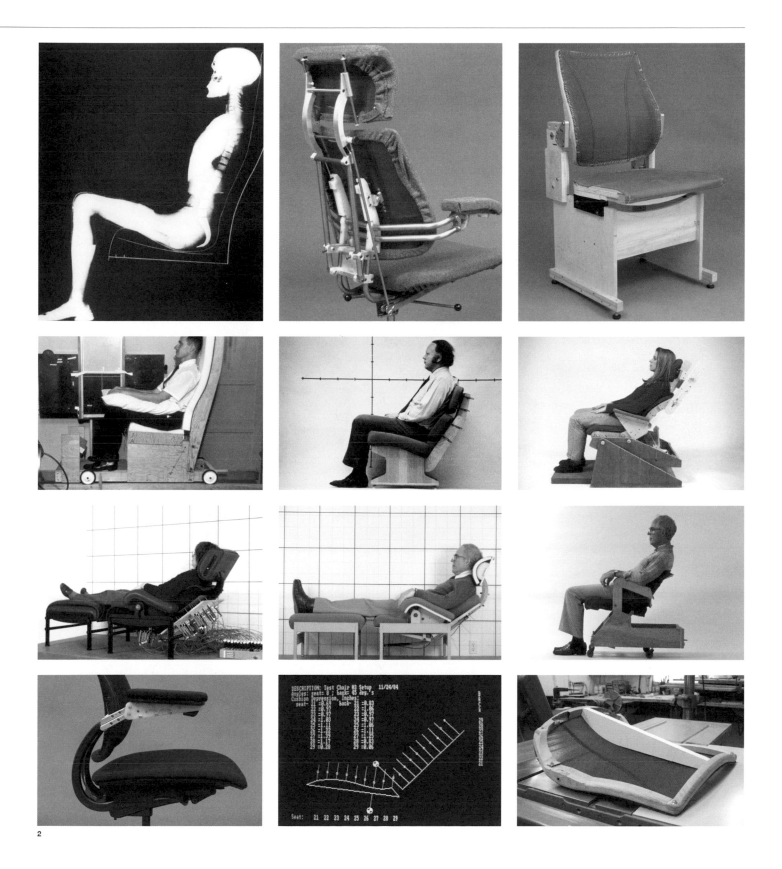

2

CHRISTOPHER DOUGLAS

MATERIAL FURNITURE
PORTLAND, OREGON

1

2

Users often become designers. Who else is a better judge of whether something functions optimally than the person who has intimate knowledge of its workings? Christopher Douglas is a self-taught designer whose former career in advertising and nomadic lifestyle contributed to his clever Knock-Down/Drag-Out (KDDO) line of collapsible furniture.

KDDO was conceived out of necessity, as Douglas moved from one cramped apartment to another and recognized the need for furniture that was easily stowable yet improved upon the plain-Jane card table and folding chair. The line includes a dining table, bench, Autopilot Station (i.e., desk), chair, end table, bed, Flipper Screen, and coffee table—enough to furnish (and dismantle) an entire apartment in under thirty minutes. Made out of three-quarter-inch-thick Europly, which has a sustainably harvested wood core and is available in an assortment of stains, most of the furniture is assembled by simply slotting the pieces together and locking them in place with hidden fasteners. The Flipper Screen has fasteners as well as heavy-duty magnets on the edge of the disks and inside the rim so that they maintain a closed position. The screen is also available in vertically laminated bamboo ply, another sustainable building material.

Douglas has taken inspiration from mid-century artists and designers like Isamu Noguchi, Charles and Ray Eames, Alvar Aalto, and Jean Prouvé, who offered eloquent and economical solutions to seating, dining, and comfortable living. Simple materials, fluid forms, and clean lines characterize Douglas's work, and KDDO fulfills a niche in a market flooded with ideas and creative thinkers. One can only imagine the prefab suburb of the future—one that is filled with Knock-Down/Drag-Out furniture inside Charlie Lazor's Flat-Pak House.

1 Knock-Down/Drag-Out Chair, 2004. Europly and maple stain. **PHOTO** Ken Anderson
2 Autopilot Workstation, 2004. Europly, maple stain, laminate surface. **PHOTO** Ken Anderson
3 Knock-Down/Drag-Out Table, 2003. Europly and maple stain. **PHOTO** Ken Anderson

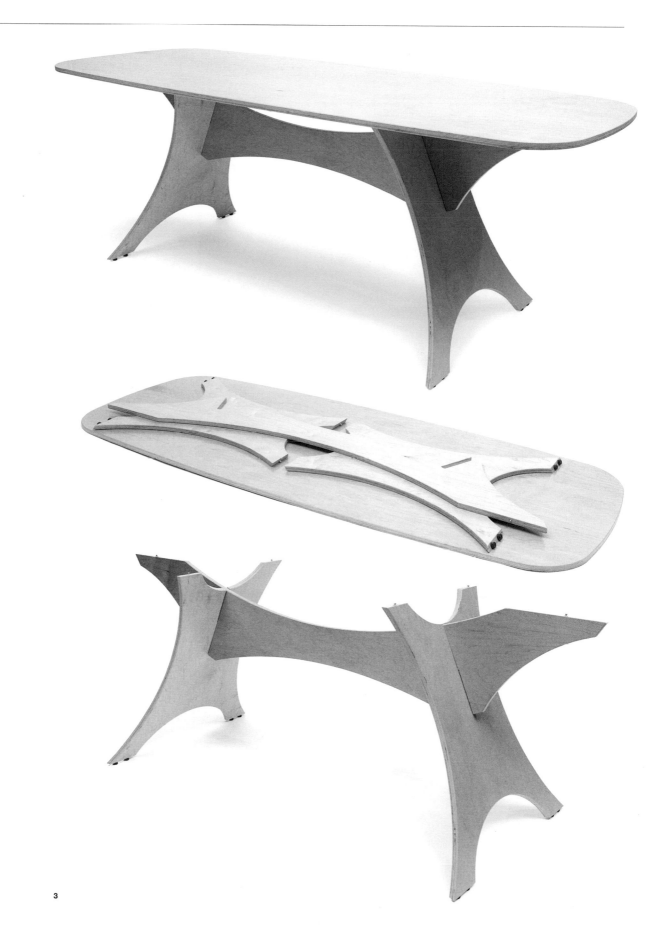

ELECTROLAND
CAMERON MCNALL AND DAMON SEELEY
LOS ANGELES, CALIFORNIA

Hailing from Los Angeles, Electroland creates interactive environments which use layers of technology to intelligently register the movement of pedestrians through public space. Walkways, entries, and faêades come alive in response to simple human actions. Founded by architect Cameron McNall and interaction designer Damon Seeley, Electroland celebrates the living, human use of public space while emphasizing the fact that everywhere we go, buildings are watching us.

Enteractive, a project in Los Angeles, produces a range of effects as visitors enter an apartment building. LED light tiles embedded in the floor of the entrance encircle visitors and follow their movements. At the same time, visitors' actions in the lobby trigger a light display across the façade, which is played back instantaneously on video monitors inside the lobby and entry areas. The combined effect is at once entertaining and uncanny, as visitors become the unwitting choreographers of an impromptu multimedia performance.

In New York City, Target Corporation commissioned Electroland to create "a branded interactive experience" in a space adjacent to the newly reopened Rockefeller Center observation decks. The ceiling and walls of the Target Interactive Breezeway are embedded with individual LED pixels and white LED backlights which trace visitors' paths and gestures, with colorful results. Target's bullseye logo is represented as light fixtures integrated throughout the glowing surfaces of the space.

In a project proposed for the new Indianapolis Airport, Electroland has designed an installation for an interior bridge which not only reacts to the movement of pedestrians, but also supports its own independent life. Covering the ceiling are luminous dots whose behavior is not wholly predictable—they might light up over a single pedestrian or suggest visual connections among several people, or they might ignore the public altogether and, in Electroland's words, "race around with each other like squirrels in a tree."

For the *National Design Triennial*, Electroland is bringing its view of design and public life to an installation that comes alive as visitors walk through it. Such projects allow the public to at once manipulate the visual environment and expose the fact that urban spaces pulse with complex activities beyond our control.

1 Target Interactive Breezeway at Rockefeller Center, New York, NY, 2005.
 DESIGNERS Electroland. **JUNIOR DESIGNER/PROGRAMMER** Eitan Mendelowitz.
 CLIENT Target Corporation. **PHOTO** Electroland
2 Enteractive (11th and Flower), Los Angeles, CA, 2005. **DESIGNERS** Electroland.
 CLIENT Forest City. Digital rendering

EMECO
HANOVER, PENNSYLVANIA

Test load per chair:

1700 lbs.!

Only 2 aluminum lightweights can take on 5 heavyweights!

Emeco's amazing heat-treatment makes these aluminum chairs **tougher than steel!**

It's the perfect way to make the perfect chair:

Make it of workable aluminum, to form without distortion in the bends.

Then **heat treat** it to incredible strength, toughness, rigidity. So it can support nearly a ton — 1700 pounds — with less than ⅛-in. permanent distortion. So just **one** chair could support those wrestlers — **and a couple of their biggest friends!**

And anodize the surface into aluminum oxide, next to diamonds in hardness.

Result: the perfect chair (available in 7 models) . . . fantastically strong, corrosion-resistant, wipeable clean, light on its feet. **Far and away the lowest in cost,** when you measure service and length of life.

Send for a sample of aluminum "before" and "after". It supports our story as surely as it takes on the heavyweights.

7110-264-5339

**AVAILABLE AS GSA STOCK ITEM
FEDERAL STOCK NO. 7110-264-5339**

**EMECO
DIVISION**
Standard Furniture Company
Hanover, Pa. 17331

Telephone E. F. Quinn, Government Administrator — (717) 637-5951

1

Little and a lot has changed since the Electrical Machine and Equipment Company (Emeco) was founded in 1944 by Wilton Carlyle Dinges III, utilizing the skills of local German immigrant craftsmen to create an aluminum chair. A great American manufacturing story, Emeco has established a design and manufacturing partnership that is both homegrown and cosmopolitan. It still manufactures the classic aluminum 10-06 (ten-o-six) Navy chair, originally developed with Alcoa for use in Navy submarines and warships, but these chairs, along with several new lines, are now used worldwide in boutique restaurants, retail shops, corporate offices, and airports. They are a design workhorse when it comes to chairs—each chair has a lifespan of 150 years—and the success of the company has as much to do with maintaining an extraordinary standard in craftsmanship as recognizing the need for modernization and public outreach.

When Gregory Buchbinder bought Emeco from his father, Jay, in 1998, he transformed the company from a government contractor to servicing the architect and design community. In 1999, he began working with renowned designer Philippe Starck to develop a full line of products based on a redesign and updating of the 10-06 chair. This has led to other collaborations, including a 2005 version of Emeco's 1951 hospital chair by Adrian van Hooydonk, Frank Gehry's Superlight, and, most recently, Sir Norman Foster's 20-06. For Gehry's Superlight chair, inspired by the extreme lightness of Italian designer Gio Ponti's 1952 Superleggera chair, a fine sheet of aluminum is draped over and joined to an open tubular frame, making a chair that is comfortable, lightweight, and strong. Weighing in at 6.5 pounds, the chair's shell and frame are easily snapped together by clear plastic clips, allowing each to flex independently and move with the sitter. Available with an industrial felt pad or in brushed/anodized aluminum, the chair is also stackable when disassembled.

The Superlight utilizes much of the same seventy-seven-step process that Emeco has been known for since its founding. With the 10-06 chair, it begins with twelve different aluminum sections welded together. After each step, the chair is ground to smooth out the welds and create a seamless look that has led people to believe it is cast in a mold. To strengthen it, the chair is then heat-treated, cooled off, and heated again in a proprietary process which causes its molecules to realign in a stronger formation, ultimately making the chair three times stronger than steel.

1 "Emeco: Test Load Per Chair: 1700 lbs.!" U.S. Government sales, 1947. © Emeco MMVI
2 Superlight chair, 2003–04. **DESIGNER** Frank Gehry. Aluminum, wool felt. **PHOTO** Mikio Sekita
3 1951 chair, 2005. **DESIGNER** Adrian van Hooydonk of BMW Group Designworks USA. Aluminum, ABS plastic. **PHOTO** Mikio Sekita
4 20-06 chair. **DESIGNER** Sir Norman Foster. Aluminum. **PHOTO** Nigel Young

2

2

3

4

FIELD OPERATIONS

JAMES CORNER
NEW YORK, NEW YORK

1

Since its founding in 1998, Field Operations has shaped a hybrid practice that, much like the projects it pursues, integrates landscape, ecology, art, architecture, economic development, and city life. The studio develops a diverse network of creative affiliations to bring unique resources and expertise to each project. Field Operations embraces design challenges at many different levels and scales, ranging from intimate garden designs to the reinvention of vast tracts of post-industrial land.

The studio's master plan for the Fresh Kills site in Staten Island, New York, is to revive a landscape of decay and detritus, turning the enormous landfill into a "lifescape" comprising 890 hectares of public parkland. The ambitious, complex project is phased over thirty years, with new park territory scheduled to open every five years during this period.

Together with architects Diller Scofidio + Renfro, Field Operations will transform Manhattan's abandoned High Line from an abandoned industrial relic into an elevated pathless landscape that will preserve its original character while creating a new zone of nature and urban activity for the city.

The master plan for the University of Puerto Rico Botanical Garden offered Field Operations the opportunity to rethink the botanical garden as a cultural type relevant for the twenty-first century. The design solution combines the garden—which traditionally opens a window into other cultures through diverse collections of exotic plants—with contemporary constructs of ecology and urbanism to give it a meaningful new identity for the city of San Juan. Since the Botanical Garden is located along the protected preserve of the city's Ecological Corridor, it has the potential to become an important new center for both leisure and research activities. Field Operations developed a hybrid graft of three organizational systems to govern the formal and material fabric of the entire site: The Botanical Forest activates the larger corridor by linking streams, open spaces, and ecological systems to create a vast, self-sustaining ecosystem. The Botanical Park maximizes the aesthetic and formal properties of plants to shape spaces and provide settings for events. Lastly, the Botanical System intensifies the urban edges of the site and embeds pedestrian and vehicular circulation alongside horticultural and nursery production and research. The three systems work together to provide a new kind of social space that places nature, education, and recreation in an exotic vegetal environment. Across the range of its projects, Field Operations has recast landscape architecture as an active, cultural practice operating in an expanded field.

1 The High Line [in collaboration with Diller Scofidio + Renfro Architects], Slow Stair and Vegetal Balcony, Gansevoort Street entry looking west, New York, NY, 2004–06. RENDERING by Field Operations
The High Line [in collaboration with Diller Scofidio + Renfro Architects], Grasslands and Planking System, Little West 12th Street to West 13th Street looking north, New York, NY, 2004–06. RENDERING by Field Operations
The High Line [in collaboration with Diller Scofidio + Renfro Architects], Overall Axonometric Drawing, preliminary design of Gansevoort Street to West 15th Street, New York, NY, 2004–06. RENDERING by Field Operations
2 Fresh Kills Master Plan, phasing timeline and photographs, Staten Island, NY, 2004–07. RENDERING by Field Operations

3 University of Puerto Rico Botanical Garden, site view showing light rail tracks and new fence, San Juan, PR, 2003–06. CLIENT University of Puerto Rico, Antonio Garcia Padilla, President. DESIGN TEAM Field Operations and Toro Ferrer Architectos: James Corner, Karen Tamir, Sierra Bainbridge, Jayyun Jung, Jean-Pierre Castillas, Justine Heilner, Lara Shihab-Eldin, Xun Li, José Javier Toro, Julián Manriquez, Applied Ecological Services, Stan Allen Architect, Gabriel Berriz and Associates. RENDERING by Field Operations
University of Puerto Rico Botanical Garden, Rio Piedras Recreation Terraces, San Juan, PR, 2003–06. RENDERING by Field Operations
University of Puerto Rico Botanical Garden, Cupey Plaza, San Juan, PR, 2003–06. RENDERING by Field Operations

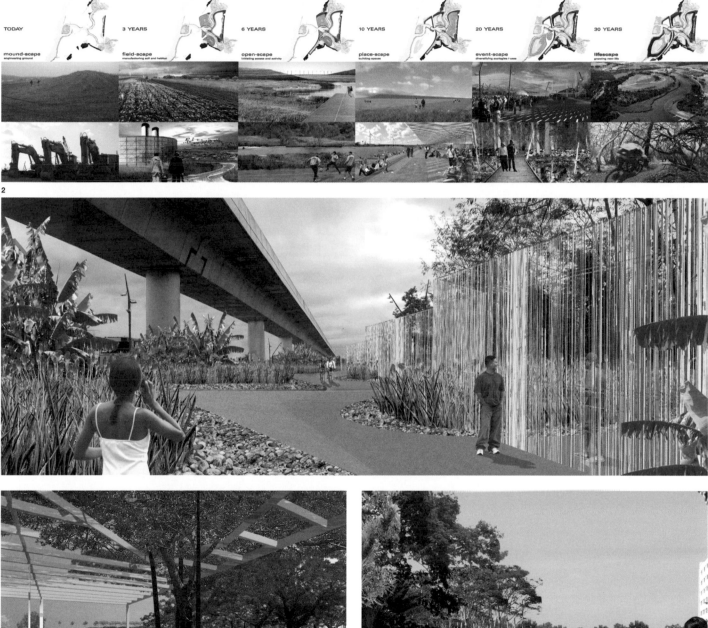

2

3

JUDY GEIB PLUS ALPHA
BROOKLYN, NEW YORK

1

2

Judy Geib is one of a new breed of independent jewelry designers who offer an idea of an exquisite jewel very different from the one presented by established houses and luxury brands. A graphic designer who also studied fine arts, Geib decided to turn her interest in making jewelry into a career in 2001.

With no formal training in jewelry design, Geib works intuitively and thinks that "not having learned what you're supposed to do" with precious stones and metals allows her the freedom to concoct her own methods of expression. Her art and graphic-design background is evident in the way she looks at stones for their color and in the intricate patterns she translates into delicate filigree compositions for bracelets, necklaces, and hair ornaments.

Geib's love of craft permeates all of her work. Her jewelry is handmade, and she insists that parures—matching sets of jewels—be displayed on the custom-fitted, crocheted wool boxes she provides to retailers. She gives each collection a whimsical name like "Especialidades" or "Xtravagant Bijoux," and presents the pieces in small handbound catalogues that recall historic specimen books of birds or wildflowers. There is a rustic charm to the pieces Geib crafts from rare gems. None of the forms are perfect; nor are the stones too polished or pristine. Gold is shaped into chunky squares and rectangles. Emeralds are clustered in settings that are rough and burnished. The hammered gold of the filigree pieces is uneven, and the forms are at times slightly off-kilter.

Geib's Sea Sounds Sea Shell bags, with their dense clusters of shells that jingle when you walk, have an exotic, almost baroque sensibility, but are, in fact, a meditative exercise in handcrafting. A hole is drilled into each shell so that it can be crocheted into the body of the bag. Geib originally made these bags for fun, but they soon became coveted by her friends, and she is now contemplating posting a do-it-yourself instruction manual on her Web site. The seemingly nonchalant mix of what Geib calls "the luxe and the brut," craft and refinement, is at the heart of her work.

1 Aureole pins, 2004. 18-carat gold. **PHOTO** Dirk Vandenberk
2 Amazon emerald and peridot parure on display case, 2006. Emeralds, peridots,
  18- and 24-carat gold and silver; wool, aluminum, cotton (box). **PHOTO** Dirk
  Vandenberk
3 Erewhon filigree parure in display case (necklace, bracelet, 3 pair earrings), 2003.
  18-carat gold; wool, aluminum, cotton (box). **PHOTO** Dirk Vandenberk
4 Sea Sounds seashell bags, 2003. *Netirina parallelina*, *Musculum lacustre*,
  Argystoma trachea, cotton. **PHOTO** Dirk Vandenberk

3

4

RON GILAD
DESIGNFENZIDER
NEW YORK, NEW YORK

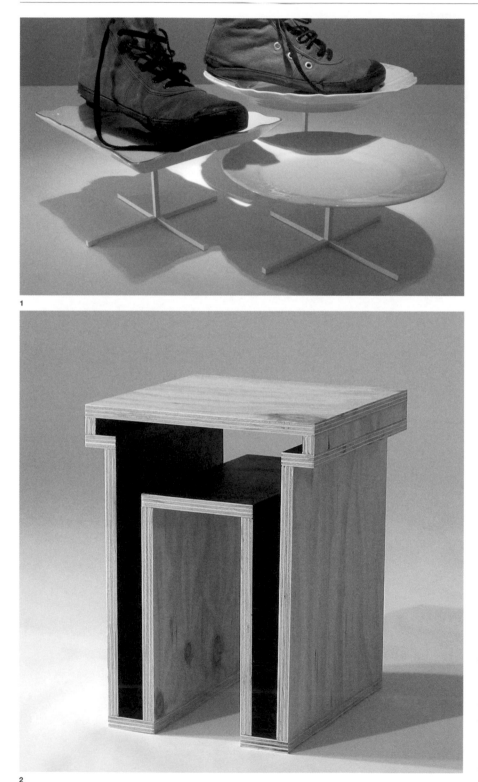

1

2

Ron Gilad's functional design objects
are conversation pieces that talk to
each other. From porcelain vases a mere
2 1/2" high to a chandelier of adjustable
task lamps, these objects share a sophisticated wit, humor, elegance, and precision that make Gilad's creations so
distinctive.

Gilad is fascinated with deconstruct-
ing the function of an object. Often it
begins with a found object that he reinterprets and ultimately transforms into
something at once familiar and jarring.
Porcelain Platters are put on a pedestal,
physically and figuratively. Water bottles,
coffee cups, and champagne glasses
become pedestals as well as vessels for
his Vase Maker and Candlestick Maker.
In isolation, the porcelain tops are use-
less; but by conjoining with a bottom
half or its "missing limb," the user can
create a unique flower- or candleholder
that defies implications of mass production. Similarly, each of Gilad's Run Over
By Car (R.O.B.C.) vases is one of a kind,
since the car's impact always leaves
slightly different curves and dimples.
As part of his recent "design through
destruction" series, R.O.B.C. explores
the results of losing control and allows
fate to rule the object's final form.

A graduate of the industrial design
department at the renowned Bezalel
Academy of Art and Design in Jerusa-
lem, Israel, Gilad formed Designfenzider
with Lior Haramaty in 2001, soon after
Gilad arrived in New York. There is a
conceptual edge to Gilad's designs in
that the object is not always an end in
itself, but sometimes cause for analysis
and reflection. His studies with porcelain
tableware, for example, are almost completely enveloped by a colored balloon,
making it functionless as a drinking
vessel but potentially a point of depar-
ture for an examination of form, material,
and color. In Dear Ingo, Gilad takes the
individual task lamp and makes it a more
communal chandelier. Both an ode to the
German lighting designer Ingo Maurer
and a contemporary update of Serge
Mouille's ceiling lamps of the 1950s, it is
like a spider crawling across the ceiling.
It can curl up into a ball or spread its
legs, allowing those underneath to be
caught in its web of light.

1 Porcelain platters, 2005. Porcelain, painted metal, silicon legs. **PHOTO** Designfenzider Studio
2 *A Void* stool, 2003. AC plywood, lacquer. **PHOTO** Designfenzider Studio
3 *Dear Ingo* chandelier, 2003. **MANFAUCTURER** Moooi. 16 task lamps. **PHOTO** Maarten van Houten
4 Candlestick Maker, 2005. **DESIGNERS** Ron Gilad, Matthew Bradshaw. Porcelain. **PHOTO** Designfenzider Studio
5 *Run Over By Car* vases, 2003. Painted metal. **PHOTO** Designfenzider Studio

3

4

5

MARSHA GINSBERG
NEW YORK, NEW YORK

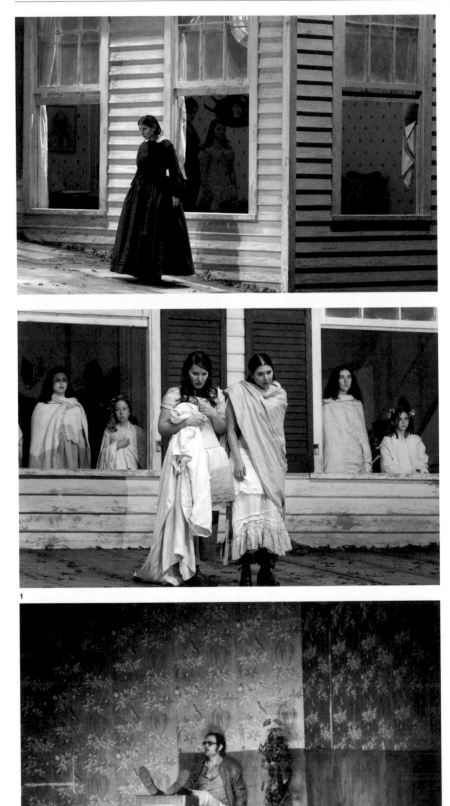

1

2

Familiar settings turn strange in Marsha Ginsberg's stage designs. A New England house, a Berlin apartment, and a maze of low-rent Brooklyn offices provide incongruous locales for works of opera and staged song. Disheveled spaces show signs of human use: peeling wallpaper, chipped paint, water-stained plaster, an unmade bed.

Ginsberg studied art at New York's Cooper Union for the Advancement of Science and Art and then the Whitney Museum Independent Study Program in the early 1980s, where she became fascinated with the media-based work of Barbara Kruger, Martha Rosler, and Hans Haacke. This intellectual background shaped Ginsberg's thinking as she pursued an MFA in theater design at New York University. Over the past five years, she has emerged as a distinctive voice in the vanguard of international theater. Ginsberg's set designs build compressed and layered spaces that close in with claustrophobic intensity on the human drama they support.

Imeneo, directed by Christopher Alden, transports George Frideric Handel's Baroque family drama onto the frigid soil of mid-nineteenth-century America. The opera unfolds on the roof of a white, somewhat battered New England house; additional action is glimpsed through its dirty windows (including a father sniffing his daughters' discarded petticoats). In Act III, the dining room is excised from the interior to sit on top of the r oof. As Ginsberg explains, "The absent fourth wall is a long-standing convention in stage design. I like to suggest a physical process of cutting away that fourth wall. The floor is cut to reveal the joists; the walls show layers of plaster and lathe."

The set for *In Mahler's Shadow*, a two-part enactment of three song cycles by Gustav Mahler, consists of a grim, windowless corner whose shabby furnishings and precisely curated hardware details such as wall plugs and light switches recreate an apartment in post-reunification Berlin. Each cycle is sung by a different occupant of the apartment in a different slice of time. For Georges Bizet's *Carmen*—set in present-day Brooklyn—Ginsberg designed a suite of generic offices, built on a turntable. Don Jose, cast as a security guard, observes his beloved Carmen from a bank of video monitors that allows the audience to participate in his voyeuristic obsessions and to peer into hidden parts of the set.

1 *Imeneo,* Glimmerglass Opera, Cooperstown, NY, 2004. Co-production with New York City Opera. **SET DESIGN** Marsha Ginsberg. **DIRECTOR** Christopher Alden. **COSTUMES** Doey Luethi. **LIGHTS** Adam Silverman. **PHOTO** George Mott

2 *Wayfarer's Song and Fourth Symphony: In Mahler's Shadow,* Ethical Culture Society, New York, NY, 2003. EOS Orchestra, Jonathon Sheffer, Conductor/ Artistic Director. **SET AND COSTUME DESIGN** Marsha Ginsberg. **DIRECTOR** Christopher Alden. **PHOTO** George Mott

3 *Carmen,* National Theater, Mannheim, Germany, 2003. **SET DESIGN** Marsha Ginsberg. **DIRECTOR** Christopher Alden. **COSTUMES** Doey Luethi. **PHOTO** Hans Jorg Michel

4 *Das Lied von der Erde: In Mahler's Shadow,* Ethical Culture Society, New York, NY, 2003. EOS Orchestra, Jonathon Sheffer, Conductor/Artistic Director. **SET AND COSTUME DESIGN** Marsha Ginsberg. **DIRECTOR** Christopher Alden. **PHOTO** Marsha Ginsberg

3

4

GOOGLE
MOUNTAIN VIEW, CALIFORNIA

1

2

3

Google has transformed the way over 400 million global users access information. Since 2003, the Google Web site has emerged as the easiest and most comprehensible, successful, and fast means to look for information. The company's mission, to organize the world's information and make it universally usable, is so successful that the word "google" is listed in dictionaries as a verb meaning to search for and find information on the World Wide Web. Google users can search data, facts, figures, images, locations, and more in over 140 languages around the world. And the company's future aspirations are vast: Google strives to be the world's largest data archive, driven entirely by computers.

Google's success rests in part on its redesign of the work environment. It fosters creativity by hiring "the most intelligent people out there" and providing them with the smartest and best tools. In 2005, the company hired an estimated eight new staff members per day. The employees, who come from varied backgrounds, including sociology, technology, engineering, mathematics, and cognitive psychology, are hired into the company rather than for any specific jobs. Most work is done in teams averaging three people, so there is room for a great deal of individual input. Google also has a fairly radical idea of utilizing staff time: every week, each employee has one day, or twenty percent of his or her week, free to work on any idea or subject.

The design of the company campus, affectionately termed the "Googleplex," reflects this investment in its employees. It is configured to assist in generating creative thinking and in making the employees feel differently about their work days. Contrary to the typical professional environment, at Google, everyone is surrounded by toys, sports, and games, with plentiful free and healthy gourmet food, massages, laundry, and dry cleaning. Many bring their dogs and children to the office; and people move among the buildings informally on Razor scooters.

The company's informal motto, "Don't be evil," reflects a moral imperative derived from the founders' intention to treat their employees, users, and company ethically. From its inception, Google went against the prevalent trend toward Flash and visual complexity in designing its Web site. Its logo and homepage remain remarkably simple, focusing on providing the most accurate and efficient way to give the viewers access to information. Proprietary software enables the millions of results from any user's search to be instantaneously sorted so that the sites containing the most comprehensive information on the subject appear at the top. Beyond researching general information, Google's simple interface provides immediate answers to specific queries on local and global weather, currency calculations, telephone and address information, definitions, quotations, comparison shopping, video, UPS/Fedex/USPS package tracking, airline flights, images, translations, books, quotations, music—just about anything that is recast as information and can be searched.

Google's new products appear at a remarkable rate, and are rapidly altering traditional economies. With Google News, computer algorithms track thousands of news sites so users can read news from varied perspectives. In 2003, Google's AdSense program generated revenue for the company by providing advertisers with highly targeted placement adjacent to relevant content at a relatively low price. This was followed by AdWords, a real-time "auction" in which hundreds of thousands of ads are compared to a user's search query, with the most profitable ad displayed. AdWords has quickly become the second-largest market ever created after the New York Stock Exchange, and it accounted for more than $6 billion in revenue in 2005. Prior to GoogleMaps and GoogleEarth, only one to two percent of the world's population had ever seen satellite imagery. Now mapping is easily available and highly interactive, with users able to drag, drop, and zoom in on any part of the map. Not only can you focus on the house where you were born, you can also see the new owner's lawn furniture.

In 2006, Google plans to spend more than $500 million on research and development, with teams working on virtually every kind of long-term technology. No one part of the Google organization is specifically focused on design; instead, the entire company focuses on users' needs. However, in its culture, employees, manner of working, Web site, and means of providing the world with instant information, Google has redesigned the way we work, learn, and think.

1 Google homepage, september 1999. Courtesy of Google.
2 Google Geodisplay. Original 2-D version by Greg Rae, Laurence Gonsalves, Lucas Pereira, and Amit Patel; 3-D version by Amit Patel. Courtesy of Google.
3 Google "Albert Einstein" doodle, March 2003. By Dennis Hwang. Courtesy of Google.
4 Google Maps, screenshot of Cable Car Museum, San Francisco, CA, February 2005. By Lars Rasmussen, Jens Rasmussen, Bret Taylor, Jim Norris, Stephen Ma, and Noel Gordon. Courtesy of Google.
5 Google Earth, June 2005. By Brian McLendon, Michael Jones, Chikai Ohazama, Mark Aubin, John Hanke, and Phil Keslin. Courtesy of Google.

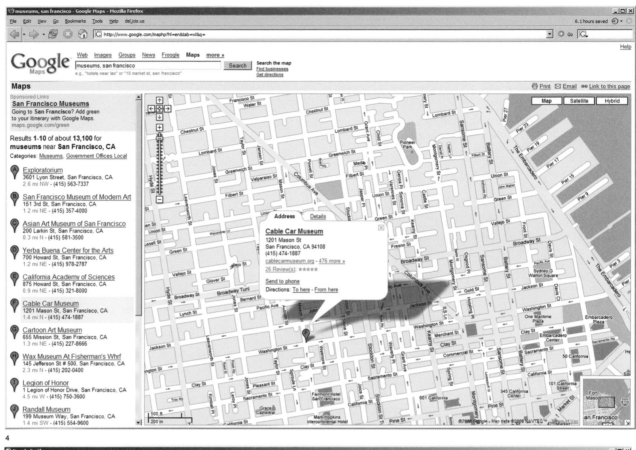

4

5

HAN FENG
NEW YORK, NEW YORK

1

From a black cashmere coat that opens to reveal a red silk floral lining to a coiled glass vase that appears to have just been removed from the furnace, Han Feng's works identify her as a twenty-first-century lifestyle designer. She puts her unique stamp on everything she designs, including fashion, product design, stage costumes, place settings, installations, and jewelry. Her aim is to be one of China's first global lifestyle brands.

Born in Nanjing, China, in 1962, Han Feng launched her first ready-to-wear collection for women and men in New York in 1993. Her fashion designs are characterized by their materials: beautifully colored silks, fine wools, and diaphanous fabrics that are minimally styled, much like her furniture. As she notes, "Today, it is all about fusion…I play with the materials…as I am trying to make something very simple."

Han Feng designs everything: richly savory meals made from a fusion of fresh ingredients, the place settings in which they are served, even the furniture and environment in which the dining takes place. In 2003, Han Feng designed a line of domestic products, including translucent, porcelain, cantaloupe-inspired melon bowls. The smoothness of the bowls' interiors contrasts sharply with their rough surface "rinds."

In 2004, noted director Anthony Minghella asked Han Feng to design the costumes for his original staging of Giacomo Puccini's opera *Madama Butterfly*, which premiered to great acclaim at the English National Opera on November 5, 2005. Han Feng's creations are an astonishing mix of fine detailing, unexpected patterns, and rich materials. They reflect a unique vision, hinting at traditional Japanese fashions, now updated for the twenty-first century. International critics raved about the "coloristic riot" of her "ravishing costumes." *Madama Butterfly*, with Han Feng's costumes, opened the Fall 2006 season of New York's Metropolitan Opera.

1 Porcelain cantaloupe bowl, 2005. Porcelain. **MANUFACTURER** Stacy Cushman, Brooklyn, NY. **PHOTO** Udom Surangsophon
2 Costumes from *Madama Butterfly,* 2005. Produced by English National Opera, Lithuanian National Opera, and New York Metropolitan Opera. Manufactured by English National Opera and Han Feng Shanghai. **PHOTO** Johan Pearsson

HANSON ROBOTICS, INC.

DAVID HANSON
DALLAS, TEXAS

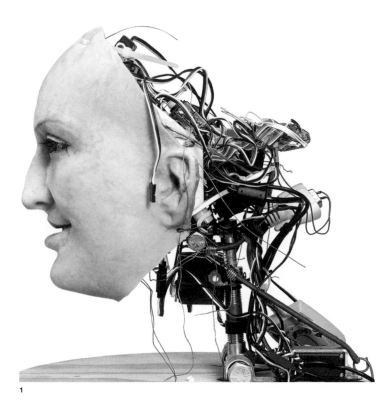

1

David Hanson's work revolves around the question "What does it mean to be human?" Although robots' capabilities currently remain far behind those in science fiction, Hanson's work demonstrates that the day of convincingly sociable robots displaying aspects of human intelligence and appearance is not far away. Combining innovations in art, science, and technology, Hanson's robots already mimic human behavior, expressions, and appearance to an unprecedented degree.

In 2003, Hanson founded Hanson Robotics after a number of years working on animatronics, or autonomous robot-like figures, for Disneyland Amusement Park. Realizing that to emulate human skin he needed a material that compresses easily, stretches with little force, and is very strong and durable, Hanson designed a patent-pending polymer "skin" called Frubber™, which moves the way real skin moves on a human face. Hanson stretched the Frubber over a frame of facial hardware he designed, with twenty to forty servomotors acting as artificial muscles underneath. The platinum-cured silicone Frubber allows the resulting face to react in one-eighth of a second with a full range of realistic and subtle expressions. Remarkably, the artificial muscles and skin run for hours on rechargeable AA batteries.

In 2005, collaborating with the artificial intelligence group of the FedEx Institute of Technology, the Automation & Robotics Institute at the University of Texas at Arlington, and the Philip K. Dick estate, Hanson created a life-size android figure of Philip K. Dick, the noted science-fiction writer whose works have been adapted into the motion pictures *Blade Runner*, *Total Recall*, and *Minority Report*. Dick often wrote about robots who thought they were human, and believed that compassionate artificial intelligence would eventually save the world. Hanson's robot not only mimics Dick's face, but his eyes contain tiny cameras that allow him to track and recognize people. Andrew Olney of the FedEx Institute of Technology added artificial intelligence and software integration to Hanson's hardware systems, electronics, and mechanisms, enabling Dick to carry on conversations with passersby. As Hanson observes, the robot "invents new ideas using a mathematical model of Dick's mind, extracted from feeding the software over 10,000 pages of his vast written texts."

Ultimately, Hanson hopes that other scientists will use robots, such as his latest replica of Albert Einstein, to test theories about how humans respond to social cues. Einstein is the first walking, talking robot with human expressions. His body was built by the Korean Advanced Institute of Science and Technology. Making both his software and robotics open-source and available to developers, Hanson believes that in the future, such "social" robots will help the autistic to learn, interpret, and respond to facial expressions, and be used in science labs and medical applications to help people with disorders that affect communication skills.

1 Vera, 3rd generation "Kbot," 2004. **DESIGNER** David Hanson. **MANUFACTURER** Hanson Robotics, Inc. **PUBLISHER** *Wired* magazine. Frubber, servos, camera eyes, AI software, electronics. **PHOTO** *Wired* magazine
2 Hubo Einstein Robot, 2005. **DESIGNERS** David Hanson, Kim Won Sup, Jun Ho Oh, Richard Bergs. **MANUFACTURER** Hanson Robotics Inc, KAIST. **COMMISSIONED BY** *KAIST*. **SPONSOR** UTA Automation and Robotics Research Institute. Frubber, facial robotics, biped walking robot, cameras, computer, AI software. **PHOTO** Hanson Robotics, Inc.

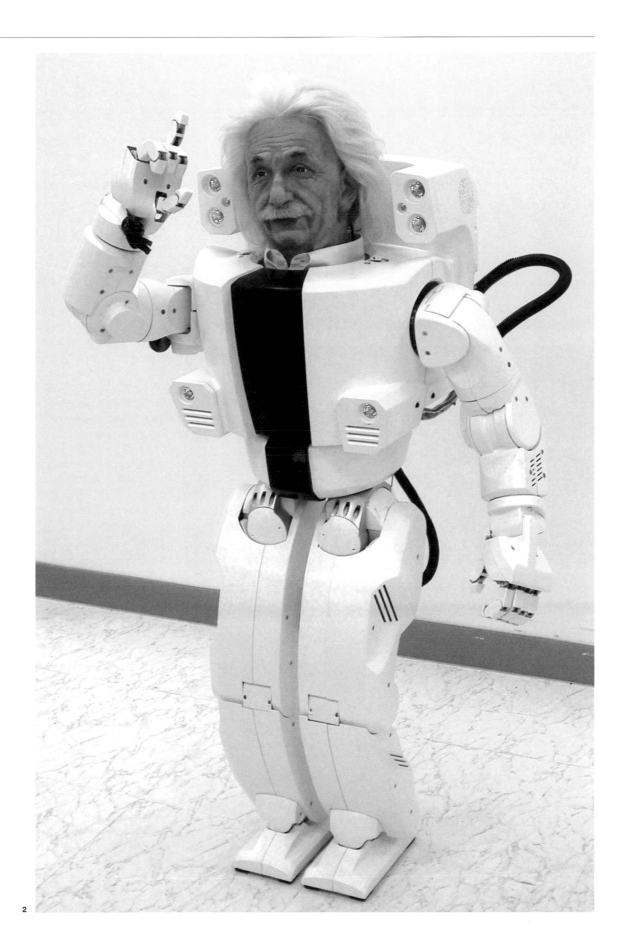

2

GRAHAM HAWKES/DEEP FLIGHT

SAN FRANCISCO, CALIFORNIA

1

2

Graham Hawkes is our twenty-first-century Jules Verne. However, rather than simply imagining future ocean travel, Hawkes has designed manned vehicles for underwater exploration. Since the first underwater craft was invented in the seventeenth century, traditional submersibles have operated like elevators, sinking to a certain depth and only then being able to move horizontally, with limited maneuverability. By contrast, Hawkes's *Deep Flight* winged submersibles represent as radical a leap in design engineering as that between the dirigible and the first fixed-wing aircraft. Hawkes's submersibles "fly" through the water, much like an airplane. For the first time, their pilots can operate and maneuver underwater at great depths while doing little potential harm to ocean life.

As Hawkes notes, water is the planet's true primary "atmosphere," but humans have first-person knowledge of only the surface skin that is lit by the sun. Scientists today believe that over fifty percent of the life forms existing in the sea's depths are completely unknown. Until now, underwater craft used by explorers, scientists, and filmmakers have invaded these pitch-dark depths with huge, slow machines and bright lights that scare away and potentially damage the eyes of creatures in this environment. Hawkes has designed *Deep Flight* with tiny lights along the wings and top to act as "bio-luminescence." This forces the user's eyes to adjust, rather than blinding the sea life. In addition, unlike traditional underwater vehicles, which are powered by fuels that pollute the surroundings—which affects sharks, for example, the way piercing horns may irritate a dog's ears—*Deep Flight* is powered by low-voltage batteries and quiet thrusters, causing much less disturbance to the surroundings. Hawkes hopes that, as a result, the deep-sea animals will gradually be curious and come toward the vehicles so they can be seen and studied. Heralding a new age of exploration, Hawkes notes that he wants to "engineer a meeting of the eyes—human, sea creatures, and camera—underwater."

With his wife and partner, Karen, Hawkes intends to continue developing his deep-sea winged submersibles at one-tenth the cost of other similar vehicles, making them more accessible to scientists and future "astronauts" of the ocean. Ultimately, as he observes, "I have a strong sense of design. Although I am initially drawn by the engineering, physics, and math, I have many levels of freedom to make these objects look beautiful, to please myself."

1 *Deep Flight I* winged submersible, 1997. **MANUFACTURER** Hawkes Ocean Technologies. Founding **SPONSOR** Autodesk, Inc. **PRODUCT SPONSORS** Ansys, Inc., Electronics Workbench, Hewlett Packard. **PHOTO** Hawkes Ocean Technologies

2 *Deep Flight I* winged submersible, 1996. **MANUFACTURER** Hawkes Ocean Technologies. Founding **SPONSOR** Autodesk, Inc. **PRODUCT SPONSORS** Ansys, Inc., Electronics Workbench, Hewlett Packard. **PHOTO** Amos Nachoum/Big Animals Photography

3 *Deep Flight 302-3* (Gen 3) winged submersible, 2006. **DESIGNER** Hawkes Ocean Technologies. **SPONSOR** Autodesk, Inc. **RENDERING** Jon Bell

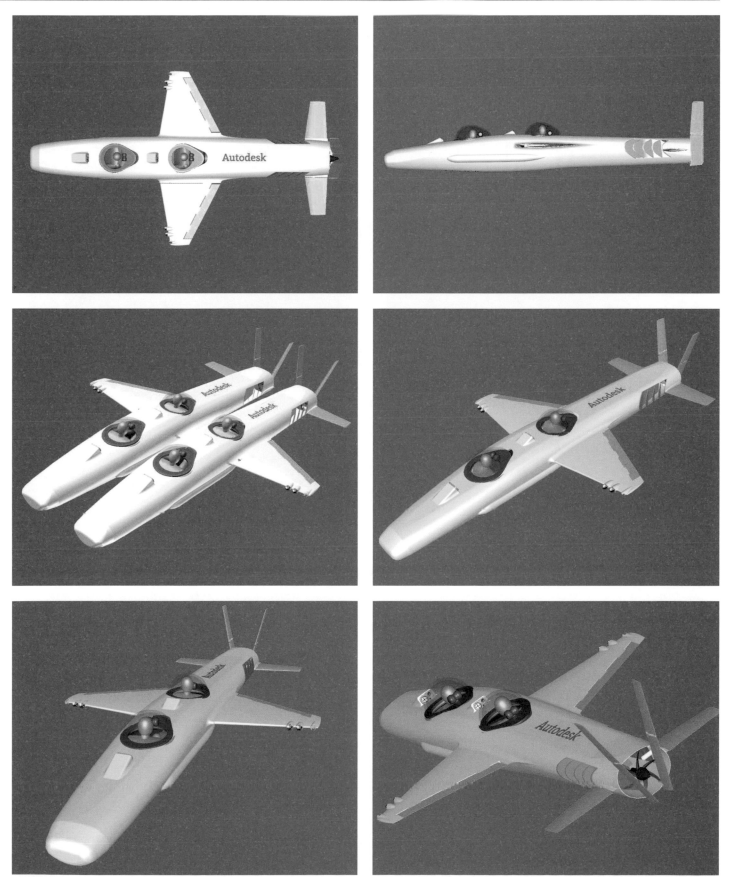

HERMAN MILLER, INC.
ZEELAND, MICHIGAN

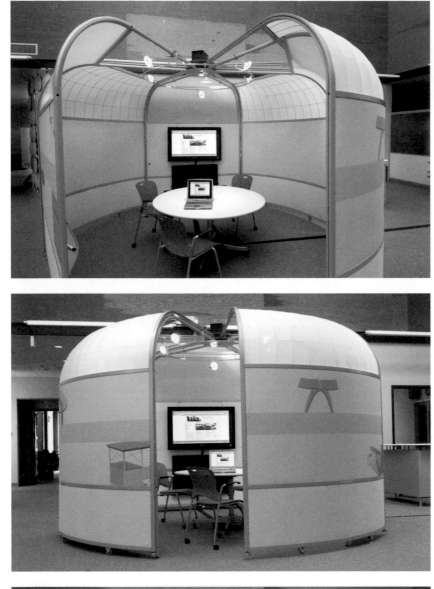

For over eighty years, Herman Miller, Inc., has designed and manufactured innovative furniture systems for work environments of all kinds. Today, the company's design and development team is rethinking the office in response to changes in how we work. In many industries, employees are increasingly unmoored from any fixed physical place, connected wirelessly to a world of mobile data and tools. The challenge for office planners is to create flexible, stimulating spaces that are an attractive destination for employees who can choose when and where they work. The dismal cubes satirized by Scott Adams's infamous Dilbert cartoon enforce a paradoxical mix of isolation and exposure, not unlike a modern prison cell: keep people in one place, and make sure they are always visible.

Herman Miller's New Office Landscape rethinks office planning within an economical open-floor plate. Borrowing ideas from New Urbanism, an urban design movement that burst onto the scene in the late 1980s and early 1990s, the New Office Landscape combines individual office spaces with more spacious shared areas—just as New Urbanist housing developments offer a greater density of homes along with public amenities such as parks, stores, and restaurants.

The Basket is a group-seating area with a woven wall that provides both privacy and permeability. The Rolling Tent feels as stable as a constructed conference room, yet as light and open as an informal community area. The rolling screens provide adjustable levels of privacy, while a fixed back wall allows integration of technologies. Unlike a traditional conference room, these systems are designed for spontaneous meetings, offering an inviting landing place for brief or extended conversations. Such works of "soft architecture" are envisioned within organic clusters of individual workspaces that break the grid of the old cubicle landscape.

Collaboration spawns creativity. Examples of people enjoying work in public and semi-public places are all around us. The design team at Herman Miller observes, "The kind of anonymity found in plain sight at Starbucks, the kind of variable stimulation found in libraries and public plazas—these are the new qualities to be fought for in work environments." As people become more connected, and thus more mobile, the office will increasingly become a place to meet, network, and share ideas—a social space.

1 Rolling Tent office furnishing system, 2005. **DESIGNERS** Ayse Birsel and Bibi Seck, Birsel+Seck. Aluminum and steel, PETG, MDF board, polyester fabric. **PHOTO** Jim Powell Photography
2 Basket office furnishing system, 2004. **DESIGNERS** David Ritch and Mark Saffell, 5D Studio. Wood, aluminum. **PHOTO** Jim Powell Photography

HOBERMAN ASSOCIATES, INC.

CHUCK HOBERMAN
NEW YORK, NEW YORK

1

2

Transformation, the changing of one form into another, is a fundamental process in the natural world. But rarely do we have the opportunity to encounter its technical and aesthetic applications in nature's counterpart, the mechanical domain. Chuck Hoberman, an inventor, artist, engineer, and designer, has dedicated over twenty years to transforming objects, including deployable or unfolding structures. From palm-size studies in paper and plastic to a seventy-two-foot-wide aluminum "theater curtain," structures Hoberman has created organize synchronous movements into a fluidly transforming whole.

When Hoberman was approached by Johnson Outdoors, a major tent manufacturer, the company had identified the need for large-scale tents that could be erected very quickly for military, emergency-response, and commercial use. Hoberman created the Rapidly Deployable Structure (RDS), an "instant shelter" that was 500 square feet, could fit in a small truck, and was capable of being set up by four people or fewer. In addition, the tent withstands winds of up to sixty-five miles per hour and snow loads of up to 4,000 pounds, and endures hundreds of sets and strikes. RDS can be set up in under three minutes, compared to other shelters that take up to eight minutes. Good ergonomic design enabled this increase in speed, as users are able to maintain a natural standing position during deployment. Special handles make final cable-tensioning and locking operations simple and easy to perform.

Johnson Outdoors pushed the innovations even further by developing new manufacturing techniques, allowing the use of advanced lightweight fabrics which operate under the harshest conditions and, for ultimate night camouflage, block all visible and infrared light from the tent. The fabric also acts as a tensioning element, which prevents distortion of the tent under high loads.

Through his years of exploration, Hoberman has pinpointed the critical parameters for the successful creation of transformative objects. The process of transformation itself must be complete and fully three-dimensional, smooth and continuous, reversible and repeatable. The explanation may be rooted in science and geometry, but the structure is a symbol of the elegant promise of technology.

1 Folding tent (U.S. Patent 4,981,732), 1993. Single sheet of corrugated polypropylene. **PHOTO** Hoberman Associates, Inc.

2 Pop-up lamp, 2003. Cast urethane, vellum, white LEDs. **PHOTO** Hoberman Associates, Inc.

3 Rapidly deployable structure, 2004–present. Developed by Hoberman Associates, Inc. and Johnson Outdoors, Inc. **MECHANICAL FRAME** Chuck Hoberman and Matt Davis. **FABRIC DESIGN** Joe Wiegnad and Trent Nelson. **STRUCTURAL ANALYSIS** Oliver Osterwind (Buro Happold). Aluminum and vinyl-impregnated polyester. **PHOTO AND RENDERINGS** Hoberman Associates, Inc.

3

HUNTER HOFFMAN
UNIVERSITY OF WASHINGTON
SEATTLE, WASHINGTON

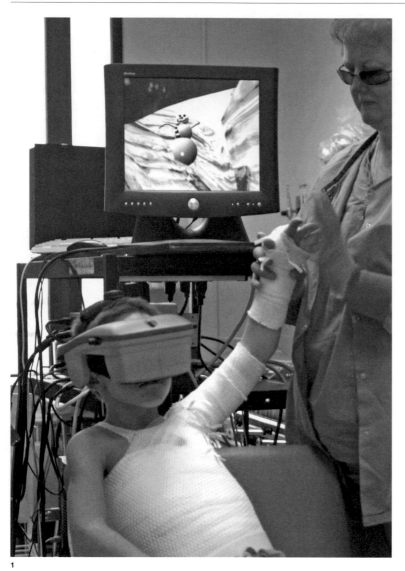

1

Imagine a design so powerful that viewing and interacting with it lower a person's pain perception by half. That is what Hunter Hoffman and his University of Washington colleagues have achieved with *SnowWorld*. Designed for use with severely wounded burn victims, *SnowWorld* is a three-dimensional virtual-reality "game."

Even with narcotic analgesic medication, burn victims can suffer excruciating pain during rehabilitation; and treatments may continue daily for weeks or months. The program lures the patient into a virtual environment. As Hoffman notes, "Pain requires conscious attention, so by taking the user's attention away from the pain...there is less attention available for the person to process the pain signals. The more the patient feels like he or she is in *SnowWorld*, the greater the pain reduction." Once inside, patients are suddenly floating through the air along a snow-covered, canyon-bordered river. They have a 360-degree view of this glacial world, where images of penguins, snowmen, igloos, woolly mammoths, and robots suddenly appear. By pushing a button, the user hits snowmen with snowballs or splashes objects into the icy river.

To study brain activity during its use, Hoffman designed virtual-reality helmets which provide the wide peripheral vision necessary for a fully immersive sensation. When they tested *SnowWorld*, Hoffman and his colleagues found 50-90% reduction in pain-related brain activity in all five pain regions of the brain. Hoffman and collaborator Dave Patterson from UW's Harborview Burn Center provide the software free to several national burn centers, which are also testing *SnowWorld's* pain control with burn victims.

Since receiving his Ph.D. there in 1992, Hoffman has worked at the University of Washington, which is internationally known for creating unconventional models of team-based research. In 2003, he became the Director of the University's Virtual Reality Research Center. His initial foray into VR therapy began with *SpiderWorld*, a program still used to desensitize people with arachnophobia. Following the World Trade Center attacks, Hunter and Manhattan therapist JoAnn Difede designed *WTC World*, a virtual post-traumatic stress disorder (PTSD) therapy program. Dr. Difede has used the program to successfully treat nine survivors of September 11th, five of whom had failed to respond to traditional therapy. Hunter has recently worked with colleagues to develop *IraqWorld* for U.S. military personnel suffering from post-traumatic stress disorder; and *BusWorld* to treat Israeli civilian survivors of terrorist attacks. Hoffman observes, "As the technology continues to advance, we can expect more remarkable applications using VR in the years to come."

1 *SnowWorld* virtual-reality pain distraction for severe burn therapy, 2006.
DESIGNER Hunter Hoffman, Ph.D. **CREATIVE WORLD-BUILDING** Ari Hollander. **VR GOGGLE SYSTEMS** Jeff Magula; optical lens system designed by Janet Crossman-Bosworth and Eric Seibel, University of Washington and Harborview Hospital. © Hunter Hoffman, U.W.
2 *SnowWorld,* 2006. Image by Ari Hollander. Programmed by Ari Hollander and Howard Rose. © Hunter Hoffman, U.W.
3 *SpiderWorld* virtual-reality exposure therapy for reducing arachnophobia, 2003.
DESIGNER Hunter Hoffman, Ph.D., in collaboration with Al Carlin and Azucena Garcia Palacios. Programmed by Ari Hollander and Howard Rose. © Mary Levin, U.W., with permission from Hunter Hoffman, U.W.

2

HOWTOONS

SAUL GRIFFITH, NICK DRAGOTTA, AND JOOST BONSEN
EMERYVILLE, CALIFORNIA, AND BOSTON, MASSACHUSETTS

Howtoons brings hands-on science education to children through a series of illustrated instructions showing how to build homemade technologies. Kids learn to use the things in the world around them to put together their own toys and create their own fun. Through the process, they develop an intuition for the physical world. The projects encourage kids to see ordinary household materials in a new light, expanding and building up a vocabulary of resourcefulness and imagination.

Howtoons was created by inventors and social entrepreneurs Saul Griffith and Joost Bonsen, who began working on the project when they were students at MIT. They were soon joined by Nick Dragotta, a professional Marvel Comics artist working in Boston, who brought the characters to life through rich illustrations and a passion for comic art. Howtoons provide the instructions for the projects within a playful narrative. Each Howtoon features a boy and a girl who inspire each other to new heights of mischief and invention; adults are rarely depicted.

Every Howtoon is family-tested, and projects range from rocket launchers and zoetropes to light benders and musical instruments. A marshmallow shooter is made from PVC plumbing pipes and connectors, pieced together into an ingenious device designed to propel marshmallows across the room. In another Howtoon, a flute can be made from a plastic turkey baster, a few rubber bands, and a glass of water. Many of the projects are available for free on the Internet, and others are now also available in a book.

Howtoons are described by the creators as "Open Kid Ware," and are part of the broader social movement to create an information commons available to everyone. It is a movement with global implications; Griffith's other inventions include a system for inexpensively testing people's vision and fabricating eyeglasses, an idea that has life-changing potential in developing countries.

1 Marshmallow shooter, Howtoons instructional graphics, 2005. **DESIGNERS** Joost Bonsen, Nick Dragotta, and Saul Griffith. **PRODUCER** SQUID Labs, Inc. Published by arrangement with Regan Books, an imprint of HarperCollins Publishers, Inc.
2 Turkey baster flute, Howtoons instructional graphics, 2005. **DESIGNERS** Joost Bonsen, Nick Dragotta, and Saul Griffith. **PRODUCER** SQUID Labs, Inc. Published by arrangement with Regan Books, an imprint of HarperCollins Publishers, Inc.

ICT LEADERS PROJECT

INSTITUTE FOR CREATIVE TECHNOLOGIES, UNIVERSITY OF SOUTHERN CALIFORNIA
MARINA DEL REY, CALIFORNIA

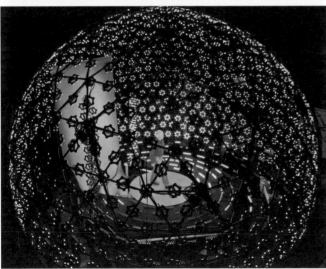

1

How does one train future military leaders to negotiate complex situations in foreign lands, understand cultural differences, and protect troops and civilians in highly populated urban areas? The United States Army enlisted Hollywood to help solve these problems. Discussions among former entertainment industry executives, academics, and officials from the U.S. Defense Advanced Research Projects Agency (DARPA) led the Army to launch the Institute for Creative Technologies (ICT) at the University of Southern California, where entertainment creatives work with computer scientists to fulfill the Army's directive: "Build us a holodeck."

Today, with much of the U.S. military's work, such as peacekeeping missions, happening away from the battlefield, soldiers need greater skills and training in diplomacy and decision-making. To accomplish this, ICT creates synthetic immersive experiences that are so compelling, the participants often react as if they were real. Through real-time training simulations, ICT is building a new generation of leadership development tools through what ICT's Creative Director Jim Korris describes as "complex interactive narrative, using highly advanced artificial intelligence (AI) capabilities and high production-value graphics. Our games look good—but they are unusually 'smart.'" Up to sixty percent of the processor resources in typical ICT-developed applications are devoted to AI, as opposed to about twenty percent in typical commercial entertainment titles.

In February 2003, ICT released *Full Spectrum Command* and, soon after, the award-winning *Full Spectrum Warrior*, training games which teach users to think and make strategic decisions three-dimensionally. In the *Leaders* program, a collaboration between ICT and Paramount Pictures, users interact with avatars to choose between two leadership decisions, each of which leads to a different storyline. In a number of these training games, AI is programmed to "learn" from the user's questions, and virtual characters can progressively adapt and answer related, but unexpected, questions.

Sergeant John Blackwell is a three-dimensional virtual character capable of spoken interaction with visitors using ICT's natural language-processing technology. ICT's Animation Lab developed techniques to drive the character's voice-synchronized mouth movements, facial animation, and eye-tracking systems. With his extensive vocabulary and AI language programming, Sergeant Blackwell can answer a wide range of visitors' questions, structuring his answers based on recognized words in the questions. Engaging and funny, Blackwell even answers open-ended questions. For example, when asked, "What time is it?" he may answer, "What am I, a clock?" Or, if asked about the weather, he may reply, "You are asking me the wrong question. What you should be asking me is…" In another ICT program, viewers must negotiate with a resolute doctor in Iraq to move his hospital to a safer area. The AI can be programmed to alter the doctor's mood, tone of voice, level of aggression, and negotiation skills. As with so many design innovations that originate from military uses, ICT's designs presage training that will be useful in all aspects of life in the future.

1 Light Stage 6, January 2006. **MANUFACTURER** Institute for Creative Technologies,
Graphics Lab. **PHOTO** Paul Debevec
2 Full Spectrum Leader 1.0 Command Interface, desktop computer training aid,
2005. **DESIGNERS** ICT/USC in partnership with Quicksilver Software, Inc.
Courtesy of RDECOM-STTC, ICT/USC, and Quicksilver Software, Inc.
3 Sergeant John Blackwell: Interactive Character, projection of real-time graphics
combined with physical props, 2004–06. **CLIENT/SPONSOR** RDECOM & Assistant
Secretary of the Army for Acquisition, Logistics, and Technology. **EQUIPMENT**
transcreen: Laser Magic Productions; projector: NEC MT1075 with short
throw lens; microphone headset: Plantronics; software: Gamebryo: Emergent
Game Technologies/NDL; SONIC: The Center for Spoken Language Research,
University of Colorado, Boulder; Elvin: Mantara software; proprietary software
developed at USC ICT. © ICT/USC

2

3

IROBOT
BURLINGTON, MASSACHUSETTS

1

2

Washing and vacuuming floors are among the most mundane aspects of life. They are also not what most of us imagined our first domestic experience with robots would involve. For the last four years, however, with new models arriving annually, the iRobot Roomba® Vacuuming Robot and iRobot Scooba® Floor Washing Robot are showing us how robots can and will clean our homes.

Founded in 1990 by Massachusetts Institute of Technology roboticists, iRobot Corporation designs behavior-based robots for consumer and military purposes. Using proprietary AWARE™ Robot Intelligence Systems, they introduced the Roomba, the first affordable vacuuming robot, in 2002. In 2005, the company introduced the Roomba Scheduler®, and the Scooba, which washes floors. Together, they offer a new level of programmable efficiency to help eliminate the drudgery of household chores.

With the Roomba Scheduler, you can program up to seven different cleaning schedules. It will clean the floor, returning to its home base to rest and repower when it has completed its job or the battery is low. An infrared receiver located at the front of the bumper "sees" the signal emitted from the home base. A patented three-stage cleaning system—a spinning side brush to clean along walls, two counter-rotating brushes that capture large debris, and a vacuum that picks up loose particles and dust—ensures a thorough job.

Roomba features a self-adjusting cleaning head that adapts automatically as it moves from one type of floor surface to another. As part of the AWARE system, a sensor located above the brushes detects the dirt and turns toward that area, so Roomba can actually identify the dirtiest areas and respond by increasing the intensity of its cleaning.

Scooba, iRobot's latest product, completely replaces the need to mop floors. It preps the floor by cleaning up loose crumbs, sand and dirt; washes it using fresh, clean solution (rather than just pushing the dirty water around like a mop); scrubs floors gently but effectively; and picks up the dirty suds, leaving the floor clean and dry. All four of these cleaning methods happen in one pass of the robot.

The AWARE Robot Intelligence System uses dozens of infrared sensors to monitor the environment, while adjusting the behavior of the robot up to sixty-seven times per second, allowing the robots to negotiate around furniture and along walls. The robots also feature a cliff sensor which prevents them from falling down stairs.

iRobot also designed the iRobot PackBot® Tactical Mobile Robot. Hundreds of PackBots are currently helping American troops in Afghanistan and Iraq.

1 iRobot Roomba® Scheduler Vacuuming Robot, 2002. PHOTO iRobot Corp.
2 iRobot Scooba® Floor Washing Robot, 2005. PHOTO iRobot Corp.

NATALIE JEREMIJENKO

X DESIGN LAB

NEW YORK, NEW YORK, AND SAN DIEGO, CALIFORNIA

Natalie Jeremijenko, who runs a research lab in the art department at the University of California, San Diego, is changing the way we think about technology. In her Feral Robotic Dog project, she works with teams of high-school students to take apart toy robots and rebuild their physiques and behavior. Armed with pollution sensors, a lowered center of gravity, and all-terrain wheels, the Feral Robotic Dogs head out across the landscape in search of toxins. Released into landfills and urban areas from Arizona to Ireland, the dogs are programmed to seek out some of the same pollutants used in their own manufacture, drawing attention to the toxic nature of high-tech industry. Whereas most consumer robots are designed to dance, yap, or vacuum the rug, the Feral Robotic Dogs are equipped with a social agenda.

Why reverse-engineer a commercial toy? Jeremijenko's "open-source" tactics aim to exploit the distribution power of the corporate toymakers, whose economy of scale makes these digital dogs an inexpensive way to get a sophisticated robotics platform into the hands of kids. Her project also helps kids recognize the consequences of consumer choices and imagine toys and technologies with a different purpose. As she explains, "Robotic toys embody a particular view of learning and entertainment. Are we equipping our children to address the technological future, or are we simply training them to push buttons in predetermined, pre-scripted interactions?"

Jerejimenko's map of the San Francisco Bay Area shows that one of the nation's most prosperous regions, and one which has set the bar worldwide for high-tech innovation, is also host to more Superfund sites—the nation's worst toxic waste sites—than any comparable geographic area in the United States, with serious consequences for public health. The Feral Robotic Dog project prepares its young participants to address one of the central challenges of our time: finding ways that technology can enrich human life without destroying the systems that sustain it.

CHIP KIDD
NEW YORK, NEW YORK

1

2

3

Chip Kidd has been creating book jackets and covers for the publishing house Alfred A. Knopf for twenty years. Entering the field almost directly out of college, he discovered a medium where his dark and clever sensibility could flourish. By the time he turned thirty, his name was recognized not only among designers but throughout the literary world.

Kidd's jackets and covers are distinctively his own, yet they adhere to no particular style. His cover for Jay McInerney's *The Good Life* features a photograph of ordinary objects covered in dust from the collapse of the World Trade Centers, exposing the intimate side of an enormously public disaster. The cover typography for *Dry* by Augusten Burroughs appears to disintegrate before our eyes, like the resolve of an alcoholic struggling to recover. Stories about the making of these and dozens of other works enliven the pages of *Chip Kidd: Book One* (2005), a monograph which uncovers Kidd's distinctive way of compressing a literary trajectory onto the body of a book.

Kidd prides himself on allowing the content of each book to suggest its own design approach, an attitude he owes to his education at Pennsylvania State University, where a quirky cast of professors promulgated a concept-based approach to graphic design. (Kidd's experience there is the basis of his comic novel *The Cheese Monkeys*, published in 2001.) The books themselves have also shaped his education, immersing him every day in writing of the highest order. The literary scene, more than the design profession, has provided the context and community for Kidd's work.

Book production engages the efforts—sometimes conflicting—of authors, editors, agents, designers, publishers, publicists, marketers, booksellers, and more. By the time it reaches the bookstore, a jacket or cover design has survived a gauntlet of approvals. Humming along beneath the fray of battle is an intense and intimate collaboration between designer and author—although very often they never meet. Working in the space of the mind rather than the corporate meeting room, the designer absorbs a book and conjures a visual interpretation that compels readers to pick it up and look inside.

1 *Chip Kidd: Book One,* 2005. **DESIGNERS** Chip Kidd and Mark Melnick. **PUBLISHER** Rizzoli International Publications. **PHOTO** Geoff Spear
2 *Dry,* book cover, 2003. **DESIGNER** Chip Kidd. **AUTHOR** Augusten Burroughs. **PUBLISHER** Picador. **PHOTO** Geoff Spear
3 *Magical Thinking,* book jacket, 2005. **DESIGNER** Chip Kidd. **AUTHOR** Augusten Burroughs. **PUBLISHER** St. Martin's Press. **PHOTO** Geoff Spear
4 *The Good Life,* 2006. **DESIGNER** Chip Kidd. **AUTHOR** Jay McInerney. **PUBLISHER** Alfred A. Knopf. **PHOTOGRAPHER** Quyen Tran
5 *Pushing the Limits,* 2004. **DESIGNER** Chip Kidd. **AUTHOR** Henry Petroski. **PUBLISHER** Alfred A. Knopf

6 *No Country for Old Men,* book jacket, 2005. **DESIGNER** Chip Kidd. **AUTHOR** Cormac McCarthy. **PUBLISHER** Alfred A. Knopf. **PHOTO** Matt Lindsay/Nonstock
7 *Father's Day,* book jacket, 2004. **DESIGNER** Chip Kidd. **AUTHOR** Philip Gaines. **PUBLISHER** Alfred A. Knopf. **PHOTO** Geoff Spear

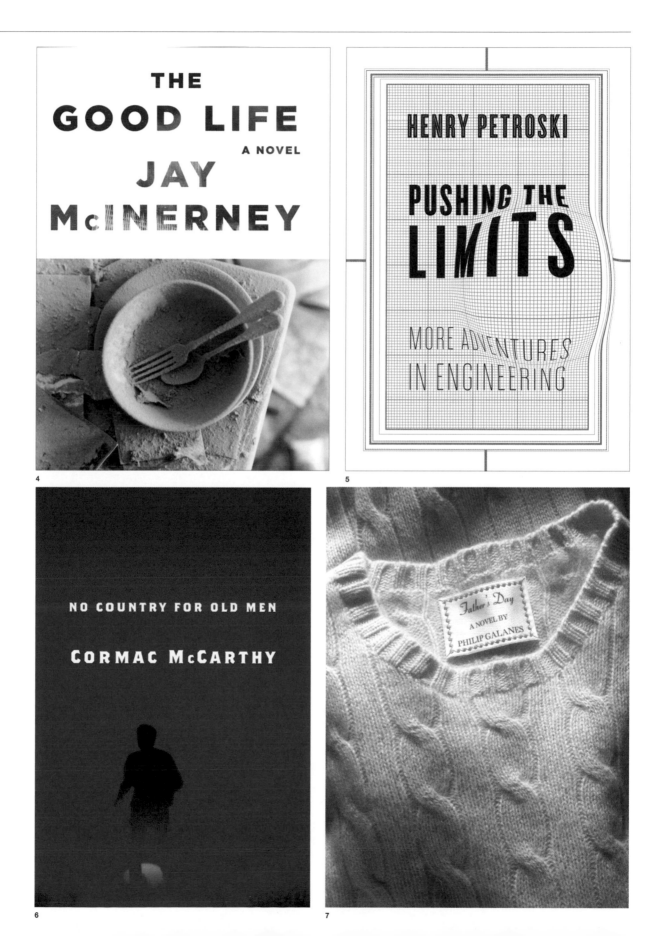

4

5

6

7

KIDROBOT
NEW YORK, NEW YORK

1

What makes a toy? Kidrobot, a creator and retailer of limited-edition art toys, defies most traditional definitions. The toys sold at Kidrobot feature urban street trends mixed with creative design and fine art to produce collectible pieces of art. Many Kidrobot toys are designed by world-renowned artists with backgrounds in graffiti, fine art, industrial design, graphic design, illustration, and music. Kidrobot is erasing the boundaries between street culture and art at an affordable cost to people of all ages.

Kidrobot owner Paul Budnitz opened his first store in San Francisco in 2002 and his second in New York's SoHo in 2003. The business began online, selling small-run designer toys, largely from Japan, by designers such as Michael Lau and Hiraru Iwanaga, who are credited with beginning the urban vinyl-toy movement. Budnitz designed the Kidrobot figure in 2001 and the infamous Dunny figure in 2003 with artist Tristan Eaton. From there, Budnitz began designing, commissioning, and selling designer vinyl toys at a rapid rate, releasing new limited editions continually at his stores and via the Kidrobot Web site. Often a single form, such as Dunny, will be customized by a number of artists, including Dalek, Huck Gee, Tim Biskup, and graffiti artists Doze Green and Tilt. Issue 44 of *Visionaire* magazine in 2005 consisted of two sets of five Kidrobot toys. Each is a small rounded figure with arms, designed in front and back by ten leading fashion designers, including Karl Lagerfeld, Jean-Louis Dumas Hermès, Domenico Dolce & Stefano Gabbana, and Marc Jacobs for Louis Vuitton. In 2005, Kidrobot began designing polo shirts sold exclusively at Barneys New York, as well as limited-edition running shoes for Nike. No longer just infiltrating the world of toys, Kidrobot is becoming a lifestyle brand of the future.

1 Ice-Bot, 2005. **DESIGNER** Dalek. Vinyl, fabric. **PHOTO** Kidrobot
2 Big Mouth Dunny, 2005. **DESIGNER** Paul Budnitz and Tristan Easton, paint design
  by DEPH. Vinyl. **PHOTO** Kidrobot
3 CYCLE Munny, 2005. **DESIGNER** Paul Budnitz and Tristan Easton, paint design
  by CYCLE. Vinyl. **PHOTO** Kidrobot

2   3

KONYK

CRAIG KONYK
BROOKLYN, NEW YORK

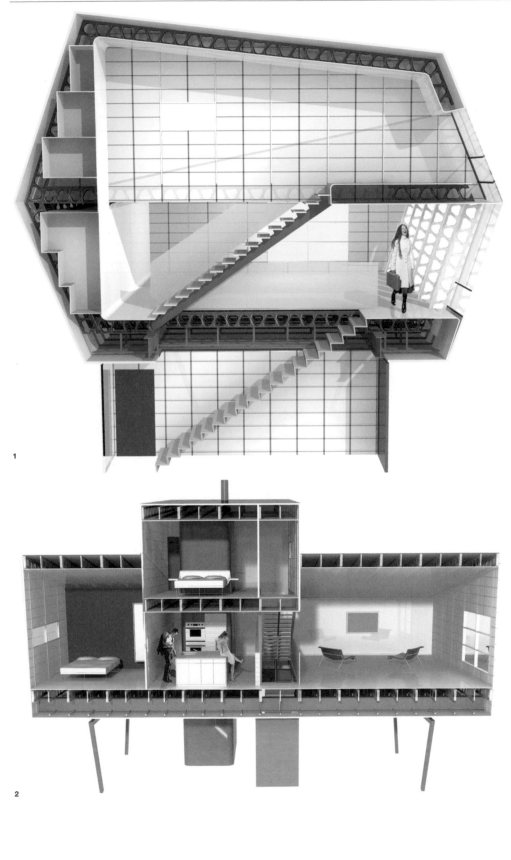

1

2

Konyk's up! house puts a new spin on the idea of prefabricated housing. Originally commissioned for *Dwell* magazine's "dwell home invitational" in April 2003, the up! house has evolved into an ongoing investigation into the morphology and ideology of prefab dwellings. Each successive generation of the design—there are now two- and three-bedroom models—features innovations in manufacturing, finishes, and custom options available to clients.

As real-estate values have skyrocketed across the country, the idea of prefabricated housing has gained a new allure. What could be more interesting, efficient, and economical than ordering your new home online and having its components shipped to your site and assembled in practically no time at all? Because most prefab dwellings are trucked to their final destination, the factory-made parts are based on a module that must fit on a flatbed truck. As a result, many prefab homes are long, low, and boxy. The up! house, however, looks to the future, as well as to futuristic projects of the past, such as Buckminster Fuller's Dymaxion House. Its architecture borrows from the world of industrial design, especially automotive design and production techniques. The main component of the structural system is its factory-welded, lightweight steel-tube "uni-frame" or "chassis," to which an exterior "body" of high gloss coated-metal panels with matching tinted glass is attached. Finishes are available in sixteen colors, and guaranteed to last twenty years. Similar to an automobile, packages of options range from power windows to a moon roof. Indeed, Konyk claims that its aim is "to make the purchase of a single-family house akin to buying a new Mini Cooper."

1 up! house 1500 prototype, section through stairs, 2003–05. **ARCHITECT** Craig
  Konyk. **RENDERING** David Fano
2 up! house 1500 prototype, cross-section, 2003–05. **ARCHITECT** Craig Konyk.
  RENDERING David Fano
3 up! house 1500 prototype, main view, 2003–05. **ARCHITECT** Craig Konyk.
  RENDERING David Fano
4 up!house 1500 prototype, view of kitchen, 2003–05. **ARCHITECT** Craig Konyk.
  RENDERING David Fano

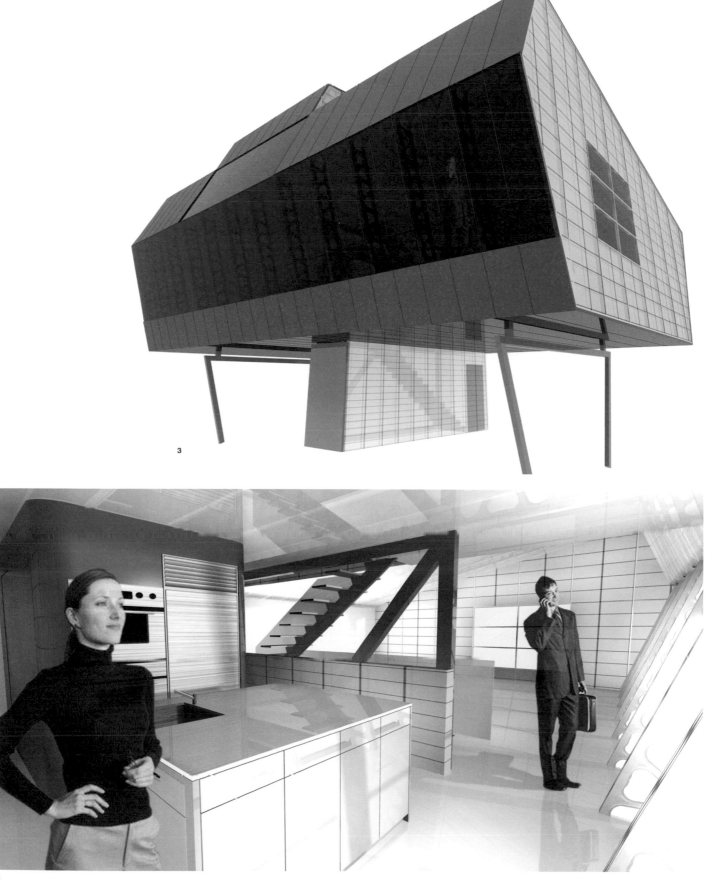

3

4

LADD BROTHERS
STEVEN LADD AND WILLIAM LADD
BROOKLYN, NEW YORK

1

2

Born in St. Louis, Missouri, the Ladd brothers spent their summers at Terre du Lac, an area characterized by thousands of acres of woods, lakes, and rivers. While a teenager, William, the younger brother, was "whisked away" into the world of high-fashion modeling. While working and traveling in New York, Paris, and Milan, he began experimenting with design and beadwork, eventually devoting years to the craft.

Five years ago, William began a close collaboration with Steven, who specialized in textile, fiber, and costume design at Rockhurst University. After several years of designing clothing, Steven studied couture handbag design. Steven and William combined their talents, with Steven crafting the handbags and William enhancing the handbags with beaded appliquìs and accessories. Steven also hand-stitches extraordinarily beautiful boxes that enclose and reveal the brothers' work.

The brothers have, to date, designed a limited number of these elaborate handcrafted works. *Shadow Tower* was based on the highly personal concepts of self-discovery and collaboration. The *Tower* is an aesthetic whole, constructed of layers that unfold as you open them to reveal unexpected, uniquely beaded riches. A single box opens to disclose a vignette of beautiful objects. In the center is a small handbag made entirely of glass beads. Shaped like a medieval slipper, its arabesque forms are beaded with colors and designs that are reflected in all of the other objects in the surrounding space.

The Ladd brothers' complementary accessories include cascading necklaces and bracelets, patterned ties and sashes, and jewel-colored "ribbons" that tie around one's neck. Each object is a luxurious, unique design, to be used or to stand alone as a work of art. Desiring not to waste any materials, the Ladds use every scrap of material left over from their creations to make scrolls of various sizes, which are then used to decorate the interior of Steven's boxes, make jewelry, or decorate the covers of hand-stitched books that they make to accompany each of their major works.

Although they usually begin the process of their works with a handbag, then design its environment, box, accessories, and book, in their tour de force, *Terre du Lac*, the brothers began with the environment, making over twenty stackable boxes whose interiors are small tableaux of three-dimensional beaded trees. On and around the branches of these miniature forests, necklaces, scarves, and handbags are draped and propped, waiting to divulge their treasures when the box lids are lifted.

1 *Terre du Lac*, 2006. **DESIGNERS** Steven and William Ladd. Silk, ultrasuede, paper, glass beads. **PHOTO** Andrew Zuckerman
2 *Fire: Purple Bag*, 2004. **DESIGNERS** Steven and William Ladd. Glass beads, ultra suede, acid-free board, metal. **PHOTO** Andrew Zuckerman

1

ABHINAND LATH

SENSITILE
DETROIT, MICHIGAN

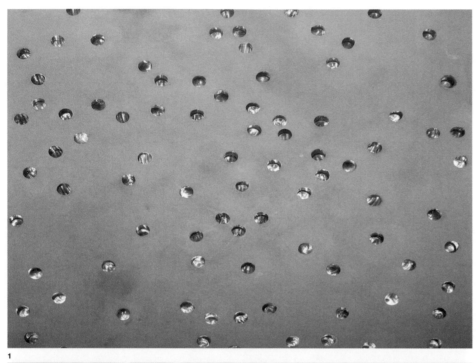

1

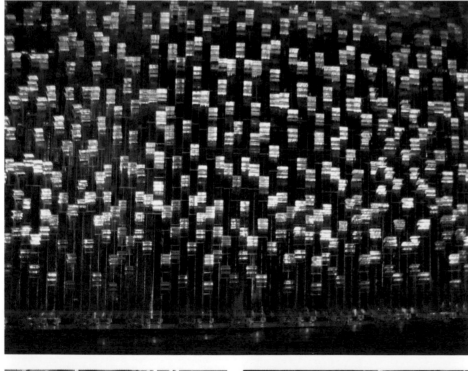

2

I repeat my vow
In unchanging colors of the
Ageless bamboo—
Which still creates ten thousand
Generations of shadows
—Gyokuran (eleventh-century
Japanese poet)

SensiTile is a material inspired by a material. When Abhinand Lath was working on a thesis about bamboo at the University of Michigan's school of architecture, he came across the Japanese poem above. He was inspired to translate the idea of light, shadow, and movement into a material based upon his previous work, which had involved embedding fiber-optics into concrete. The end product was SensiTile, a material with kaleidoscopic arrays of color, a passive system which responds to existing light sources so that the more active the movement of light or an object, the more rapidly the surface changes.

SensiTile technology is composed of a light-conducting matrix and a substrate within which the matrix is embedded. It transports light from one surface point to another by total internal reflection—the same principle that makes fiberoptics possible. SensiTile either reconfigures the shadows that fall on it or redirects and scatters any oncoming light. In an environment with ambient light, any movement around the material that casts shadows will produce a set of "ripples" on the material's surface; while in darker environments, any beam of light falling on a SensiTile is redirected to emerge from another part of its surface.

The light-conducting matrix can be combined with a range of materials including concrete (Terrazzo), polymer (Scintilla), and resin (Sensi-Tile Volatile), and has been incorporated into flooring, walls, façades, countertops, and partitions. At a time when it has become common-place to see everything from rose petals to metal grillwork embedded into resin wall systems, SensiTile creates an alternative—a "material as dynamic as light."

1 Terrazzo, 2004. **MANUFACTURER** SensiTile Systems. Concrete and cast acrylic. **PHOTO** SensiTile Systems
2 Scintilla, 2005. **MANUFACTURER** SensiTile Systems. Cast PMMA acrylic. **PHOTO** SensiTile Systems

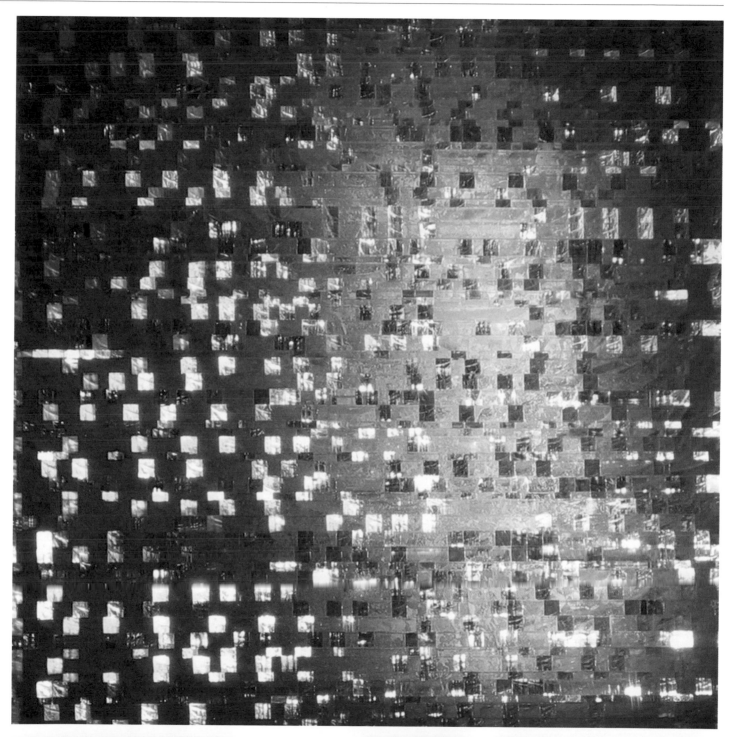

LAZOR OFFICE

CHARLIE LAZOR
MINNEAPOLIS, MINNESOTA

1

2

Charlie Lazor's FlatPak House is perhaps the most successful, and resolved, of the prefabricated housing efforts currently available. Lazor, who trained as an architect, cofounded Blu Dot, a company devoted to affordable, modern furniture design, with Maurice Blanks and John Christakos. In 2003, motivated by his frustration at not being able to find an affordable modern home for himself, Lazor returned to his architect's drawing board. With FlatPak, Lazor put to good use his knowledge of furniture design, manufacture, and assembly methods. The result is a remarkably flexible, affordable, and user-friendly system.

On FlatPak's Web site, clients can explore a range of floor-plan configurations and exterior and interior finishes. The site, a crucial part of the FlatPak experience and a key to its success, is colorful and graphically clean, and its straightforward instructions are communicated step by step with wit and humor. Currently, four different prototypes, each with a different floor-plan configuration, are available. FlatPak's flexible kit-of-parts system, based on an eight-foot-wide, one-story wall module, consists of three basic components: concrete wall panels; wood-framed panels with wood, metal, or cement-board siding; and wood frames with large expanses of glass.

By undertaking all elements of the FlatPak process himself—from design to manufacture and construction—and living in it with his family, Lazor has delivered an efficient and refined kit of parts that is no longer a dream but a reality.

1 FlatPak House, view of main façade, Minneapolis, MN, 2004. **DESIGN TEAM** Charlie Lazor, Robert Ewert, Patrick McGlothlin, Meredith Molli, Peter Cornue. **PHOTO** Joel Koyama
2 FlatPak House, kitchen, Minneapolis, MN, 2004. **DESIGN TEAM** Charlie Lazor, Robert Ewert, Patrick McGlothlin, Meredith Molli, Peter Cornue. **PHOTO** Joel Koyama
3 FlatPak House, exterior view, Minneapolis, MN, 2004. **DESIGN TEAM** Charlie Lazor, Robert Ewert, Patrick McGlothlin, Meredith Molli, Peter Cornue. **PHOTO** Joel Koyama
4 FlatPak House, master bedroom, Minneapolis, MN, 2004. **DESIGN TEAM** Charlie Lazor, Robert Ewert, Patrick McGlothlin, Meredith Molli, Peter Cornue. **PHOTO** Joel Koyama

3

4

TOM LEADER STUDIO
BERKELEY, CALIFORNIA

1

2

Tom Leader takes his work seriously—but not too seriously. His studio works comfortably with advanced technology and the humble materials of everyday life alike, in projects ranging from an interwoven network of pedestrian plazas in Shanghai, China, to a 2004 installation of hay bales and screen doors at the Cornerstone Festival of Gardens in Sonoma County, California. Wit, playfulness, and experimentation are a vital part of the collaborative studio's work, which always acknowledges the importance of the community that will activate and inhabit the places it creates.

After a number of years spent "rolling with the punches" in the business of making landscape architecture, Leader decided that it was time to get less serious. *Break Out*, Leader's project at Cornerstone, elicits a laugh, but not because it is a one-liner. Walls made of bales of hay surround a maze of screen doors that creak and slam as visitors and the wind pass through, evoking barnyards, porches, and the vernacular culture of rural California. The spirit of Johnny Cash inhabits *Break Out* as scratchy fragments of his songs intermingled with bugzapping sounds play on speakers throughout the site. The project, which has a dark side—its title and maze refer to incarceration and tough times —inspired a new project, a temporary garden made of shipping containers, catwalks, and scaffolds at the Fresno Museum.

Leader's work is not always gritty and humorous, but as the studio takes on more sophisticated large-scale projects, such as the Railroad Reservation Park in Birmingham, Alabama, it tries to keep experimentation and unpredictability an important part of its working process.

1 Railroad Reservation Park, master plan, Birmingham, AL, 2005–06. **DESIGN TEAM** Akiko Ono, Sarah Gerhan, Rachel Johnston. **CLIENT** City of Birmingham Mayor's Office. **PROJECT MANAGERS** Renee Kemp Rotan and H. B. Brantley. **COLLABORATORS** Consultecon, Tom Martin. **RENDERING** Akiko Ono/TLS
2 ASK Fresno Temporary Landscape (in collaboration with Michael Maltzan Museum Architecture), Fresno Museum of Art, Fresno, CA, 2005. **DESIGN TEAM** Akiko Ono, Matthieu Jacqmin, Christina Abreu. **PHOTO** Matthieu Jacqmin/TLS
3 Breakout, Cornerstone Festival of Gardens, Sonoma, CA, 2004. **DESIGN TEAM** Ryosuke Shimoda, Michelle Dubin, Sarah Gerhan, Christina Abreu. **CONSTRUCTION** David Aquilina. **SOUND DESIGN** Roderick Wylie. **PHOTO** Richard Barnes

GREG LYNN FORM
VENICE, CALIFORNIA

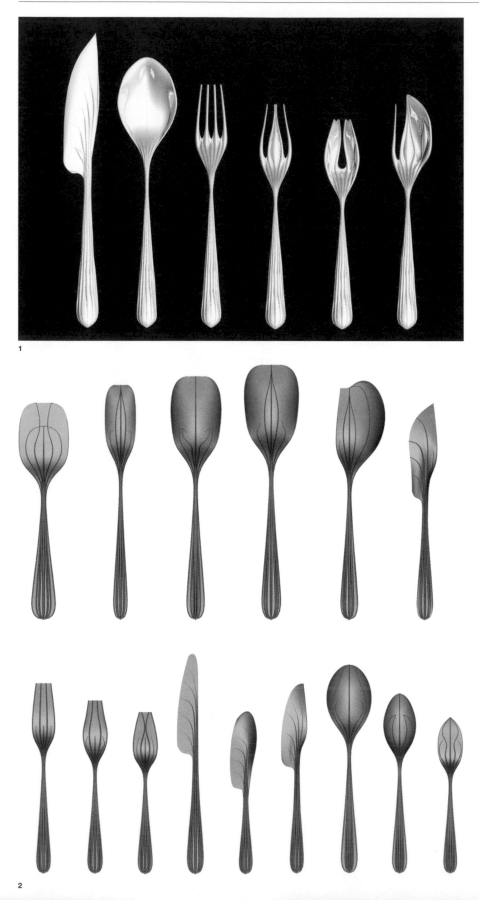

1

2

When Greg Lynn relocated his architecture practice to Venice, California, in 1998, it was to take advantage of the presence of Southern California's advanced design and manufacturing technologies for use in aeronautic, automotive, and product design. Lynn, one of contemporary architecture's most provocative thinkers, constantly searches for new technologies and manufacturing methods to make his complex architectural forms a reality. Recently, he has turned his talents to product design as well.

Lynn combines his exploration of advanced digital design with a strong belief in craftsmanship. Greg Lynn FORM was one of the first design studios to invest in a computer-controlled milling robot that can shape foam, plastic, wood, and aluminum into physical models at various scales. The studio specializes in converting digital form into coded paths which direct advanced manufacturing tools to generate physical models and prototypes. As a result, Lynn is able to fully articulate his formal and ornamental vocabulary of intricate textures and voluptuous curves.

In 2003, renowned Italian design company Alessi commissioned Lynn and a number of other architects to design coffee and tea services. The flower-like form of Lynn's prototype, which Alessi produced in a limited edition in 2003, echoes forms he explored on an architectural scale in projects such as the Ark of the World Museum in Costa Rica. While Lynn's exceptionally innovative forms may, in many cases, be too advanced for current building and construction methods, they lend themselves perfectly to the scale of product design. The Alessi coffee and tea service inspired Lynn to develop other products for the company. His Supple Cups, made of bone china, launched in November 2005, are deceptive: their bulging amorphous shapes look as if they are made of a malleable material distorted by the imprint of a human hand or the liquid volume contained inside. Lynn's Alessi flatware and grill are in the prototype stage. The flatware, due to be launched in 2006, recalls the sinuous tendrils of Art Nouveau, with the shape of each utensil suggesting a stem, leaf, or flower.

1 Alessi flatware. Flatware prototypes, resin painted white, 2006. **DESIGN TEAM** Greg Lynn FORM, Brittney Hart, Chris Kabatsi, Andi Kranier, Helen Lee, Elena Manferdini. **RENDERING** Greg Lynn FORM
2 Alessi flatware, 2006. **DESIGN TEAM** Greg Lynn FORM, Brittney Hart, Chris Kabatsi, Andi Kranier, Helen Lee, Elena Manferdini. **RENDERING** Greg Lynn FORM
3 Alessi grill prototype, 2006. **DESIGN TEAM** Greg Lynn FORM, Chris Kabatsi, Elena Manferdini. **RENDERING** Greg Lynn FORM
4 Alessi Supple Cups, 2005. **DESIGN TEAM** Greg Lynn FORM, Jackilin Bloom, Brian Ha, Chris Kabatsi. Bone china. **RENDERING** Greg Lynn FORM

3

4

133

MAKE MAGAZINE
SEBASTOPOL, CALIFORNIA

Make is an action-packed response to the growing interest in do-it-yourself design. Subtitled *Technology on Your Time*, this "mook" (book/magazine hybrid) is directed at readers who like to hack, tinker, build, and take things apart. The magazine's compact, easy-to-hold format is based on *Popular Mechanics* and other geek classics of the 1950s, recast in bright, crisp pages of photographs and instructional illustrations.

In addition to reporting on the work of renegade inventors, artists, and engineers, *Make* features such ingenious projects as an aerial, kite-born photography system, a video stabilizer to keep your digicam from shaking, and a megaphone that lets you throw your voice via loudspeaker up to thirty feet away. Warning: basic electronics skills are required.

Mass-customization was a progressive design paradigm in the 1990s, allowing customers to pick their own features and finishes before a product was put together in the factory. Today, DIY customization is launching a fresh assault on uniformity, as an outspoken vanguard of users seeks to get under the hood of products in order to reinvent their function—or simply fix them when they break. While manufacturers of everything from cars to software have been sealing off the inner workings of goods, a new wave of consumers is determined to break through the barriers and understand the stuff they use.

Make is the brainchild of publisher Dale Dougherty, who has dedicated his career to demystifying software. As cofounder, with Tim O'Reilly, of O'Reilly & Associates, Dougherty created a line of no-nonsense software manuals revered by coders everywhere. *Make's* editor in chief, Mark Frauenfelder, a veteran writer, illustrator, and blogger, and designers David Albertson and Kirk von Rohr pull it all together by making the magazine fresh and readable.

The Maker's Bill of Right's (vol. 04) nails the magazine's philosophy with such commonsense commandments as "Screws better than glues" and "Ease of repair should be a design ideal, not an afterthought." As more consumers demand abidance to these principles, products will have longer and more varied life spans.

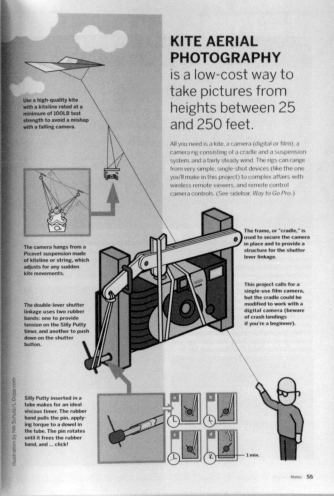

PROJECTS: KITE AERIAL PHOTOGRAPHY

HAVE YOU EVER WANTED TO TAKE PICTURES FROM THE SKY?

Kite aerial photography (or KAP for short) bridges the gap between taking pictures from a ladder and taking them from an airplane. Within this elevation spectrum, you can capture landscapes, objects, architecture, and people in entirely new ways.

In the pages that follow, I'll give you step-by-step instructions for building a very low-cost rig consisting of a camera cradle made of craft (popsicle) sticks and model airplane plywood, a shutter-button timer mechanism that uses rubber bands and Silly Putty, and a camera-stabilizing suspension.

Following the step-by-step section, I'll recommend some kites and other equipment you can use for the project, and then run you through your first flight with the rig.

Charles C. Benton (arch.ced.berkeley.edu/kap/kaptoc.html) is an inveterate tinkerer from Berkeley, California, where he serves as a Professor of Architecture for the University of California, Berkeley. Benton's research in Building Science often involves the design and construction of prototype devices.

KITE AERIAL PHOTOGRAPHY
is a low-cost way to take pictures from heights between 25 and 250 feet.

All you need is a kite, a camera (digital or film), a camera rig consisting of a cradle and a suspension system, and a fairly steady wind. The rigs can range from very simple, single-shot devices (like the one you'll make in this project) to complex affairs with wireless remote viewers, and remote control camera controls. (See sidebar, *Way to Go Pro*.)

Use a high-quality kite with a kiteline rated at a minimum of 100LB test strength to avoid a mishap with a falling camera.

The frame, or "cradle," is used to secure the camera in place and to provide a structure for the shutter lever linkage.

This project calls for a single-use film camera, but the cradle could be modified to work with a digital camera (beware of crash landings if you're a beginner).

The camera hangs from a Picavet suspension made of kiteline or string, which adjusts for any sudden kite movements.

The double-lever shutter linkage uses two rubber bands: one to provide tension on the Silly Putty timer, and another to push down on the shutter button.

Silly Putty inserted in a tube makes for an ideal viscous timer. The rubber band pulls the pin, applying torque to a dowel in the tube. The pin rotates until it frees the rubber band, and ... click!

1 min.

Illustration by Nik Schulz/L.Dopa.com

MICHAEL MEREDITH

CAMBRIDGE, MASSACHUSETTS

1

2

3

Architects are the designers of our environment. The good ones can make something small seem monumental, and transform marginal spaces into center-pieces for cultural activities. Michael Meredith accomplished both in the Huyghe + Corbusier: Harvard Project. In collaboration with French artist Pierre Huyghe, Meredith designed and constructed a temporary puppet theater to house three live performances com-memorating the fortieth anniversary of the Carpenter Center for the Visual Arts at Harvard University, designed by the Swiss architect Le Corbusier. The the-ater, located in an uninviting sunken courtyard underneath the Carpenter Center, was made of 500 prefabricated polycarbonate panels that were all unique. Foam inserts stiffened each panel and provided a surface to which living moss could adhere. Meredith took his inspiration for the structure from the site itself, framing a tree on one end and the puppet stage on the other. The live, spongy green mass provided a counter-point to the stark masonry of the loom-ing building overhead.

In his recently completed Shed in upstate New York, Meredith inserted a forty-foot-long perforated metal box into a bucolic green landscape. The effect is totally unexpected: the shed virtually disappears as one stands at a distance looking through the perfo-rated growth patterns stamped on the metal to the landscape behind—a magic mirror that does not reflect, but allows a view to the other side.

Meredith, an assistant professor of architecture at Harvard University's Graduate School of Design, likes to be engaged in interdisciplinary work rang-ing from art to technology. His recent design for coat hooks have the same organic and tactile qualities as Soft Cell, an installation of cast rubber and silicone mats that have been described as "three-dimensional drawings." The mats are meant to seem alien in a room, but nevertheless invite visitors to touch, sit down, and lie on the rubber pile sur-face. The coat hooks and mats seem to spread like spores over the walls and floor, creating an environment that is both engaging and unsettling.

1 "ivY" coat hooks system, 2005. **PROJECT TEAM** Michael Meredith, Andrew Atwood, Jessica Rosenkrantz. **MANUFACTURER** Crowley Jones, LP. ABS plastic. **PHOTO** Hilary Sample

2 *Soft Cell*, installation at Henry Urbach Architecture, New York, NY, 2005. **PROJECT TEAM** Michael Meredith, Temple Simpson. Silicone rubber. **PHOTO** Florian Holzherr

3 Shed, Ancram, NY, 2005. **PROJECT TEAM** Michael Meredith, Hilary Sample, Jaron Lubin. Perforated aluminum. **PHOTO** Michael Varhnewald

4 Huyghe + Corbusier: Harvard Project, Cambridge, MA, 2004. **PROJECT TEAM** Michael Meredith, Hilary Sample, Geoff von Oeyo, Chad Burke, Zac Culbreth, Elliott Hodges, Fred Holt. **PHOTO** Florian Holzherr

4

THOMAS MEYERHOFFER
MONTARA, CALIFORNIA

1

2

Thomas Meyerhoffer designs products in the areas of sports, technology, and furniture. His early success as the designer, in 1997, of Apple's eMate, the predecessor to the colorful Apple computer designs of the late 1990s, set the stage for his later career. Since starting his own company in Montara, California, in 1998, Meyerhoffer has completed many projects for companies such as Cappellini, Scott, and SonyEricsson. In recent work, Meyerhoffer combines technology and forward-thinking ideas into sculptural, widely accessible design. Most recently, Meyerhoffer has been applying his sensibility to his passion for surfing.

The results are two very different designs: The first is a surfboard with interchangeable tails, for which Meyerhoffer's goal was to design "the most advanced tool in the surf culture." With it the rider can change the tail section from a pin-tail—a rounded "V" shape that channels the water in a single stream and essentially holds the board in its line—to a swallow-tail (the shape of the letter W), which breaks the flow of the water running from the bottom of the board, thereby slightly lifting the tail and making it easier to turn. This easy adjustment enables surfers to instantly customize their ride to maximize their performance while eliminating the need to carry boards of different sizes. Meyerhoffer's second, less performance-oriented surfboard design is an experiment to express the experience of surfing in the design of the board. The BooSoo board, a longboard with a sculptural, hourglass shape, enables the rider to make tighter turns that are usually possible only on a shortboard. Meyerhoffer says that this innovative form delivers a new experience and dimension of gliding for to the rider. Both of these designs combine the high-tech computer programming that Meyerhoffer applies to all of his work with the intricate craftsmanship required to create a surfboard.

Progio is another example of his ability to synthesize technology with modern functionality for a high-tech performance experience. This handheld, sleek device with an organically inspired shape is a multimedia platform for interactive personal coaching in any sport.

1 The narrative act of surfing waves, Legozoo, Soomatic, Boosoo, and Codrod, 2005. Foam, fiberglass, tinted polyster resin. **PHOTO** Marcus Hanschen
2 Progio, 2005. Injected molded plastic and injected molded translucent rubber. **PHOTO** Marcus Hanschen
3 Surfboard with interchangeable tail, 2005. Foam, fiberglass, polyester resin, polycarbonate. **RENDERING** Meyerhoffer

3

JASON MILLER
BROOKLYN, NEW YORK

1

2

3

4

5

Jason Miller designs imperfect home furnishings. Drawing inspiration from the basements, attics, and family rooms of suburban America, he plays with form, function, tradition, and modernism to create fresh and surprising objects. His fabricated illusions of wear-and-tear evoke fictional biographies, while his unconventional materials suggest the labors of an eccentric hobbyist. Challenging typical notions of desirability, Miller's work celebrates the humility of everyday things.

Miller received his MFA in painting from the New York Academy of Art. Shortly thereafter, while painting still lifes of personal household effects, he realized his deeper interest lay in the objects themselves—tables, dishes, appliances—rather than in their pictorial representations. Permanently shelving his paints, he began working in the studios of Jeff Koons and Karim Rashid before founding his own studio in 2001. He currently lives and works in Brooklyn, where he is part of a burgeoning design community inspired by the area's industrial history.

Premeditated flaws and do-it-yourself aesthetics permeate Miller's work. Beautifully Broken is a collection of cracked vases that have been mended with colored epoxy to highlight their damage. His Scotch Magic series of shattered mirrors are restored with a glass product that looks like tape. Miller also simulates duct-tape repairs using leather strips to suture wool-upholstered armchairs. Rebelling against propriety, his Dusty Tables are permanently soiled with trompe l'oeil dust.

The materials and aesthetics of childhood find a second life in Miller's objects: he casts porcelain vases from Lego forms and molds containers from homemade Play-Doh. For his Glassicle lamps, Miller obsessively glues glass popsicle sticks into sparkling, architectonic fixtures.

Miller's designs emulate personal belongings not suitable for public display, but nonetheless privately enjoyed. The wit and simplicity of his work remind us that beauty can take many forms, and that an intriguing personality is more desirable than a perfect face.

1 Scotch Magic, 2006. **MANUFACTURER** Jason Miller Studio. Laminated glass and mirror. **PHOTO** Jason Miller Studio
2 Ogel vases, 2004. **MANUFACTURER** Jason Miller Studio. Stoneware. **PHOTO** Jason Miller Studio
3 Little Gift cupcakes, 2004. **MANUFACTURER** Jason Miller Studio. Porcelain. **PHOTO** Jason Miller Studio
4 Can of Play-Doh, 2004. Play-Doh. **PHOTO** Jason Miller Studio
5 Dusty Tables, 2006. **MANUFACTURER** Jason Miller Studio. Wood. **PHOTO** Jason Miller Studio
6 Duct Tape Lounge Chair, 2006. **MANUFACTURER** Jason Miller Studio. Upholstery over wood. **PHOTO** Jason Miller Studio

6

141

MOORHEAD & MOORHEAD

ROBERT MOORHEAD AND GRANGER MOORHEAD
NEW YORK, NEW YORK

The Moorhead brothers belong to a growing cadre of architects and designers interested in reappropriating industrial techniques and materials to make everyday objects. Relying on Granger's expertise in architecture and Robert's knowledge of industrial design, they aspire to maintain a practice which allows design exploration at a variety of scales. Their collaboration over the last five years has produced a consistently refined group of furniture, from chairs and lighting to room dividers, ready for production and distribution to the home.

Tape Wound Borne, resembling an oversized ball of twine, is a fiber-reinforced bench/table made using tape-winding, an automated manufacturing technique commonly employed for products ranging from golf-club shafts to aircraft fuselages. Thermoplastic tape is heated and applied to a mandrel in a continuous wrapping pattern. Once the plastic has cooled, the mandrel is removed, leaving a lightweight latticework structure. As Granger explains, "Part of what makes our design process special is letting a material create a language of its own....When we design objects we look at it more as an engineering project."

In Cargo Wall, the Moorheads cleverly utilize polypropylene webbing, commonly used in backpacks and dogleashes, formed into loops to create a room divider and giant vertical storage. The use of webbing in a wall was partially inspired by the webbed chairs of Jens Risom, but also derives from the brothers' particular interest in finding a lightweight means of support. The frame system for Cargo Wall is an adjustable tensioning system that allows it to be held in place by the floor and ceiling. The first test of the wall was with their competition-winning design for the *Metropolis* magazine booth at the 2005 International Contemporary Furniture Fair, where the designers created an animated face to the booth using issues of the magazine. Like Moorhead & Moorhead, Cargo Wall bridges the gap between furniture and architecture.

1 Tape Wound Borne, 2004. **DESIGNERS** Robert Moorhead and Granger Moorhead.
Fiber-reinforced polypropylene. **PHOTO AND RENDERINGS** Moorhead & Moorhead
2 *Metropolis* magazine booth, ICFF, New York, NY, 2005. **DESIGNERS** Robert
Moorhead and Granger Moorhead. Polypropylene and wood. **PHOTO AND
RENDERINGS** Moorhead & Moorhead

TOSHIKO MORI ARCHITECT
NEW YORK, NEW YORK

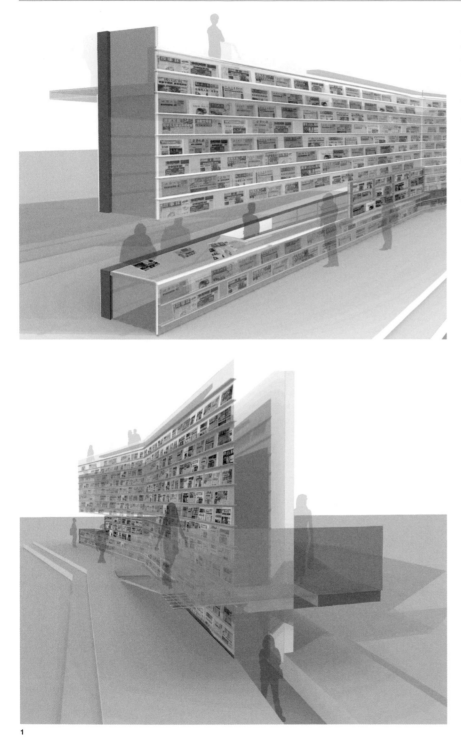

1

As an architect and chair of the School of Architecture at Harvard University's Graduate School of Design, Toshiko Mori has sought to reestablish the architect's direct involvement in the study of material properties and research into fabrication processes. By practicing what she preaches and teaches, Mori has created a diverse group of exemplary works since opening Toshiko Mori Architect (TMA) in 1981. From exhibition installations—such as *Josef and Anni Albers: Designs for Living* and *Extreme Textiles: Designing for High Performance* at Cooper-Hewitt—and storefronts to residences and institutions in the United States and abroad, TMA integrates new and traditional materials and techniques into extraordinarily varied architectural contexts.

At Frank Lloyd Wright's Darwin D. Martin House, the Visitors' Center, designed by TMA, is at once respectful to Wright's masterpiece and sufficiently assertive to overcome its off-street location. Its design inverts Wright's ground-hugging, masonry construction house into a transparent and uplifting glass box. It ultimately reflects TMA's interpretation of Wright's "organic architecture" as "an integral architecture that embraces technological advancements in materials, mechanical and structural systems for sustainability, together with expressive intentions that inspire the human spirit." TMA's Syracuse Center of Excellence in Environmental and Energy Systems, an elegant, minimal 80,000-square-foot space for laboratories, classrooms, and offices, further tests these ideas by incorporating sustainable building concepts such as strategic building disposition, high-performance glazing and insulation, brown water collection and usage, hydronic heating and cooling system, and energy-efficient airflow. The transparent south façade opens up to the surrounding community, visually communicating the research taking place within the laboratories.

In the Newspaper Café, one of sixteen new structures designed by international architects for an architecture park in Jinhua City, China, TMA created a vertical reading room offering hundreds of daily newspapers printed in China. The structure is a lesson in restraint and vibrancy, singular subject matter and infinite variety—as the newspapers change daily, so does the architecture.

1 The Newspaper Café, Jindong New District Architecture Park, Jinhua City,
  China, 2004–06. **DESIGNER** Toshiko Mori. **PROJECT TEAM** Jolie Kerns, Sonya Lee.
  CLIENT Jindong New District Constructing. **RENDERING** Toshiko Mori Architect
2 Syracuse Center of Excellence, Syracuse, NY, 2005–present. **DESIGNER** Toshiko
  Mori. **PROJECT TEAM** Josh Uhl, Tilmann Schmidt, Ashley McGraw Architects
  (associate architect). **CLIENT** Syracuse Center of Excellence. **RENDERING** Toshiko
  Mori Architect

NASA'S HYPER-X PROGRAM
X-43A PLANE
HAMPTON, VIRGINIA

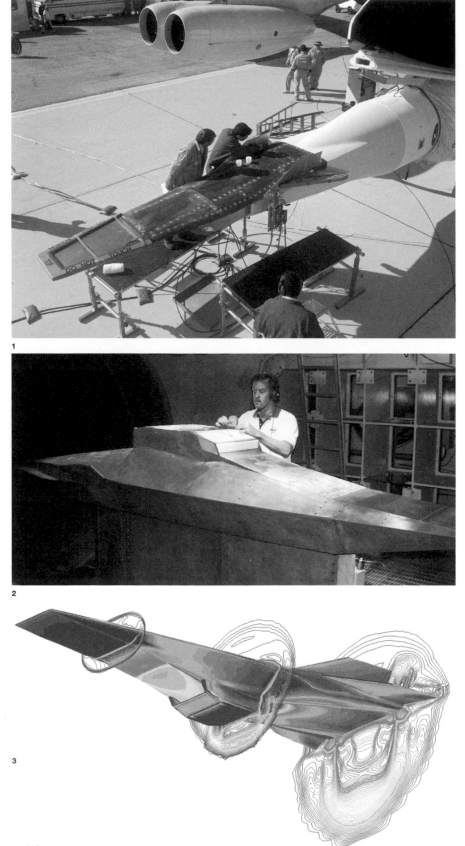

1

2

3

On November 16, 2004, the NASA X-43A scramjet, an unmanned experimental aircraft designed to test beyond high-supersonic flight speeds, broke the world speed record for an air-breathing (jet) air-craft, traveling at Mach 9.8, nearly 7,000 miles per hour, at an altitude of 110,000 feet. Before the X-43A flights, the previous air-breathing record of Mach 5 was held by a missile, and the previous speed record for any form of winged aircraft had stood since the rocket-powered X-15 flights in 1967 reached nearly Mach 7—a remarkable span of thirty-eight years. The only manmade winged object that has traveled faster than the X-43A is NASA's Space Shuttle, which did so outside the earth's atmosphere.

These amazing speeds are achieved through a distinctive wedge-shaped design and the employment of a super-sonic combustion ramjet, or scramjet. The scramjet has no moving parts, and achieves its thrust by compressing air at very high speed into a constricted tube. Such a design is necessary for hyper-sonic flight, where conventional jet engines cannot function.

The X-43A was carried aloft by the old-est B-52 on flying status, and launched from an altitude of 40,000 feet. A rocket booster then carried the X-43A to an alti-tude of over 100,000 feet and accelerated to test-condition speeds. The rocket booster then fell off, and the X-43A flew under its own power for approximately ten seconds on a programmed flight pro-file. Afterwards, the craft made a planned crash landing in the Pacific Ocean.

NASA originally built three X-43A air-craft. One was lost in 2001 when it spun out of control after dropping from the B-52 carrier plan. The second X-43A flew successfully on March 27, 2004, and set a speed record of Mach 7. The third X-43A achieved the current speed record, cover-ing approximately two miles per second.

The X-43A is part of the X-plane series of aircraft dating back to the 1947 X-1, the first aircraft ever to beak the sound bar-rier. NASA's Hyper-X program involved ATK GASL, Boeing, and Orbital Sciences Corporation. Hyper-X is conducted jointly by the Langley Research Center in Hampton, Virginia, and the Dryden Flight Research Center in Edwards, California.

X-43A Research Vehicle, 2000–04. **DESIGNERS** NASA, ATK GASL, Orbital Sciences Corp., Analytical Mechanics Associates, The Boeing Company, DCI, Dyncorp, SAIC, Swales Aerospace, Zeltech, and Analytical Sciences & Mechanics
1 X-43A Research Vehicle prepared for test flight, March 27, 2004. **PHOTO** NASA/Dryden Flight Research Center
2 X-43A Research Vehicle engine before test firing. **PHOTO** NASA/Langley Research Center
3 X-43A Research Vehicle at mach 7 with engine operating. Computational Fluid Dynamics Image. Courtesy of NASA/Dryden Flight Research Center

4 X-43A Research Vehicle after separation from Pegasus booster. Capture from animation video. Courtesy of NASA/Dryden Flight Research Center and Langley Research Center
5 Hyper-X Research Vehicle, artist's concept in flight with scramjet engine firing. Courtesy of NASA/Dryden Flight Research Center

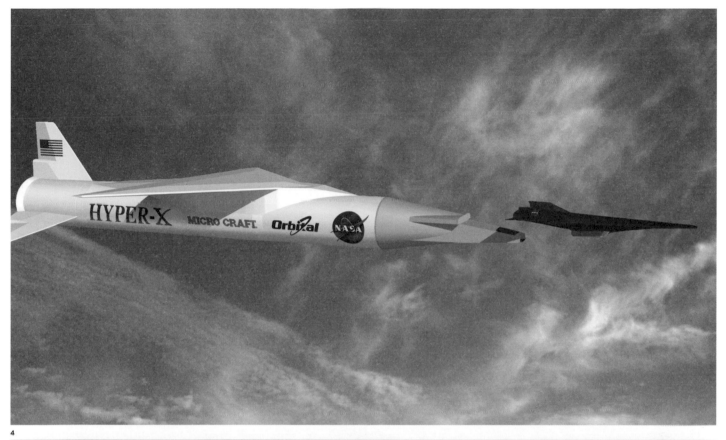

4

5

NASA'S JET PROPULSION LABORATORY

MOBILITY AND ROBOTIC SYSTEMS GROUP
PASADENA, CALIFORNIA

1

2

3

4

Lemurs are small, arboreal primates found in Madagascar. Their name, Latin for "spirits of the night," most likely refers to their large reflective eyes and nocturnal habits. One of the most recent and innovative robotic devices at NASA's Jet Propulsion Laboratory, the *Legged Excursion Mechanical Utility Rover* (*Lemur*) is inspired in part by this primate's ability to use its limbs for mobility and manipulation. It is one of dozens of robots that JPL is working on for use in various types of space exploration.[1]

The robot's role in space is by now a well-accepted fact; researchers have been working for years on developing robots that can substitute for as well as assist humans in space. The enormous success of *Spirit* and *Opportunity*, the rovers which have been on the surface of Mars for over two years transmitting images and data back to Earth, has only reinforced the potential for such technology. But unlike the rovers, whose "life" expectancy was initially measured in months, scientists and engineers are working toward systems that can be permanently installed in space, providing long-term, continuous information and data feedback. This requires a robot which possesses a high level of operational flexibility relative to mass and volume, dexterity, significant processing and sensing capabilities, and the ability to be easily reconfigured, both physically and algorithmically.

Lemur IIa, one of the most significant developments in this area, is intended to expand the operational envelope of robots in its size category (about 10 kg). Specializing in small-scale assembly and the maintenance of macro-space facilities, it consists of six limbs arranged around a hexagonal body platform composed of high-strength, lightweight carbon-fiber and Nomex composites. The limbs have a special feature that allows a rapid change-out of its tools, including a walking/poking tool, LED task light, video camera, and rotary tool. The stereo camera set sits on a track and is propelled around the circumference of the body, allowing omnidirectional vision. The advanced materials used in the *Lemur* keep mass to a minimum—its chassis only weighs 0.5 kg—while providing a rigid base for mobility and manipulation operations. According to JPL, the *Lemur* is the "Swiss Army knife of six-limbed primates."

1 The information for this text came from a public document about the *Lemur*: "The Lemur II-Class Robots for Inspection and Maintenance of Orbital Structures: A System Description," Brett Kennedy, Avi Okon, Hrand Aghazarian, Mike Garrett, Terry Huntsberger, Lee Magnone, Matthew Robinson, Julie Townsend at the 8th International conference on Climbing and Walking Robots, Sept 13-15, 2005, London, England.

1 Artist's concept of Mars Exploration Rover. Digital rendering. Courtesy of
  NASA's Jet Propulsion Laboratory
2 Cahokia Panorama, Mars, taken by Mars Exploration Rover *Spirit,* 2004.
  Photomosaic of 470 panoramic images. **PHOTO** *NASA/JPL/Cornell University*
3 Mars Exploration Rovers 1 and 2 with predecessor *Sojourner* Rover, 2003.
  PHOTO NASA's Jet Propulsion Laboratory
4 Mars Exploration Rover 2 with lander, Kennedy Space Center, 2003.
  PHOTO NASA/JPL/KSC
5 *Limbed Excursion Mechanical Utility Rover (LEMUR) IIa,* 2004–present. **DESIGN
  TEAM** Brett Kennedy, Hrand Aghazarian, Mike Garrett, Lee Magnone, Avi Okon.
  Aluminum, nylon, graphite, Nomex composites. **PHOTO** NASA's
  Jet Propulsion Laboratory

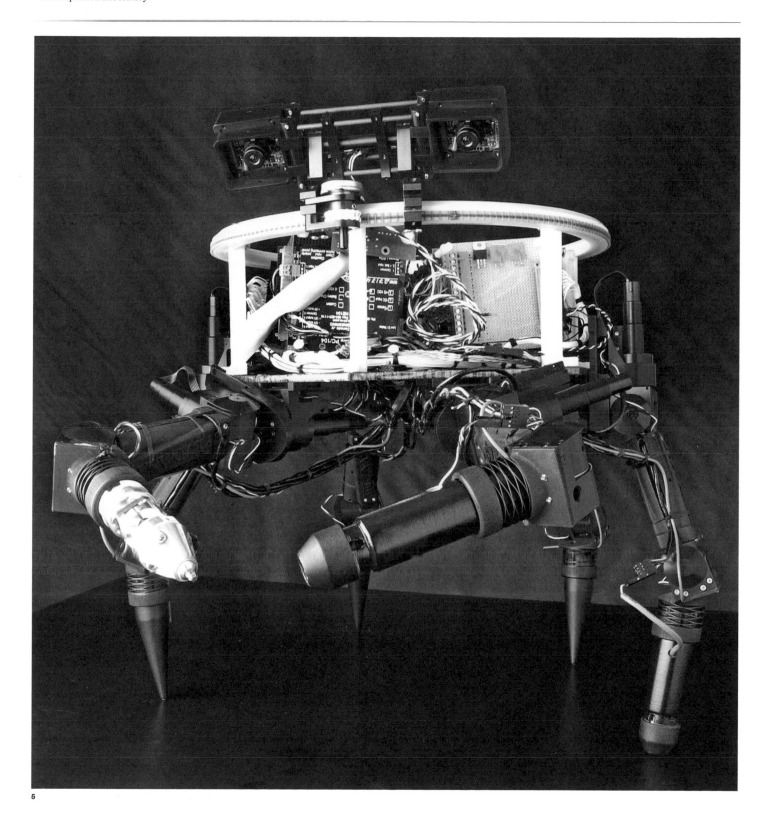

5

NIKE, INC.
PORTLAND, OREGON

1

2

Over the last several years, there has been considerable attention paid to "smart" design as it relates to integrating electronics into apparel. In the sports arena, it has been especially rampant, with companies designing, for example, motion-control running shoes embedded with microprocessors to analyze foot impact and adjust the cushioning with each stride. But some companies like Nike, embracing a "less is more" attitude, are producing shoes that do not inhibit or restrict the foot's own movement, thus allowing the foot to function more naturally. The Nike Free 5.0 is a shoe that behaves like you are not wearing a shoe at all.

Nike's years of testing and observation have shown that as shoes become more protective, feet end up more restricted and, ultimately, weaker. When Nike researchers observed athletes running barefoot, they found that "during propulsion and landing, athletes have more range of motion in the foot and engage more of their toes. Their feet flex, spread, splay, and grip the surface, meaning less pronation and more distribution of pressure." At the start, Nike used a zero-to-ten scale to analyze prototypes, with zero being barefoot and ten being the most structured and protective shoe it makes. The goal was to achieve a five—hence the 5.0—which offered enough cushioning and protection, but put the foot in control. After eleven prototypes had been fully tested at the Nike Sport Research Lab, including workouts with athletes, the Nike Free was launched in 2004.[1]

Innovation Kitchen, Nike's think tank for shoes and other athletic wear, is the heart and soul of the company, and reflects the mission to innovate that has guided the company since it was founded over thirty years ago. The designers and engineers find inspiration in everything from Mexican embroidery and Dutch design to nature. They collect these artifacts and ideas, translate the essentials into their own language, and process them for future application.

Apparel designers of the Advanced Innovation Team at Nike followed a similar approach in creating Nike Sphere React, a line of "electronic-free" smart apparel which responds to changes in the body or environment. The designers of the textiles in Sphere React were inspired by biomimetics—the study of the formation, structure, or function of biologically produced substances, materials, and processes, with the goal of reproducing them artificially—and wanted to "create a personal atmosphere for the wearer," much like feathers allow a bird to be insulated from variable weather conditions.[2] The new materials react to changes in the wearer's environment, such as reducing cling to help keep athletes dry, promoting increased airflow to keep athletes cool, and making a more breathable garment while protecting the athlete from outside weather. Together with Nike Free 5.0, it makes for one smart athlete.

1 Interview with Tobie Hatfield, Senior Engineer for Advanced Products, Innovation Kitchen, on January 17, 2006.
2 Interview with Jordan Wand, Global Director, Advanced Innovation Team, on January 23, 2006.

1 Nike Sphere React, 2005. **DESIGNER** Jordan Wand. Dri-FIT, polyester, Spandex. **PHOTO** Nike, Inc.
2 Rafael Nadal wearing Nike Sphere React apparel. **PHOTO** Nike, Inc.
3 Nike FREE 5.0, 2004. **DESIGNER** Tobie Hatfield. Nylon, synthetic microfiber, rubber. **PHOTO** Nike, Inc.

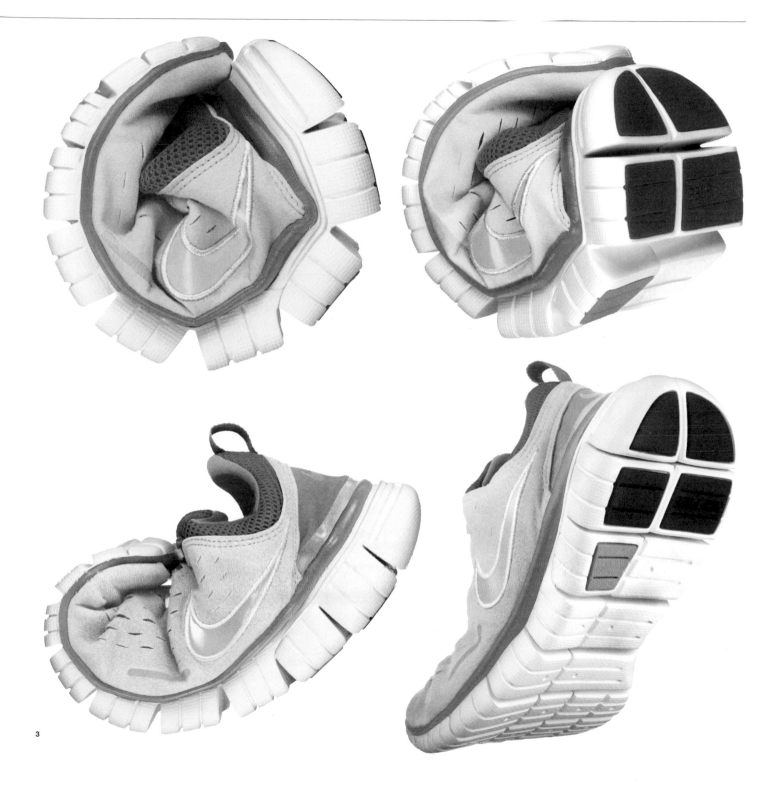

3

OMA / REM KOOLHAAS

OFFICE FOR METROPOLITAN ARCHITECTURE
ROTTERDAM, THE NETHERLANDS, AND NEW YORK, NEW YORK

1

2

The new Seattle Central Library is truly a library for the twenty-first century, remarkable for its stunning architecture as well as for the extraordinary research process that shaped not only its program but also the building that houses it. The first freestanding building in the United States by Rem Koolhaas's architecture firm OMA (Office for Metropolitan Architecture), the new library not only redefines the way we think about libraries, it is a significant new civic building and public space for the city.

OMA is known for the vast amount of research it conducts for every project. Upon receiving the design commission, the architects spent three months trying to define what a contemporary library could, and should, be. They interviewed and received input from librarians, publishers, technology experts, and business leaders, among others. After a thorough examination of the library's program, they assigned a color to each form of media and activity and reorganized them into spatial compartments, which they arranged and rearranged to establish the building's overall form.

Two significant conclusions are at the heart of the design concept. OMA determined that, contrary to popular thinking, books are here to stay, but they need to coexist with other sources of information, such as the Internet. In addition, libraries in general are experiencing a rise in nontraditional responsibilities, such as classroom teaching, Internet access, public meetings, and social gatherings. These findings pointed the way to a new system of flexible design, which divides the library's program into stable areas for predictable functions and unstable areas for unpredictable functions. These areas take physical form in the floor platforms that shift from side to side and create the strikingly asymmetrical cantilevered form of the building. At the core is the Books Spiral, which provides a flexible space for the library's collection to grow without overtaking other programmatic areas. Rather than separating books by category and floor, the Spiral winds its way up through the entire building. The structural mesh skin of the building creates light, airy, inviting interior spaces. Plants are brought into the ground floor, and colorful carpets of abstracted plant forms reinforce the connection between the inside and outside. The building's design incorporates many other innovative features, including the use of bright colors and a computer-guided book circulation system.

152

ORGAN RECOVERY SYSTEMS

LIFEPORT (DESIGNED WITH IDEO)
DES PLAINES, ILLINOIS

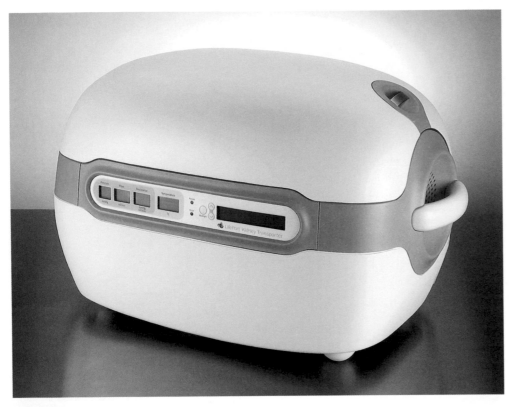

Today, the number of people in America who need, and may not receive, donated human organs has reached startling levels. More than 68,000 critically ill patients are currently waiting to receive kidneys. This crisis is not only due to scarcity of the organs, but also to the extreme difficulty of keeping donated organs viable until they can be transplanted.

To begin solving this problem, Organ Recovery Systems designed the LifePort® Kidney Transporter, which received the Food and Drug Administration's approval in 2003. The LifePort design represents a new, state-of-the-art standard of care and ease of transport for transplantable kidneys; and uses proprietary, integrated, precision-engineered technology.

The LifePort's exterior is sleek and compact, with a display that continuously monitors the organ's performance data in real time. Its one-touch keypads offer streamlined operation. The interior is outfitted with hoses to continually pump tissue-nourishing fluids through the kidney, and includes a microprocessor to monitor vital signs. Recent studies have shown that kidneys transported in the LifePort survive at least seventeen hours longer than those transported the standard way, doubling the viability time of the organs. On March 22, 2006, LifePort was featured in a episode of *CSI: New York*, a television show noted for its use of the latest forensic medical techniques and equipment.

The company is currently in the last stages of design and development for LifePort Transporters for the heart, liver, and pancreas. Each will offer portability for long-range transport and substantially improved organ-assessment capabilities and preservation time. As a result, thousands of lives will be saved.

LifePort® Kidney TransPorter, 1998–2003. **DESIGNERS** David Kravitz, John Brassil, and Douglas Schein (Organ Recovery Systems); Dickon Isaacs and Jerry O'Leary (IDEO). Cast polyurethane housing, expanded polystyrene insulation, injection molded polycarbonate cassette, cannulas, and tube frame, lithium ion batteries, proprietary single board controller and real time firmware, OEM-supplied pumps, valves, sensors, LCD displays, and components, polyester membrane key panels, EtO sterilized disposable set. **PHOTO** Tom Petrov, © 2003 Organ Recovery Systems, Inc.

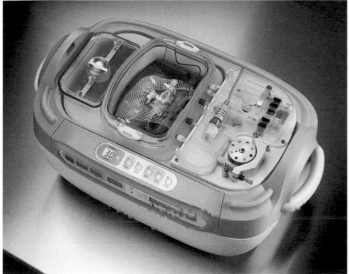

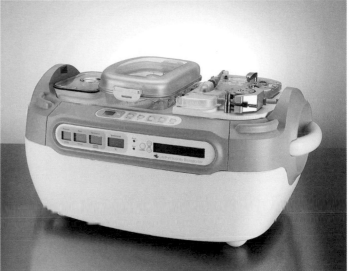

PANELITE
EMMANUELLE BOURLIER AND CHRISTIAN B. MITMAN
NEW YORK, NEW YORK, AND LOS ANGELES, CALIFORNIA

1

2

Panelite's composite panels are not only attractive, but their exceptional strength and structural integrity make them perfect for a wide range of architecture and design applications. Made using a sandwich construction method typically found in the aerospace industry, each panel consists of a cellular honeycomb core, faced on both sides with either prefabricated or cast polyester resin sheets reinforced with fiberglass.

Panelite was originally founded in 1998 by two young architects, Emmanuelle Bourlier and Christian Mitman, who developed this innovative material as a solution to a design problem. Deeply committed to material research and development, Panelite has tapped the potential of its initial concept to develop a full array of ingenious variations on the first generation of panels. Honeycomb cores made of different materials—PET, polycarbonate, or aluminum—and different cellular configurations provide a range of surface patterns, textures, and visual effects that modulate both light and vision. Recently, the company developed Panelite Insulated Glass Unit (IGU) panels, which are strong and weather-resistant enough to be used for exterior applications. The Laminated and Cast Polymer series are interior-grade composite panels, and the Cast Polymer panels can be custom-tinted to match any paint chip or color specification, and have been used by many architects to create colorful and translucent interior walls and surfaces.

Rem Koolhaas's OMA used Panelite products throughout the interior and exterior of the McCormick Tribune Center at the Illinois Institute of Technology in Chicago. OMA also collaborated with Panelite to develop furniture for the building, including the Workstation, a sleekly minimal table made entirely of Cast Polymer Panelite, and which makes use of new technology developed by the company to curve the panels, expanding the material's potential even more. In keeping with its core purpose of transforming the possibilities of building through ongoing innovation, Panelite developed an interlocking system called ITL which takes full advantage of the structural strength of the honeycomb core of the panels to eliminate the need for any additional support. ITL, like Panelite's other products, is highly customizable and allows design freedom and efficiency all at once.

1 View of exhibition *Translu-city: Panelite in Architecture and Design*, UCLA Perloff Gallery, Los Angeles, 2003. **PHOTO** Panelite

2 Panelite Workstations 2.0, at Illinois Institute of Technology's McCormick Tribune Campus Center, Chicago, IL, 2003. PE/RC Panelite™ Cast Polymer Series™ panels (polymer honeycomb core with un-tinted resin facings). **PHOTO** Panelite

3 PE/RO Panelite™ Cast Polymer Series™ panels. Polymer honeycomb core with orange resin facings. **PHOTO** Panelite

4 PE/RVLBMLA Panelite™ Cast Polymer Series™ panels. Polymer honeycomb core with very light blue resin facings and amber mica laminated to one face. **PHOTO** Panelite

5 Falcón Headquarters, Mexico City, Mexico, 2004. **DESIGNER** Rojkind Arquitectos. **EXTERIOR GLAZING** IGU Panelite™ Insulating Glass Unit. **PHOTO** Panelite

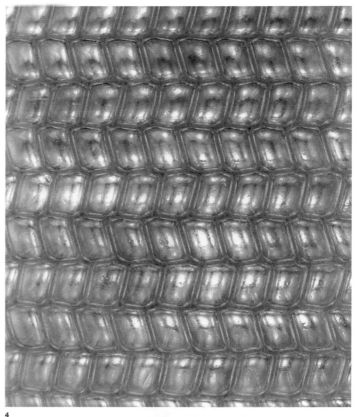

3

4

ORLANDO PITA
NEW YORK, NEW YORK

1

Hair has carried sacred and spiritual connotations throughout history. It was the source of Samson's strength in the Bible, and the route by which Rapunzel's visitors came to call. Hair lends its wearer an aura of sexual virility, seduction, and health. It is one of the few parts of our body we can play with, change at will without incurring permanent damage, and "dress" to reflect our personality, chosen identity, and momentary moods.

Orlando Pita is a hair design magician. For the last two decades, he has been a master of hair styles and fashions, the theatrical as well as the more realistic. Chances are that everyone who is reading this has seen numerous examples of his work. Pita styles hair for celebrities from Madonna and Janet Jackson to Gwyneth Paltrow and Julianne Moore. His work has graced magazine covers such as the Italian, French, British, and American editions of *Vogue*, *W*, *Harper's Bazaar*, and *Allure*, and he has worked with such noted fashion photographers as Richard Avedon, Irving Penn, and Mario Testino.

Many of his most extreme and fabulous hair designs were created for the fashion runway. Pita has created looks for Michael Kors, Versace, Prada, Miu Miu, Christian Dior, Valentino, Gucci, Narcisco Rodriguez, Tommy Hilfiger, and Dolce & Gabbana, and has also designed hair for rising designers such as Proenza Schouler and Derek Lam. Pita has worked with John Galliano for over six years; and it took him three days to create the incredible, flat, square hairstyle worn by models for the 2004 Egyptian-themed Dior Couture show.

Declaring that he missed actually cutting hair, Orlando Pita opened his own salon in January 2005, in New York's meatpacking district.

PIXAR
EMERYVILLE, CALIFORNIA

Until Pixar Animation Studios began releasing feature films, the terms *authenticity* and *animation* seemed oxymoronic. However, since it was founded in 1998 by Steve Jobs and Ed Catmull, Pixar has revolutionized animation through its technological innovations, remarkable spatial illusionism, sculptural reality, and emphasis on authenticity in its stories, set designs, and characters. Its success is based on three factors: its pioneering proprietary software; its talented staff, who work in small collaborative teams; and its belief in and support of traditional animation artistry. In seven full-length films as well as groundbreaking shorts during the last decade, Pixar has replaced the traditional method of photographing individually framed celluloid or paper drawings with the most advanced digital technology available today.

Pixar's technical and creative teams developed three core proprietary software systems—Marioneet, Rightmaster, and RenderMan—all of which have significantly advanced motion-picture rendering. The process of creating a Pixar film, however, begins largely by hand. The company employs artists, painters, sculptors, and animators; teams of up to twenty people work on the front end of a film before any technology is used. As Brad Bird, director and voice of the *Incredibles* character Edna, observes, the main job of the technology is to "find a way to do" whatever is necessary to create a believable, engaging story. Once that is achieved, everything else follows.

Each film involves months of research and brainstorming before any commitment is made toward a specific drawing style or character. Creative teams go to great lengths to understand every aspect of the film's subject matter, often taking acting classes to learn how to convincingly communicate what a character is thinking. During research for the film short *Boundin'*, Pixar artists learned to shear sheep; and for *Ratatouille*, they took culinary lessons from a chef and kept live rats in their studios to study the animals' movements and gestures.

Characters are first drawn in two dimensions—resulting in thousands of drawings, sketches, and collages of each. Simultaneously, another group of artists paints oil and pastel paintings of the various landscape locations and contexts in which the action will take place. Once the illustrators and director choose the best angle to shoot each sequence, the storyboards are locked into place; the characters are translated from two to three dimensions (individually modeled by Pixar sculptors); and lighting, shading, and texture are added.

The goal is not hyperrealism, but believability—to capture the "essence" of life rather than record every tiny facial hair and blemish. As Bird observes, although they have the ability to do the latter, they have found that "what you think it looks like is often more 'realistic' in perception than the actuality." For *Finding Nemo*, the Pixar team replicated the *look* of ocean water, but found that, when reproduced on the screen, it looked dead. So they started over, this time trying to replicate how water *feels*, with extraordinarily life-like results.

Pixar's commitment to authenticity extends to each film's sets and costumes. For example, there were ninety-five costume changes in *The Incredibles*. The technology teams learned how to wrap flat clothing patterns around three-dimensional animated bodies. The film's set designers watched James Bond films and *The Jetsons* cartoons before designing the 1960s-style fashions; and they included Ludwig Mies van der Rohe furniture, George Nelson clocks, and 1960s stereo equipment in the main characters' living room. For *Ratatouille*, Pixar teams toured the sewers of Paris and sampled each recipe Ratatouille teaches the young chef to make in the film. The story, of a young adult rat who initially doesn't "fit" in his environment, and slowly learns what he was meant to do with his life, is not just geared toward children, but, like other Pixar films, also resonates with adults.

With its emphasis on authenticity of detail, gesture, character, sets, costumes, and actions, an engaging story, and creative blending of human judgment with innovative technology, Pixar continues to lead the field.

1 Edna Mode (a.k.a. "E"), from *The Incredibles*, 2004. **ARTIST** Teddy Newton.
  Collage. Courtesy of Pixar Films
2 Edna Mode (a.k.a. "E") House, from *The Incredibles*, 2004. **ARTIST** Paul Topolos.
  Digital rendering. Courtesy of Pixar Films
3 E living room, from *The Incredibles*, 2004. **ARTISTS** Mark Holmes and
  Bryn Imagire. Digital rendering. Courtesy of Pixar Films
4 Gusteau's Kitchen lighting study, from *Ratatouille*, 2006. **ARTIST** Dominique
  Louis. Digital painting over computer model. Courtesy of Pixar Films
5 Omnidroid development sketch, from *The Incredibles*, 2004. **ARTIST** Lou Romano.
  Pencil. Courtesy of Pixar Films
6 Mr. Incredible vs. Omnidroid, from *The Incredibles*, 2004. **ARTIST** Lou Romano.
  LAYOUT Don Shank. Gouache. Courtesy of Pixar Films

5

6

PLANET PROPAGANDA
MADISON, WISCONSIN

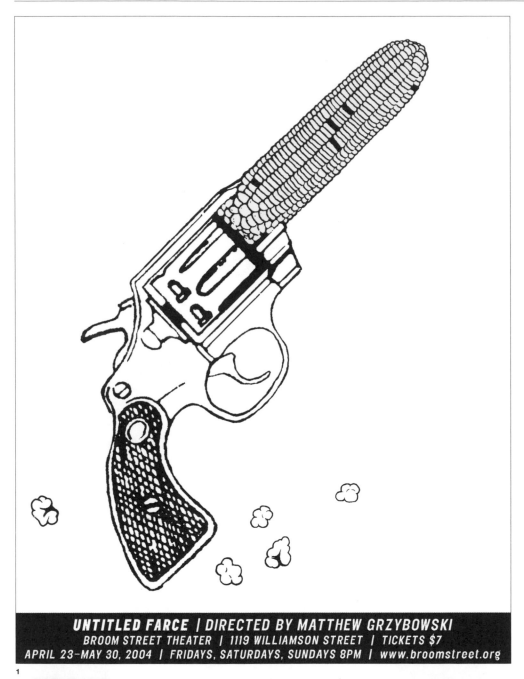

UNTITLED FARCE | DIRECTED BY MATTHEW GRZYBOWSKI
BROOM STREET THEATER | 1119 WILLIAMSON STREET | TICKETS $7
APRIL 23–MAY 30, 2004 | FRIDAYS, SATURDAYS, SUNDAYS 8PM | www.broomstreet.org

1

2

Although its name mockingly evokes delusions of totalitarian grandeur, Planet Propaganda is a design agency that approaches a diverse range of media with commonsense thinking and carefree creative energy.

Founded in 1989 as Planet Design Company by designers Kevin Wade and Dana Lytle, the firm was renamed Planet Propaganda in 2000, marking its transformation from a traditional graphic-design firm to a full-service design, advertising, and interactive company. Its client list has ranged from national companies such as Rollerblade, Target, and Miller Brewing to the Wisconsin Film Festival and the local Broom Street Theater.

A direct, real-life sensibility pervades Planet Propaganda's diverse body of work. Hand-drawn illustrations deliver blunt, immediate humor: in a theater poster, the barrel of a gun is made of popcorn; to promote a show by P'elvis, a band featuring Wade, at the local Anchor Inn, a classic ship's anchor becomes a pelvic bone. The pleasure taken in well-written copy shines through in direct, down-home advertising and branding for Jimmy John's Gourmet Sandwiches, a national chain of high-quality fast-food restaurants.

Planet Propaganda extends its attitude to motion graphics, creating unforgettable campaigns for Gary Fisher Mountain Bikes and other clients. Planet's third principal, John Besmer, established a film division, P Star Pictures, in 2004, dedicated to developing and marketing original features, shorts, and films. Prepare for world domination, as Planet Propaganda brings the cool humor that has helped reap success for the Wisconsin Film Festival and other clients to its own independent media productions.

1 *Untitled Farce*, poster, 2004. **CREATIVE DIRECTOR** Kevin Wade. **DESIGNER** Jim Lasser. **CLIENT** Broom Street Theater. Courtesy of Planet Propaganda

2 Jimmy John's Gourmet Sandwiches, advertising, packaging, brand identity, 2002–04. Creative **DIRECTOR** Kevin Wade. **DESIGNERS** Dan Ibarra, Jim Lasser, Kelly English, Travis Cain. **WRITERS** Seth Gordon, John Besmer. **CLIENT** Jimmy John's Gourmet Sandwiches. Courtesy of Planet Propaganda

3 *The Alabaster County Little League Beauty Pageant*, poster, 2003. **CREATIVE DIRECTOR AND DESIGNER** Kevin Wade. **CLIENT** Broom Street Theater. Courtesy of Planet Propaganda

Broom Street Theater

1119 WILLIAMSON STREET | TICKETS $7
FRIDAYS, SATURDAYS, SUNDAYS | 8PM
WWW.BROOMSTREET.ORG

THE ALABASTER COUNTY LITTLE LEAGUE beauty pageant

WRITTEN & DIRECTED BY SCOTT FEINER
PERFORMANCES JUNE 6TH – JULY 13TH

PLANET PROPAGANDA

PREDOCK FRANE ARCHITECTS

HADRIAN PREDOCK AND JOHN FRANE
SANTA MONICA, CALIFORNIA

1

2

Predock Frane is an emerging architecture firm featuring a collaborative research and development studio, in which it explores "analogues, environmental intelligence, oppositions, and the erosion of traditional boundaries." Conceptually complex yet time-sensitive, these pursuits, translated into building form, are extraordinarily elegant, thought-provoking, and functional.

In its design for the Central California History Museum, to be located in downtown Fresno's new cultural district, Predock Frane addresses the crucial agrarian landscape and water systems that have been part of the 15,000-year story of human presence in this region. The building is layered like a landscape: the lower level is the most earthbound, and uses thickened earth and heavy materials; the upper levels seem to float, with a perforated copper skin which changes appearance under different lighting conditions. Archival materials embedded in wall elements stitch the floors together.

For the Center of Gravity Foundation Hall, a teaching and meditation hall for the Bodhi Mandala Zen Center in New Mexico, light itself structures the space. Predock Frane's design traces the course of the sun during the day, integrating this information within its scheme. Embracing oppositions, the architects juxtapose heavy rammed earth with light polycarbonate, creating an ideal environment for the various rituals that take place inside and out.

Predock Frane studies the confrontation of human and natural forces with "Acqua Alta, or Just Add Water," using the city of Venice as its context. Chosen to be one of six architects to represent the United States in the 2004 Venice *Architecture Biennale*, it evoked water and marsh patterns and the complex geometries of piers that underpin this environmentally vulnerable city. In its mesmerizing installation of nearly 6,000 strands of monofilaments, each monofilament was hung from the ceiling and held in position by lead weights, creating a transparent linear forest. To grasp a bunch of strands would have been tempting, but this urge underscored the fragility of the environment that we have created, and how easily it can be destroyed.

1 The Central California Museum of History, Fresno, CA, 2002–present. **PROJECT TEAM** Hadrian Predock, John Frane, and Max Frixione. **RENDERING** Predock Frane Architects

2 Center of Gravity Foundation Hall, Jemez Springs, NM, 2003. **PROJECT TEAM** Hadrian Predock, John Frane, and Max Frixione. **PHOTO** Jason Predock. **RENDERING** Predock Frane Architects

3 *Acqua Alta or Just Add Water*, Venice Architecture *Biennale*, 2004. **PROJECT TEAM** Hadrian Predock, John Frane, Elizabeth Grace, Morgan Maclean, Jodi Batay-Csorba, and Max Frixione. **PHOTO** Predock Frane Architects. **RENDERING** Predock Frane Architects

PROCESSING

BEN FRY AND C. E. B. REAS
CAMBRIDGE, MASSACHUSETTS, AND LOS ANGELES, CALIFORNIA

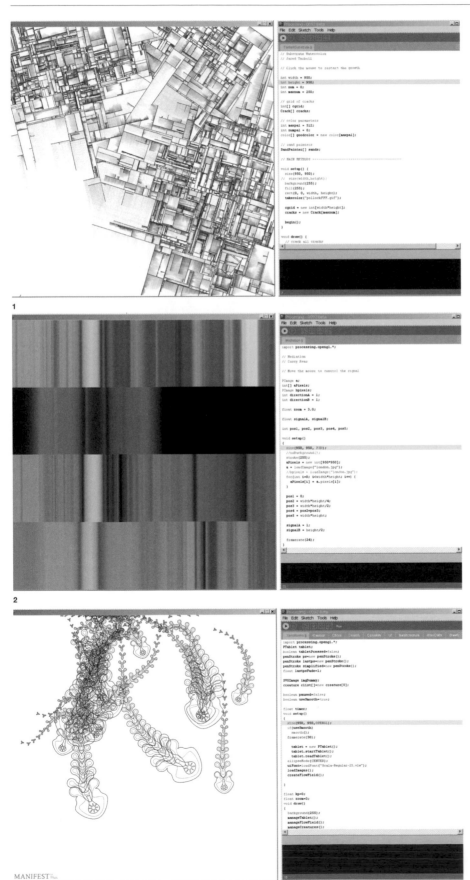

1

2

Processing is at once a digital tool, an online community, a teaching environment, and a powerful medium of visual expression. Created by Ben Fry and Casey Reas, graduates of the MIT Media Lab, Processing is the language behind a body of visual projects produced by artists and designers around the world. This open-source application can be downloaded for free at www.processing.org, a Web site where a global network of users meets to shape the life of the program and share the results of its work.

With its direct syntax and elegant interface, Processing enables users with minimal programming experience to create simple, rule-based animations and interactive or self-evolving works. Whereas most commercial animation programs such as Flash employ a familiar palette of drawing tools—brush, pen, paint bucket—and a graphic timeline for organizing elements sequentially, drawing in Processing is entirely code-based, requiring the designer to write instructions for generating a mark on the screen and defining its behavior.

Despite its simplicity of use, Processing supports ambitious interactive pieces and intricate self-generating compositions. Professional designers such as the architects Morphosis in Santa Monica, California, and the interactive media designers Art+Com in Berlin, Germany, are using the program as part of their research and production process. In addition, Fry, in collaboration with scientists, is using Processing to visualize the human genome at the Broad Institute of MIT and Harvard University.

As artists, both Fry and Reas use Processing to create complex automated drawings. Reas's project *Articulate* generates a field of elements that spontaneously interact, resembling a cloud of spores or a bed of lichen—shrinking, growing, merging, clustering, disintegrating. Fry's *Disarticulate* takes written code from Reas's piece and traces its repetitive routines with dense furls of machine-drawn lines. These two works reflect a new role for the designer: to define a point of origin and a set of conditions, then step back and watch life take over.

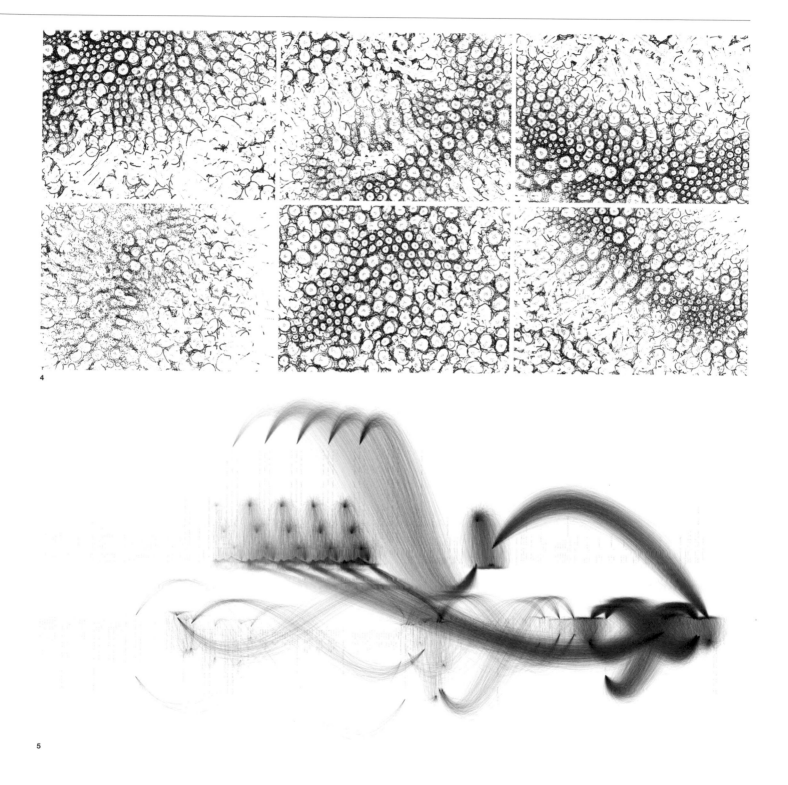

1 *Substrate*, 2003. **DESIGNER** Jared Tarbell. Processing designed by Benjamin Fry and Casey Reas. Digital drawing generated with Processing code and interface. Courtesy of Processing

2 *Mediation*, 2003, 2006. **DESIGNER** Casey Reas. Processing designed by Benjamin Fry and Casey Reas. Digital drawing generated with Processing code and interface. Courtesy of Processing

3 *Manifest*, 2005. **DESIGNER** Michael Chang. Processing designed by Benjamin Fry and Casey Reas. Digital drawing generated with Processing code and interface. Courtesy of Processing

4 *Process 6 (Image 4)*, 2005. **DESIGNER** Casey Reas. Digital drawing generated in Processing. Courtesy of Processing

5 *Process 6 (Disarticulate)*, 2005. **DESIGNER** Benjamin Fry. Digital drawing generated in Processing. Courtesy of Processing

4

5

PSYOP
NEW YORK, NEW YORK

Q

What is the place of graphic design within the worlds of advertising and animation? Each of these realms has its own visual tradition, business culture, and technical methodology. Surprising results, however, emerge when design takes the lead in an ad campaign or an animated spot, as evidenced by the painterly work of PSYOP.

At this multimedia design firm, the creative process begins with still imagery generated by a team of designers and composed from drawn illustrations as well as photographs. These initial images, often built from dozens of layers of color, texture, and image, are then interpreted as a moving sequence. As PSYOP explains, "It's become a bit of a game between design and production. Our design team keeps trying to come up with styles and images that seem nearly impossible to translate into motion, which ends up inspiring our animators and technical team even more."

Consider, for example, PSYOP's Internet spot *Drift* for Bombay Sapphire, an eerie and seductive thirty-second film whose scrolling narrative combines live action and animated imagery. While the flattened aesthetic of Japanese prints establishes the piece's overarching visual reference, the camera seeks out spatial depths within the landscape, revealing subtle three-dimensional effects that are a hallmark of PSYOP's work. The Bombay spot ends with a bottle of gin, but the rest of the piece functions as an engaging narrative in its own right. A similar attempt to treat advertising as independent entertainment is seen in *Run Wild*, a forty-second spot for the popular shoemaker Merrill, in which a fierce bunny with a running shoe for a heart overtakes his forest friends in a race.

PSYOP borrowed its name from the U.S. government's Psychological Operations division, and the company has cheekily adopted the agency's slogan as well: "Persuade, Change & Influence." At a time when consumers are bombarded with more messages from more media than ever before, PSYOP seeks to win over the hearts and minds of the public through creative content that people willingly seek out and enjoy.

1 *Merrell: Run Wild*, Web and cinema spot (40 seconds), 2003. **DESIGNERS** Todd Mueller and Kylie Matulick. **FLAME ARTIST & SENIOR ANIMATION** Eben Mears. **AGENCY** Jager Di Paola Kemp Design. **AGENCY ART DIRECTOR** David Covell. **CLIENT** Merrell. Courtesy of PSYOP

2 *Bombay Sapphire: Drift*, Web spot (60 seconds), 2003 **DESIGN AND ANIMATION** Todd Mueller and Kylie Matulick. **EXECUTIVE PRODUCER** Justin Booth-Clibborn. **PRODUCER** David Rosenbloom. **TECHNICAL DIRECTOR** Todd Akita. **FLAME ARTIST AND COMPOSITING** Eben Mears and Roi Werner. **ANIMATION ARTISTS** Todd Akita, John Clausing, Tom Cushwa, Kevin Estey, Eric Borzi, and Kent Seki. **SOUND DESIGN AND PRODUCTION** Singing Serpent. **AGENCY** Margeotes Fertitta + Partners. **AGENCY CREATIVE DIRECTOR** Fritz Westenberger. **AGENCY EXECUTIVE PRODUCER** Annette Suarez. **AGENCY PRODUCER** Meagan MacDonald. Courtesy of PSYOP

RANSMEIER & FLOYD

LEON RANSMEIER AND GWENDOLYN FLOYD
EINDHOVEN, THE NETHERLANDS

1

2

The objects of Leon Ransmeier and Gwendolyn Floyd are direct, yet poetic, responses to everyday situations. The Crop bookshelf, for instance, features horizontal flaps that serve to even out the staggered skylines created by rows of books. According to these rising design stars, "If an object can present an intelligence of manufacture and design while provoking people to actually think about it, that is good design."

Although Ransmeier and Floyd's partnership officially began in 2004, when the pair opened their studio in the Netherlands, these two young American designers first met in a hardware store in Providence, Rhode Island, when Ransmeier was studying in the furniture program at the Rhode Island School of Design and Floyd was immersed in cultural theory at Brown University. After moving to the Netherlands, Floyd studied at the Design Academy Eindhoven. The team's joint design venture is creating furniture and products for Artecnica, BALS Japan, Danese, Droog, Mawa Design, Serien Lighting, Vlaemsch, and other companies.

Ransmeier & Floyd's Gradient dish rack consists of flexible polypropylene rods positioned like blades of grass, progressively more crowded from one end to the other. This arrangement accommodates flatware and thin glasses where the rods are dense, and dishes and larger items where they grow sparse. Clean aesthetics meet informal living in other pieces as well, from the D.I.Y.M. lamp shade, which slips on and off any bare hanging bulb without the need for additional hardware, to a portable countertop kitchen hood modeled after a task lamp. The work of this remarkable design team expresses a new functionalism, one that rejects the glamour and luxury of sleek, seamless assembly to focus on the realities of human use and physical construction.

1 D.I.Y.M. (Do-It-Yourself-Modern) lamp shade, 2005. **DESIGNER** Gwendolyn
Floyd. **MANUFACTURER** Droog Design. Polypropylene. **PHOTO** Ransmeier & Floyd
2 Snow shelf prototype, 2006. **DESIGNER** Leon Ransmeier. Steel, road-marking
paint. **PHOTO** Ransmeier & Floyd
3 Gradient dish rack, 2005. **DESIGNERS** Gwendolyn Floyd, Leon Ransmeier.
MANUFACTURER Royal VKB. Polypropylene. **PHOTO** Ransmeier & Floyd
4 Hood countertop hood prototype, 2005. **DESIGNER** Gwendolyn Floyd. Steel,
plastic, fan, and light components. **PHOTO** Ransmeier & Floyd
5 Crop bookshelf prototype, 2005. **DESIGNER** Gwendolyn Floyd. Beech, plywood,
laminate. **PHOTO** Ransmeier & Floyd

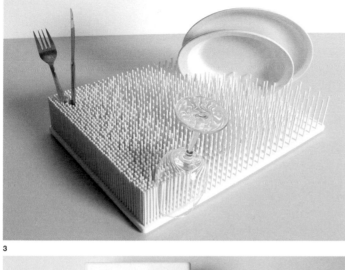

3

4

5

READYMADE MAGAZINE
BERKELEY, CALIFORNIA

1

ReadyMade magazine's tag line is "Instructions for Everyday Life." On the surface, it is a publication about how to make things out of stuff that already exists, crafting clever constructions from the by-products of consumer waste. A closer reading, however, exposes the magazine for what it really is: a manifesto for life in the twenty-first century.

Founded in 2001 by Shoshana Berger and Grace Hawthorne, *Ready-Made* speaks to a new generation of consumers and post-consumers concerned with both the ethics and aesthetics of domesticity. Many readers of *ReadyMade* will never actually build a CD rack from a FedEx tube or a chandelier from VOS water bottles, but they are drawn to the magazine's view of design as an inclusive, hands-on enterprise. Shopping is not enough; people want to actively engage their environments, finding personal pleasure and social virtue in putting together the pieces of their own physical lives.

Just as *Martha Stewart Living*, the masterwork of do-it-yourself lifestyle publishing, has always served to inspire as well as explain, *ReadyMade* delivers a message that runs more deeply than the projects that make up its core content. *ReadyMade* speaks of self-empowerment, self-education, and self-determination. A series of interviews called "How Did You Get that F*&%ing Awesome Job?" explores the career paths of creative people—from artist Andrea Zittel to filmmaker Mike Mills—and helps readers think about their own ambitions and how to realize them.

Berger and Hawthorne started the magazine with credit cards, playing a risky shell game with no-interest financing deals. They lived to tell the tale, and tell it with plucky charm in their new book, *ReadyMade: How to Make Almost Anything*. Like the magazine, the book mixes detailed project descriptions with humorous, pointed discussions of ecology and detailed advice about life skills, from starting a business to telling a story—two things Berger and Hawthorne certainly know how to do.

1 Water-Bottle Chandelier, book spread, 2005. **PROJECT DESIGN** Grace Hawthorne/ReadyMade. **AUTHORS** Shoshana Berger and Grace Hawthorne. **BOOK DESIGN** Eric Heiman. **PHOTO** Jeffery Cross

2 Bird Buffet, book spread, 2005. **PROJECT DESIGN** Grace Hawthorne/ReadyMade. **AUTHORS** Shoshana Berger and Grace Hawthorne. **BOOK DESIGN** Eric Heiman. **PHOTO** Jeffery Cross

3 FedEx CD Rack, book spread, 2005. **PROJECT DESIGN** Grace Hawthorne/ReadyMade. **AUTHORS** Shoshana Berger and Grace Hawthorne. **BOOK DESIGN** Eric Heiman. **PHOTO** Jeffery Cross

4 Cold Storage, magazine spread, July/August 2004. **PROJECT DESIGN** Rodrigo Pantoja and Brian M. Kelly. **PHOTOGRAPHER** Rebecca Miller. **ILLUSTRATOR** Kate Francis. **ART DIRECTOR** Eric Heiman. **EDITOR** Shoshana Berger. **PUBLISHER** Grace Hawthorne

MARTINI BIRD BUFFET

Got some scratched, chipped, or otherwise unclassy wineglasses you're looking to get rid of? Make a fancy feast for feathered friends by gluing a few stems together and hanging them from a nearby branch. The shape was inspired by the bubbly champagne waterfalls you see at gala events, but our version spills over with seed instead. Many hummingbird feeders are made of glass, so don't fear rigging your crystal outdoors. (When set close together, they double as wind chimes!) The birds will flock, eat themselves into a full-bellied stupor, and sing like drunken sailors.

2

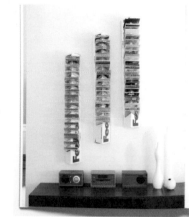

FEDEX CD RACK

Compact discs: the great storage problem of our day. The used sections of music stores are bulging to capacity. Indian reservations won't take them. If dumped at sea, they'll just bob upon the waves. Plus, discs might come back into fashion. (We can hear the kids of tomorrow saying, "You have the original CD?!") If we've convinced you at all to keep your collection, you'll need an expandable storage solution. Most racks have that style-starved "I'm not a sculpture but I play one on TV" look. Here's an overnight idea—cut slits into FedEx tubes and hang as many of them as you need to house your listening library.

3

RE-STORE

Cold Storage

Add Pop to Your Living Room
by Rodrigo Pantoja and Brian M. Kelly

Pepsi paid Britney and Madonna millions to shape our perception of the world's second most popular soft drink. Now, a group of architecture students at Drury University in Springfield, Missouri, are giving Pepsi new cred for class credit! Pupils stripped away the soda's mass-market image and gave it new meaning and function. Behold the new generation.

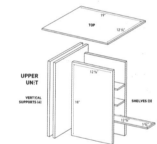

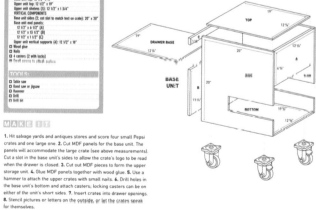

CRATE UNIT

$45

INGREDIENTS:
- ☐ 4 small old Pepsi crates, about 12" x 16" x 4 1/2"
- ☐ Large old Pepsi crate, about 12" x 16" x 12"
- ☐ 4' x 8' x 1/2" MDF (medium-density fiberboard) sheet with the following cuts:
  HORIZONTAL COMPONENTS
  Base unit bottom: 12 1/2" x 19 1/2"
  Base unit drawer base: 12 1/2" x 19"
  Base unit top: 12 1/2" x 19"
  Upper unit top: 12 1/2" x 19"
  Upper unit shelves (3): 12 1/2" x 1 3/4"
  VERTICAL COMPONENTS
  Base unit sides (2, cut slot to match text on crate): 20" x 20"
  Base unit end panels:
  12 1/2" x 6 1/2" (A)
  12 1/2" x 13 1/2" (B)
  12 1/2" x 1 1/2" (C)
  Upper unit vertical supports (4): 12 1/2" x 16"
- ☐ Wood glue
- ☐ Nails
- ☐ 4 casters (2 with locks)
- ☐☐ ☐☐☐ ☐☐☐☐ ☐☐ ☐☐☐☐ ☐☐☐☐☐

TOOLS:
- ☐ Table saw
- ☐ Band saw or jigsaw
- ☐ Hammer
- ☐ Drill
- ☐ Drill bit

MAKE IT

1. Hit salvage yards and antiques stores and score four small Pepsi crates and one large one. 2. Cut MDF panels for the base unit. The panels will accommodate the large crate (see above measurements). Cut a slot in the base unit's sides to allow the crate's logo to be read when the drawer is closed. 3. Cut out MDF pieces to form the upper storage unit. 4. Glue MDF panels together with wood glue. 5. Use a hammer to attach the upper crates with small nails. 6. Drill holes in the base unit's bottom and attach casters; locking casters can be on either of the unit's short sides. 7. Insert crates into drawer openings. 8. Stencil pictures or letters on the outside, or let the crates speak for themselves.

July/August 2004_ReadyMade **23**

4

173

NARCISO RODRIGUEZ
NEW YORK, NEW YORK

1

Narciso Rodriguez's love of modern architecture is at the core of his elegantly minimal womenswear designs. When asked to name his favorite architect, Rodriguez answers, without hesitating for a second, Ludwig Mies van der Rohe. The influence of van der Rohe and other early twentieth-century modernists does not appear in Rodriguez's work as direct architectural references, but in the way he develops his forms from an innate understanding and appreciation of structure and material. In his iconic Seagram Building, van der Rohe exposed and emphasized the simple beauty of the building's structural I-beams, expressing his belief that less is often more. Rodriguez shares that belief: he strips his garments of any extraneous detail and lets the seams of his meticulously constructed clothes serve as the only form of ornament. He also uses seaming for structure and to create interesting lines and shapes, and will spend hours obsessively draping and fitting a garment on a live model, marking, taping, and retaping fit lines until the shape and proportions are perfect. A bold graphic sensibility is another important aspect of Rodriguez's work. He designs primarily in black and white for this reason, and uses the contrast to achieve a sharp, clean silhouette. Seams are highlighted in a contrasting color, and pieces of fabric are inserted or extracted from a garment to mark points on the body—waist, hips, bust, and back. Shifts in materiality or color underline a garment's architectonic construction.

Several seasons ago, Rodriguez introduced greater volume in his clothes; while tops remained sculptural and precise, skirts made of flowing fabrics draped softly in a more overtly feminine way. Sexy and prim, bound and unbound—Rodriguez successfully incorporates both ends of the spectrum in the way he blends the classic with the modern. He describes his style as American (the practical streamlined tailoring) with a European influence (the tradition and craftsmanship of haute-couture fashion) and a Latin heart (his own Cuban-American heritage).

1 Violet coat, autumn/winter 2005–06. Wool bouclé. **PHOTO** Narcisco Rodriguez
2 Coral dress, spring/summer 2005. Silk. **PHOTO** Narcisco Rodriguez

RALPH RUCCI
NEW YORK, NEW YORK

"Invisible luxury" best describes the creations of fashion designer Ralph Rucci. Rucci, who studied philosophy and literature before focusing on fashion, opened his business in 1994 and decided to call it Chado, after the traditional Japanese tea ceremony. He chose this name because it embodies respect, tranquility, grace, and integrity—qualities he wishes to evoke through his fashion designs.

In 2002, France's prestigious Chambre Syndicale de la Haute Couture invited Rucci to show his haute-couture collection in Paris; he was the first American to earn this honor since Mainbocher in the 1930s. Rucci has always concentrated on luxurious womenswear, and his work on one-of-a-kind, lavishly detailed garments serves as a laboratory where he tests ideas and techniques that cross over into his ready-to-wear line. Eschewing the theatrical spectacles and bells and whistles of other haute-couture designers, Rucci focuses instead on the quiet and steady development of his collections, the strength of which lies in their impeccable craftsmanship, luxurious fabrics, and subtle embellishments.

In Rucci's office, photographs, drawings, and an assortment of beautiful objects provide clues to the things that fuel his imagination: a close-up of a woven Japanese basket; Irving Penn's famous photograph of a highly abstracted wedding gown by Balenciaga; paintings by Twombly, Bacon, and Gottlieb. He describes himself as a sponge, soaking up rich references that inspire the textures, forms, and ideals he develops as a conceptual basis for each collection.

Together with a dedicated staff, Rucci produces all of his designs in his New York atelier, giving couture-level attention to every garment. The cut and construction of Rucci's clothes are architectural, and almost every garment features complex seaming, both inside and out. Some garments take 300 hours to make, others as many as six months; and often the most intricate and involved workmanship is on the inside of a garment, as in an evening skirt that has a box pleated ruffle on the inside to hold the shape. This intensive labor is virtually invisible in his gowns and dresses, which paradoxically appear simple and pure.

1 Orange double-faced wool/silk dress with pailloné belt, spring 2005 haute-couture collection. Double-faced wool, silk. **PHOTO** Dan and Corina Lecca
2 Trellis dress, fall 2004 haute-couture collection. Double-faced wool crepe with printed infanta chiffon underlay. **PHOTO** Dan and Corina Lecca
3 Black duchessc satin suspension infanta with olive embroidered insets, fall 2005 haute-couture collection. Duchesse satin with embroidered insets. **PHOTO** Dan and Corina Lecca
4 Black wool crepe and leather dress, fall 2004 haute-couture collection. Wool crepe and leather. **PHOTO** Dan and Corina Lecca
5 Degradé suspension tailleur, fall 2005 haute-couture collection. White to beige double-faced cashmere. **PHOTO** Dan and Corina Lecca

177

LENI SCHWENDINGER

LIGHT PROJECTS, LTD.
NEW YORK, NEW YORK

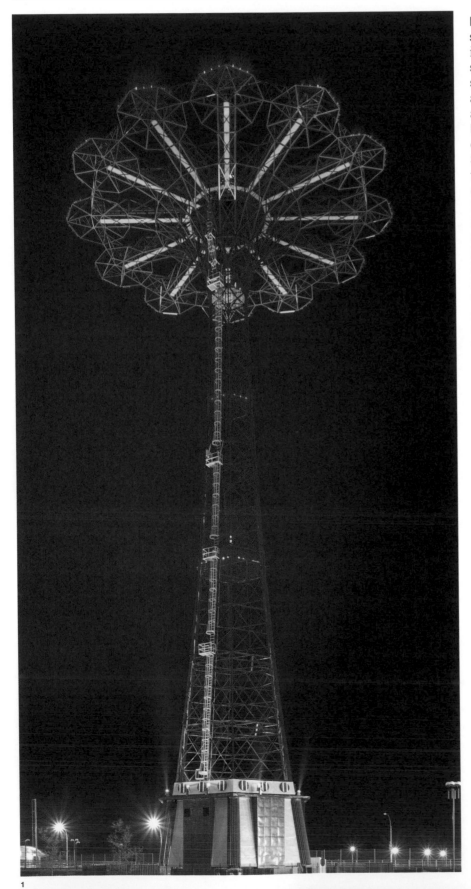

Leni Schwendinger understands the special characteristics of light that enable it to change a mood, invigorate public spaces, sculpt the perception of dimensions, and connect people to each other and to their surroundings. For more than a decade, Schwendinger's firm, Light Projects, Ltd., has attracted many multidisciplinary collaborations and clients. She brings together project-specific teams staffed by architects, graphic designers, engineers, who employ the latest technologies to create uniquely beautiful instillations. In *Chroma Streams: Tide and Traffic*, a dynamic lighting system on the underside of the busy Kingston Bridge in Glasgow, Scotland, sensors tracking traffic congestion feed data into a computer program that in turn activate swathes of light on the bridge: yellow indicates a smooth flow, while red indicates a traffic jam. At the same time, green and blue hues are synchronized with the tide cycles of the Clyde River below. Both systems run concurrently, with the colors reflecting in the water offering a double-sided wash of colored light.

Schwendinger's clients have included performing-arts centers, event planners, architecture firms, museums, and state and municipal agencies. For the Marion Oliver McCaw Hall in Seattle, Light Projects projected a program of colored light onto nine metal scrims, thirty feet tall and sixty feet long, arching across the Hall's entry promenade. Schwendinger adapted musical scoring techniques to sequence the complex changes in colored lights. The resulting spatial and temporal light installation evokes a synesthesia-like metaphor.

In 2005, Light Projects designed the illumination for the *Fashion in Colors* exhibition at Cooper-Hewitt. Working with Tsang Seymour Design, the exhibition's designers, Schwendinger and her team conceptualized and designed specific room installations of glowing ambient light—black, multicolor, blue, red, yellow, and white—surrounding groupings of matching fashion from the eighteenth through the twenty-first centuries. The results allowed visitors to experience the materiality of color and articulated color's emotional, cultural, and psychological associations.

1 Coney Island Parachute Jump Illumination, July 7, 2006. **DESIGNER** Leni Schwendinger/Light Projects, Ltd. **CONTRACTORS** 4 Wall Entertainment, CAN Resources, Electronic Theater Controls, Phoster Lighting, Martin Professional, LINCO Electric, Turner Construction. **COMMISSIONED BY** New York City Economic Development Corporation. **CLIENT** STV Inc. Metal halide automated lighting fixtures, LEDs, DMX signal programming. **PHOTO** © Charles Denson

2 *Chroma Streams: Tide and Traffic*, July 2005. **MANUFACTURERS** Martin Professional, Strand, Smartek, BP Solar Panels, Trichord Data Collection Software. **INSTALLERS** James Young Ltd, JM Architects, Normand & Thomson Ltd, Northern Light, Mott MacDonald Civil Engineers. **COMMISSIONED BY** Glasgow City Council. Stainless steel, metal halide automated light fixtures, DMX wireless transmitter/receiver. **PHOTO** Steve Hosey

3 *Dreaming in Color, a Three-dimensional Color Field*, Kreielsheimer Promenade at Marion O. McCaw Hall, Seattle, WA, 2003. **MANUFACTURERS** Coemar, Electronic Theatre Controls, Cascade Coil Drape. Nine coil-drape scrims, 20 panoramic color changing light fixtures, computerized lighting playback control system. **PHOTO** ArchPhoto

2

3

TOM SCOTT
NEW YORK, NEW YORK

1

Tom Scott's work blurs the line between garment and accessory. A scarf, a T-shirt, or a sweater—at times it is hard to tell, and his creations can often be more than one of the above. A cardigan can be transformed into a pullover. A shrug's sleeves are held together by the thin neckband of a V- or crewneck sweater, but the rest of the sweater is missing. One end of a scarf becomes a sleeve.

Scott, who began his career as an accessories designer for Ralph Lauren, designs knitwear that expands and challenges our notions of this most traditional of crafts. Since Scott launched his own line of accessories in 2000, followed by knitwear in 2002, his seasonal collections have drawn on an eclectic and eccentric range of sources for inspiration, including medical reference books, knitting history books, vintage dress patterns, the human anatomy, and topographical maps. "I don't really find inspiration from what's in fashion," he says. "I look more at things like the architecture of the human body, while experimenting with knit construction."

Scott developed his fresh and unconventional approach when, as a student, he bought his first knitting machine and became obsessed with the ways he could use it to manipulate textiles into unexpected shapes and forms. He is intrigued by distortion at all scales, from the form of an archetypal garment to individual stitches. He experiments and tests the limits of technology, materials, and craft, and his elegantly distorted forms often occur purely by accident, the result of a fortuitous mistake with a stitch or a pattern. Scott's interest in architectural constructions is evident in his Vertebrae scarf. Inspired by the bones in the human back, the scarf's soft ruffled edges are anchored by a more thickly knitted spine, which provides structure to the piece. Its complex geometry is most apparent when draped around a neck, falling in an undulating spiral that becomes at once ruff, shawl, and scarf. With his quirky and elegant knits, Tom Scott shows us that sweaters and scarves don't have to be dowdy and utilitarian.

1 Diagonal seam muscle tee w/ sleeves, worn with reverse pointelle shrug, spring/
summer 2005. Cotton jersey tee, cashmere/cotton shrug. **PHOTO** Mathias Kessler
2 Rib lace cowl tank, spring/summer 2006. Cashmere/cotton. **PHOTO** Stephen Rose
3 Double front tank worn with cardigan jersey shrug, spring/summer 2006. Cotton/
steel tank with cashmere/cotton shrug. **PHOTO** Stephen Rose
4 Sheer mohair moss-stitch pullover, autumn/winter 2006. Knit mohair. **PHOTO**
Stephen Rose
5 Vertebrae scarf, autumn/winter 2006. Cashmere. **PHOTO** Mathias Kessler

2

3

4

5

SHOP
CHRISTOPHER R. SHARPLES, WILLIAM W. SHARPLES, COREN D. SHARPLES,
KIMBERLY J. HOLDEN, AND GREGG A. PASQUARELLI
NEW YORK, NEW YORK

1

2

SHoP is a New York design firm that has been instrumental in a reevaluation of the entire building process. A leader in the current digital generation of architects, SHoP employs digital technology as a tool to build efficiently while creating structures that reflect architecture's precision and worksmanship.

In 2005, SHoP completed its first digitally designed, computer-fabricated building, in the village of Greenport, New York. The Camera Obscura ("dark room" in Latin) is a 350-square-foot building that acts like a camera. A live image of the Camera's surroundings is projected through an optical lens and a mirror onto a flat circular table that is raised or lowered to adjust focal depth. It can focus on all the buildings and elements in Mitchell Park and across Long Island Sound.

The Camera is composed of 750 custom parts accompanied by a set of instructions, much like a model-airplane kit. Primary aluminum and steel components were laser-cut using digital files directly extracted from the computer model, with crucial information etched into the components for ease of fabrication. SHoP employs the same 3-D software as its engineers and fabricators, allowing them to communicate with each other more directly and seamlessly.

Most of the fabrication took place offsite and the pieces later bolted into the concrete foundation and to each other. The subtly warped exterior skin, milled in a single morning, makes the entire structure look like a hovering horseshoe crab.

SHoP was founded in 1996 by five graduates of Columbia University's School of Architecture whose education and experience encompass architecture, fine arts, structural engineering, finance, and business management. Although Camera Obscura is a relatively modest project compared to others currently in its office, including Brown University's Jonathon Nelson Fitness Center and the academic building and master plan for New York's Fashion Institute of Technology, it exemplifies SHoP's strong commitment to research and development as well as built work. The firm is incorporating leading-edge technologies that ultimately enable them to do more with less.

1 Camera Obscura, Mitchell Park Phase 2, Greenport, NY, 2005. **ARCHITECTS** SHoP Architects, P.C.: Christopher R. Sharples, William W. Sharples, Coren D. Sharples, Kimberly J. Holden, Gregg A. Pasquarelli. **PROJECT TEAM** Mark Ours, Reese Campbell, Jason Anderson, Keith Kaseman, Basil Lee. **PHOTO** Seong Kwon
2 Competition model, Busan, Korea, 2006. **ARCHITECTS** SHoP Architects, P.C.: Christopher R. Sharples, William W. Sharples, Coren D. Sharples, Kimberly J. Holden, Gregg A. Pasquarelli. **PHOTO** SHoP Architects PC

JESSICA SMITH
DOMESTIC ELEMENT
SEATTLE, WASHINGTON

Specializing in the design of textiles, wallpaper, and china, Jessica Smith uses elements of domestic design to explore contradictions. Although her products seem innocuous enough at first glance, upon further study, they often contain highly ironic commentaries on contemporary life, remixed within well-known historic textile patterns.

Smith combines traditional, intricate weaving techniques, including matelassì, Jacquard, and damask, with highly decorative scenic designs emulating eighteenth-century French toile de Jouy and nineteenth-century American chintz. Within historical motifs such as rococo flourishes, landscapes, chinoiserie, and natural florae and faunae, Smith blends in banal elements of suburban life, including garbage trucks and track housing.

Each of Smith's designs offers a mini-narrative which the designer hopes the users or occupants can "finish from their own memory." In one series, for example, sea monsters eat Apache helicopters. Her contemporary toile *Trash Day* depicts the familiar ritual of leaving the trash out on the curb. Smith's contemporary chintz *Suburban Garden* is informed by the history of the pattern. Block-printed on hand-woven, glazed cotton, chintz was imported from India in the eighteenth century, and its characteristic patterns were of flowers, animals, and decorative devices. Although stylistically similar to its earlier incarnations, Smith's chintz contains images of contemporary suburban flowers, each one representing a narcotic.

Traditional chinoiserie designs on textiles and wallpaper reflected the wave of European imitation and interpretations of Chinese styles—or those perceived to be Chinese—during the seventeenth and eighteenth centuries. The intricate and elaborate decorations on Smith's *Spying on China*, however, convey a distinctly contemporary edge. American military surveillance planes fly among the traditional Asian-style motifs. This overtly political statement emphasizes the complicated history between Asia and the West.

Through Smith's designs, our homes become a reflection of our contemporary psyche, and offer a unique opportunity for self-expression and commentary. As the Seattle-based designer notes, "While often ironic in its interpretation, I intend for my [artwork] to make a more inclusive statement. I hope to make work that sets a stage for thoughtful conversations."

1 *Sea Monsters Eating Apache Helicopters*, 2004. **PRINTING** EFS Designs. **FINISHING** Domestic Element. Hand-printed linen. **PHOTO** Jessica Smith, © Domestic Element
2 *In Pursuit of Leisure*, pattern design for Jacquard tapestry, 2004. **MANUFACTURER** Beljen Mills. **PHOTO** Jessica Smith, © Domestic Element
3 *Goldilocks Meets the Jones*, Woven Fiber Art House, West Chester, PA, 2004. **MANUFACTURERS WALLPAPER** Studio Printworks, LLC. **TEXTILES AND CERAMICS** Domestic Element. Hand-printed wallpaper (Studio Printworks, LLC), hand-printed fabric, digitally printed decals on ceramic dinnerware. **PHOTO** Jessica Smith, © Domestic Element

3

KEN SMITH LANDSCAPE ARCHITECT

NEW YORK, NEW YORK

1

Ken Smith is a *camoufleur*—he uses splashes of color, foliage, earth, grass, artificial rocks and plants, and water to disguise and conceal. He can make a blank wall into a field of daisies, a railyard into a picnic grove, and a blacktop roof into a fanciful garden. A landscape architect of urban areas, Smith is convinced that "creating livable, renewable, and inspiring urban areas is one of the best ways to limit sprawl and the waste of natural resources."

When Smith was asked to design a rooftop garden at The Museum of Modern Art in New York, the design considerations read like a laundry list of disallowances: no irrigation, no structural attachments, no live plants, no heavy planters, maintenance-free, low-budget; he also had to incorporate black and white stones that the museum had already purchased. Moreover, the garden was to be physically and visually inaccessible to the museum public; only people in surrounding buildings could see the garden due to its location. After several designs, the museum settled on a scheme that started from a skateboarder's camouflage pants, and followed with a palette of mostly natural or recycled materials, including recycled black rubber, crushed glass, sculptural stones, and artificial boxwood plants. Finished in 2005, the result is a cross between a Japanese Zen garden and a Jean Arp relief sculpture.

According to Smith, "Landscape architecture has always been about making synthetic nature." Central Park, once a rocky, swampy, and muddy site transformed into a vast green urban oasis, is as much about artifice as Smith's synthetic plants and pinwheels. But the whimsy and joy of the compositions Smith creates with his 99-cent store discoveries have the same effect as a "day at the park." For example, his installation at the Cornerstone Cafì, part of the Cornerstone Festival of Gardens in Sonoma, California, is a colorful spray of artificial flowers and ferns that sprouts from the wall. The installation is Smith's contemporary version of flowered wallpaper—three-dimensional camouflage which conceals an imperfect wall. Called *Wall Flowers*, it is intended to both blend in and stand out.

Currently on the boards for Smith is the thirteen-acre Santa Fe Railyard Park. Part of a large urban-redevelopment area, the design is based on water harvesting to create a community park that requires little or no municipal water. It will include an open field, rail gardens, performance terrace, and picnic grove. It fits Smith's modus operandi perfectly: the chance to do a lot with a little.

1 *Wall Flowers*, Cornerstone Café, Sonoma, CA, 2005. **INSTALLATION TEAM** KSLA: Ken Smith, Elizabeth Asawa; Cornerstone: David Aquilina. **PHOTO** Ken Smith. **RENDERING** Ken Smith Landscape Architect
2 The Museum of Modern Art Roof Garden, New York, NY, 2003–05. **PROJECT TEAM** Tobias Amborst, Elizabeth Asawa, David Hamerman, Rocio Lastras, Ken Smith, Judith Wong, Christian Zimmerman. **PHOTO** Peter Mauss/ESTO

SPEAK UP

ARMIN VIT AND BRYONY GOMEZ-PALACIO
BROOKLYN, NEW YORK

1

2

Founded in 2002, as blogs were emerging as a potent, independent mode of communication, Speak Up is the brainchild of Armin Vit, a graphic designer who saw an opportunity to build a new mode of design criticism. Taking root in the emerging blogosphere, Speak Up quickly became an influential forum for graphic designers, known not only for its constantly changing, sharply opinionated content, but also for its refined and accessible visual format.

Since its inception, Speak Up has explored the social and technical possibilities of the medium, keeping its interface alive, its typography crisp, and its content constantly refreshed. Among Speak Up's distinctive features is WordIt, a visual archive edited by Vit's wife and Speak Up author and co-manager Bryony Gomez-Palacio, which invites designers to submit visual comments on a particular word each month. Contributions are constrained in size and resolution—and self-promotion and blatant hatefulness are strictly prohibited—otherwise, WordIt is uncensored.

While WordIt contributions can come from anyone, Speak Up's articles are published via invitation only. These writers are paid nothing for their contributions; blogging is an act of love, narcissicism, and public service. (Not surprisingly, Vit and Gomez-Palacio both have day jobs as graphic designers; Vit works for Pentagram, and Gomez-Palacio is a freelancer.) Both were born in Mexico City, Mexico, where they studied design before coming to the United States to study, teach, and practice design—and to change its discourse through their vibrant work as independent publishers.

Speak Up has a voice in print as well: *Stop Stealing Sheep* is a series of small-format booklets featuring snippets from the Web site, selected from both the authored articles and the spontaneous threads of comments spinning out from them. In 2005, Vit and Gomez-Palacio launched a new project, the online Design Encyclopedia (www.thedesignencyclopedia.org), employing "wiki" technology—software that allows users to freely create and edit the site's content from their own browsers. Such projects are expanding a design community that, just a few years ago, was dominated by a handful of magazines and a "senior class" of professional commentators. That era has come to a close.

1 Viva La Political Correctness, Web page, 2005. **DESIGNER AND AUTHOR** Armin Vit. **PUBLISHER** UnderConsideration
2 Word It (Quick), Web page, 2004. **DESIGNER** Armin Vit. **PUBLISHER** UnderConsideration
3 Word It: Blah, visual blog post, 2005. **DESIGNER** Jeff Gill. **PUBLISHER** UnderConsideration
4 Word It: Blah, visual blog post, 2005. **DESIGNER** Ben Scott. **PUBLISHER** UnderConsideration
5 Word It: Blah, visual blog post, 2005. **DESIGNER** Robb Smigielski. **PUBLISHER** UnderConsideration
6 Word It: Blah, visual blog post, 2005. **DESIGNER** David Gilliaert Werner. **PUBLISHER** UnderConsideration

3

4

5

6

SUZANNE TICK, INC.
NEW YORK, NEW YORK

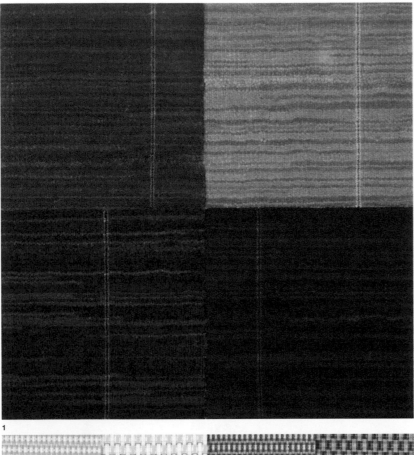

1

2

Suzanne Tick combines her love for texture with a curiosity for new technology to create textile products that are elegant, natural in appearance, and functional. Integrating the natural with the manmade is at the foundation of her work. The Open Plane carpet is just one example: wanting to represent the irregularities of natural fiber like sisal as well as the variegations that occur in the hand-dyeing of wool, Tick and her partner in Tuva Looms, Terry Mowers, have created a carpet which, through a combination of conventional weaving equipment and the careful manipulation of dyeing, is reproducible in manufacture but not in appearance.

Until 2005, Tick was creative director for Knoll Textiles, where she created an exceptional range of textiles, from the contract-furnishing market to the home; she continues to design for the company. Her Imago, introduced in 2000, embedded fabric for the first time into a high-performance resin, and this spirit of ingenuity continues with her line of flat-tape wallcoverings, Adaptation and Aperture. Tick's manufacturing technique is different from the conventional process for making flat tape for the outdoor furniture market. Tick creates a flat-tape extrusion by dragging two threads of polyester fiber through a heated channel of melted PVC, in which the fiber acts as a support for the melted plastic. The tape is cooled down in a water channel and then put on cones ready for weaving. Special equipment is required to hold the tape in place as it is drawn across the loom. The result is both a functional and visually dynamic wallcovering in the spirit of legendary Bauhaus textile designer Anni Albers, who was known for innovative textiles that fulfilled both aesthetic and practical requirements for everyday use.

Tick is constantly looking for new and challenging materials to work with, and her latest challenge is fiberoptics. She has been experimenting with handweaving monofilament and fiberoptics to create soft, sculptural lamps. Woven as a double cloth to make the three-dimensional cruciform shape, this material is especially difficult to weave because of its tendency to get tangled.

Tick counts as her influences both textile designers such as Boris Kroll and Junichi Arai and architects such as Ludwig Mies van der Rohe and Santiago Calatrava. Like them, Tick displays a versatility and passion for experimentation which enable her to constantly question and push the boundaries of her medium.

1 Open Plane carpet, 2003. **DESIGNERS** Suzanne Tick, Terry Mowers.
  MANUFACTURER Tuva Looms, Inc. Woven nylon velvet. **PHOTO** Carter LeBlanc
2 Adaptation and Aperture wallcovering, 2005. **MANUFACTURER** Knoll Textiles.
  Woven vinyl. **PHOTO** Sean Kearnan
3 Crossform lighting, 2004. **MANUFACTURER** Suzanne Tick Design Studio. Double
  woven fiber optics and monofilament. **PHOTO** Carter LeBlanc

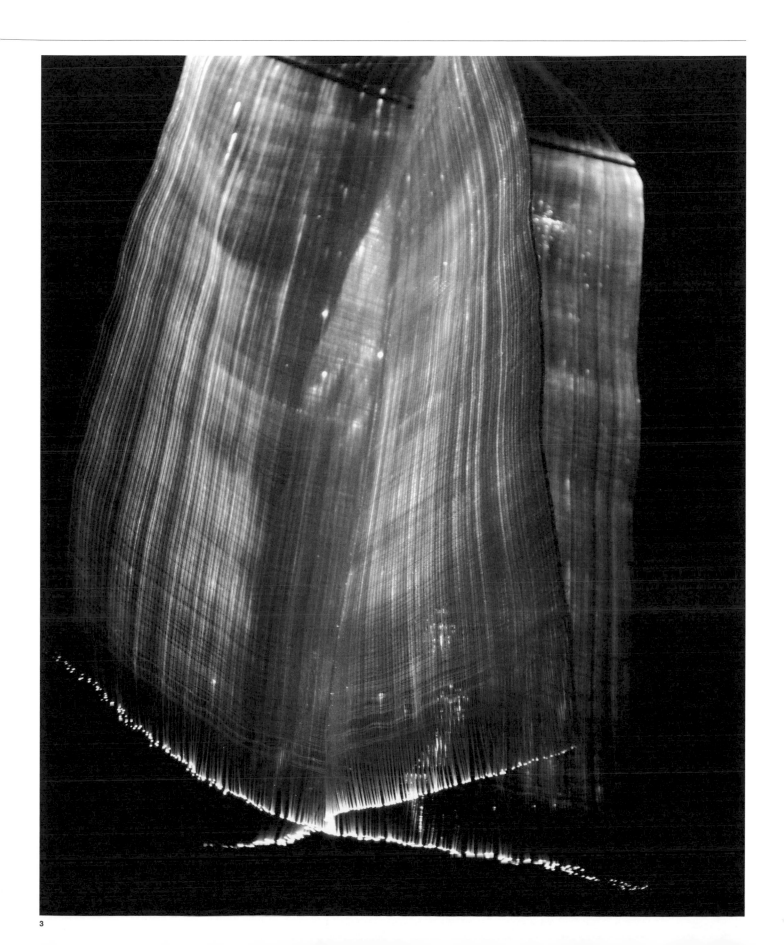

TROLLBÄCK & COMPANY

JAKOB TROLLBÄCK
NEW YORK, NEW YORK, AND LOS ANGELES, CALIFORNIA

1

What makes one television network different from another? What personality does a network hope to convey, and—above all—who does it hope is listening? The most sought-after demographic is aged eighteen to forty-nine, that broad cut of viewers who have become adults but do not yet qualify for a senior discount. Often enlisted to help networks reach this precious market is Trollbèck & Company, a visual and conceptual creative studio founded by the self-trained, Swedish-born Jakob Trollbèck in 1999.

For clients such as TCM, AMC, TNT, HBO, Lifetime, Court TV, and TV Land, Trollbèck & Company has created station identities that are clean, direct, and always inventive, saying more with simple means. No exploding rainbow backdrops or liquid metal logos for these designers; every project is framed by a solid concept executed through strong, purposeful typography, reflecting Trollbèck's lifelong respect for the work of the Swiss designer Josef Mÿller-Brockmann and the German typographer Jan Tschichold.

A painterly sensibility pervades much of Trollbèck's work. Sculpting light out of darkness, the firm's designers and directors incise the screen with glowing bits of text and image. For TCM, Trollbèck devised navigational spots that list the evening's offerings against the gridded office buildings of New York City. The project quietly recalls the film-noir era, known for its distinctive use of light and shadow and grim view of human frailty. As Jakob Trollbèck explains, "The graphics reflect our passion for architecture and typography merged with film-making, producing a mood that incidentally resonates with the neo-noir of David Lynch." A similar approach illuminates many of Trollbèck's opening titles for feature films, including *A Beautiful Mind* and *Vanity Fair*, in which imagery emerges from blackness.

Trollbèck's work has moved offscreen into print advertising, magazine design, environmental graphics, and more. A campaign for Court TV infiltrated New York City with "ambient" advertisements that imply that any person, place, or thing in town could be secretly engaging in a crime or undercover operation. A phone booth becomes "The Lookout," a taxi is a "Getaway Car," and a bus provides "Witness Relocation." Such projects bring home the fact that design—as well as crime—can turn up absolutely anywhere.

1 Court TV ambient advertising campaign, 2005. **DESIGNERS** Joe Wright, Pamela Olecki, Emre Veryeri. **CREATIVE DIRECTORS** Jakob Trollbäck and Joe Wright. **COPYWRITERS** Anne Geri, Andy Ure. **CLIENT** Court TV
2 TCM Menus station identity, 2004. **DIRECTORS** Jakob Trollbäck, Nathalie de la Gorce. **DESIGNERS** Nathalie de la Gorce, Justin Meredith. **CREATIVE DIRECTORS** Jakob Trollbäck and Joe Wright. **EDITOR** Nicole Amato. **PRODUCER** Elizabeth Kiehner. **CLIENT** Shannon Davis Forsythe, TCM Network
3 *Vanity Fair* film credits, 2004. **DIRECTOR** Joe Wright. **DESIGNERS** Joe Wright, Jakob Trollbäck, Tesia Jurkiewicz. **CREATIVE DIRECTORS** Jakob Trollbäck and Joe Wright. **EDITOR** Cass Vanini. **DIRECTOR OF PHOTOGRAPHY** Declan Quinn. **PRODUCER** Elizabeth Kiehner. **CLIENT** Mira Nair, Focus Films

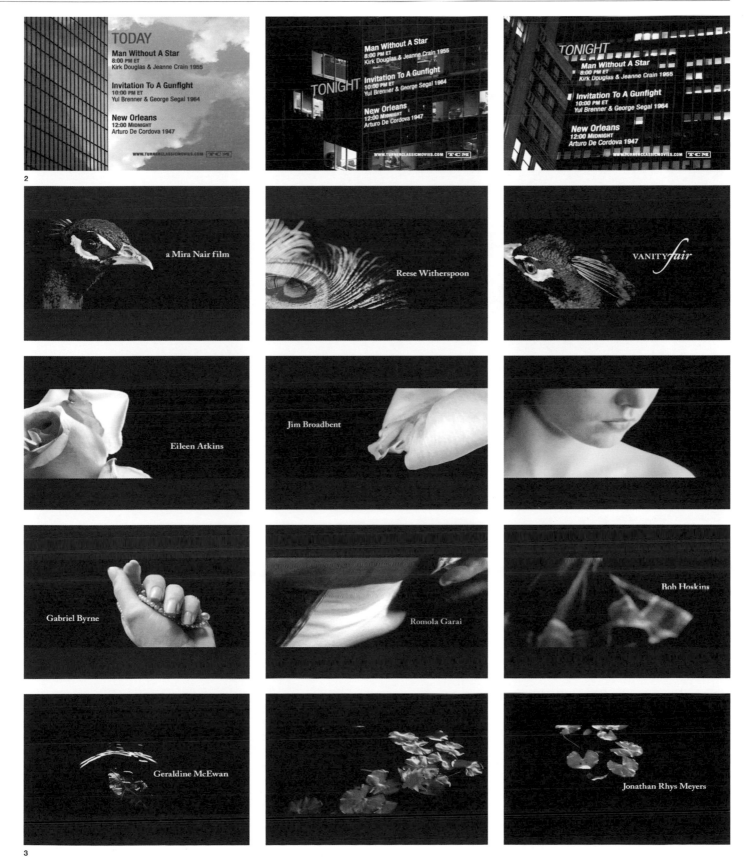

BERNARD TSCHUMI ARCHITECTS

NEW YORK, NEW YORK, AND PARIS, FRANCE

1

2

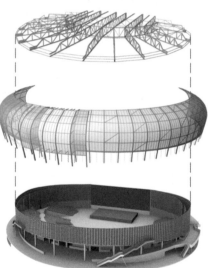

Bernard Tschumi's architecture "is not simply about space and form, but also about event, action, and what happens." This idea, derived from his influential *Manhattan Transcripts*, a series of drawings and photographs done in the late 1970s, encapsulates his most recent body of work. From small residences to urban interventions, Bernard Tschumi Architects is interested in exploring unlikely confrontations.

Inherent in each of Tschumi's projects is a theoretical discourse which often questions certain building conventions and relationships. For example, in his most recent book, *Event-Cities 3: Concept vs. Context vs. Content*, Tschumi discusses the relationship between context (location) and concept (the overarching idea) and the circumstances under which one might override the other; and whether concepts precede content or the programmatic requirements of the building take precedence.

In the sleek factory and headquarters for Vacheron Constantin, the architect's concept is based on the idea of a thin, flexible envelope. The exterior surface is formed from an immense and pliant metallic sheet which unrolls over the building like a conveyor belt, connecting the taller administrative tower with the shorter factory. Context and content are neutral; it is the concept that becomes key. Conversely, the University of Cincinnati Athletic Center stands as a "contextual free-form," using an unusual boomerang shape to maximize space within the tight site constraints. Other contextual constraints contributing to the architectural concept include the trusses needed to provide the clear spans, and which ultimately become a diagonal patterning and the faêade's mullion structure.

With the Concert Hall in Limoges, France, Tschumi reintroduces the general envelope concept, but recontextualizes it and offers material substitutions. Limoges is based on his concert hall in Rouen, France, but instead of concrete, the hall in Limoges uses an exterior skin of wood because of its location within a large forest. This powerful body of work, realized over the last several years, gives physical form to an architectural discourse that has made Tschumi a leading theorist of his generation.

1 University of Cincinnati Athletic Center, Cincinnati, OH, 2006. **PROJECT ARCHITECT** Glaserworks. **PROJECT TEAM** Bernard Tschumi, Kim Starr, Phu Hoang, Robert Holton, Jane Kim, Nicolas Martin, Eva Sopeoglou, Joel Aviles, Chong-zi Chen, Irene Cheng, Jonathan Chace, Adam Dayem, William Feuerman, Thomas Goodwill, Daniel Holguin, Matthew Hufft, Michaela Metacalfe, Valentin Bontjes van Beek, Allis Chee, Justin Moore; Glaserworks: Art Hupp, Kevin Morris, Dave Zelman, Mark Thurnauer. **CLIENT** University of Cincinnati. **PHOTO** Bernard Tschumi Architects

2 Limoges Concert Hall, Limoges, France, 2003. **PROJECT TEAM** Bernard Tschumi, Véronique Descharrières with Joel Rutten, Alex Reid, Jean-Jacques Hubert, Antoine Santiard, Matthieu Gotz, Dominic Leong, Sarrah Khan, Anne Save de Beaurecueil, Chong-zi Chen, Michaela Metcalfe, Alan Kusov. **CLIENT** Communauté d'agglomération Limoges Métropole. **RENDERINGS** Bernard Tschumi Architects

3 Vacheron Constantin headquarters and watch factory, Geneva, Switzerland, 2004. **PROJECT TEAM** Bernard Tschumi, Véronique Descharrières with Joel Rutten, Alex Reid, Matteo Vigano, Cristina Devizzi, Jean-Jacques Hubert, Antoine Santiard, Yann Brossier, Ludovic Ghirardi, Nicolas Martin, Phu Hoang, Jane Kim, Jonathan Chace, Adam Dayem, Rogert Holton, Valentin Bontjes van Beek, Michaela Metcalfe, Justin Moore, Allis Chee, Joel Aviles, Liz Kim. **CLIENT** Vacheron Constantin, Richemont, Int. **PHOTO** Christian Richters. **DRAWING** Bernard Tschumi Architects

HITOSHI UJIIE
PHILADELPHIA, PENNSYLVANIA

Throughout history, textile designs have been tailored to the production methods in use, and each technological innovation has led to a change in the visual vocabulary. Most printed textiles today are made by rotary screen printing. Since each color requires its own engraved screen, the number of colors in an image is reduced to a manageable number, usually eight to twelve. The pattern size or "repeat" can be no larger than the screen, and the level of detail is limited by the pore size of the mesh used.

Hitoshi Ujiie's work is an exploration of the aesthetic implications of digital inkjet printing for textiles, which is bringing about profound changes in the design approach for this medium. Working in the virtual realm has allowed artists and designers to collect, produce, and manipulate images in new ways, playing freely with detail and focus, color effects, and combined or layered images. Working from photographic and video sources combined with hand-manipulation, Ujiie exploits the full range of effects that can be achieved by digital technology, yet his work maintains a profoundly delicate aesthetic. The fineness of line exhibited in his etched plant forms in *Botanical* are the result of the higher resolution available in digital printing.

Digital technology also eliminates the need for repetition or repeat in textile design, and Ujiie turns his attention instead to a sense of movement, or rhythm without repetition, either through engineered patterns or randomization of pattern, or both, over extended lengths. *Branch* has an academic treatise on digital printing as a background. The subtle tonal gradation and sense of transparency showcased in *Virtual Fruit* are only possible with inkjet technology. While it is theoretically possible to print millions of colors with a four-color printing process, Ujiie uses this color precision instead in the creation of layered dimensional effects and subtle blending of color.

RICK VALICENTI
THIRST
BARRINGTON, ILLINOIS

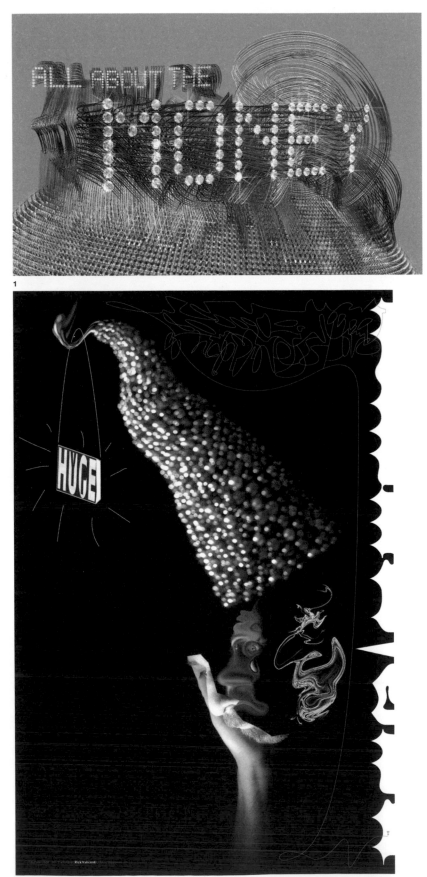

1

2

For over twenty-five years, Rick Valicenti has practiced graphic design from an experimental, deeply personal point of view, while at the same time running a successful design firm that makes business itself a mode of experiment. His career makes good on the potential—achieved by so few practitioners—to mobilize design both as an independent undertaking driven outward from self-defined problems and as a functional tool that can serve up commercial messages with stunning bravura.

Valicenti lives and works in Barrington, Illinois, forty miles northwest of Chicago. Since the mid-1980s, his company, Thirst, has dealt primarily with design-industry clients based in the Midwest, from the furniture maker Herman Miller, Inc., to Detroit's College for Creative Studies. Thirst's self-published projects include *Intelligent Design*, a translation of the Book of Genesis into zeroes and ones, representing each digit with a can of Coke Zero or Pepsi One. For the book *Suburban Maul*, Valicenti sent T. J. Blanchflower, an intern from Old Dominion University in Norfolk, Virginia, to photograph super-sized McMansions within a five-mile radius of Thirst's home base as well as the signage on any store he recognized from Virginia; Blanchflower then matched up each big-box brand with a big-box home. Both self-published works project Valicenti's voice as a cultural critic.

Valicenti has always insisted on keeping his commercial work as raw and independent as his personal endeavors. While his long-term clients love him, some casual shoppers can't take the heat. An editorial illustration commissioned by *ESPN* magazine proclaims in huge, 3D-rendered letters, "It's all about the money." Simulated strands of steroid-enhanced golden jewelry settings suspend the rhinestone-studded text against a Tiffany-blue sky, providing what Valicenti calls "a suburban white male's version of the pixel pusher/gangsta aesthetic." The magazine chose to reproduce only a tiny segment of the full image, but Valicenti shows the whole deal in his 2005 book *Emotion as Promotion*, a large-scale monograph overflowing with dialogues, rants, and visual work. For Valicenti, the book is a manifesto for reinvigorating a field deadened by its own professionalism. He declares, "Civilization will forever be served when we find what we have forgotten we have lost: our reason for being. We must serve, honor, and respect human presence by design." Valicenti's intense, vigorous work is flush with just such presence.

1 *It's All about the Money*, editorial illustration, published cropped 2001, reproduced in full 2005. **PROGRAMMER** Matt Daly, Luxworks. Courtesy of Rick Valicenti/Thirst

2 *Love and Happiness* poster, 2004. **PHOTO** William Valicenti

3 *Intelligent Design: Creating an Evolved Red vs. Blue State of Mind*, 2005. **CONCEPTUAL DESIGNER** Rick Valicenti. **GRAPHIC DESIGNERS** Rick Valicenti and John Pobojewski. **PHOTOGRAPHY AND DIGITAL IMAGING** Gina Vieceli-Garza. **JAVA SCRIPT FOR PAGE COMPOSITION** Robb Irrgang. Fox Starwhite Flash, 100#T. **PUBLISHER** Rick Valicenti, Thirst

MICHAEL VAN VALKENBURGH ASSOCIATES, INC.

CAMBRIDGE, MASSACHUSETTS, AND NEW YORK, NEW YORK

1

2

3

Landscape architects work on many different scales, from garden design and institutional landscapes to public parks. Each firm possesses a unique design philosophy: some combine the manmade and the natural, leaving the imprint of the designer on the land; others remediate industrial sites, removing the traces of man's presence. Michael Van Valkenburgh and his firm deftly draw from their extensive knowledge of plants and flowers to leave the parklands and gardens they design looking as natural as if they had grown that way over time.

Teardrop Park, completed in 2004 in Manhattan's Battery Park City, is a small jewel of a park which, through the firm's choreography of rustic materials, thoughtfully and assertively represents nature in an urban setting. Drawing inspiration and material from the dramatic tectonic geology of the Hudson River Valley, Van Valkenburgh, in collaboration with artists Ann Hamilton and Michael Mercil, crafted over 3,000 tons of bluestone into craggy walls and outcroppings that serve as a backdrop for a delicate and complex planting inspired by upstate New York's woodland ecology. In summer, water runs off the massive, layered stone wall at the heart of the park which, in winter, becomes a rugged wall of ice.

The master plan for Brooklyn Bridge Park, due to begin construction in 2008, is one of the firm's largest and most ambitious projects to date. Over the eighty-acre site facing Manhattan from across the East River, a variety of uses and materials is woven together to combine the visceral memory of the site's industrial and maritime history with an in-vitro verdant landscape to create a third park condition which syncopates the site's history with cultivated lawns and new pieces of "wildscape." Playgrounds, promenades, floating walkways, a marina, and recreation areas such as a ten-acre safe-water zone for kayaking will bring new life to Brooklyn's waterfront and no doubt become a magnet for residents of all of New York's boroughs.

At Wellesley College's Alumnae Valley, Van Valkenburgh restored a parking lot into a five-acre wetland firmly connected to the past, present, and future life of the college. Situated in a low-lying valley that was once part of Frederick Law Olmsted, Jr.'s original vision for the campus, the site combines generous open areas and intimate spaces linked by a network of pedestrian paths.

1 Brooklyn Bridge Park, view of Pier 1 walkway Brooklyn, NY, 2003–08. **PROJECT TEAM** Michael Van Valkenburgh, A. Paul Seck, Matthew Urbanski, Gullivar Shepard, Dorothy Tang, Nate Trevethan, Robert Rock, Justine Heilner, Nikki Johnson, John Zack, Eric Brightman, Nyunny Kim, Michael Smith. **ASSOCIATE LANDSCAPE ARCHITECT** Mathews Nielsen Landscape Architects. **ARCHITECTS** Maryann Thompson Architects, James Carpenter Design Associates. **CLIENTS** The City and State of New York and the Brooklyn Bridge Park Development Corporation. Digital rendering. Courtesy of MVVA, Inc.
2 Brooklyn Bridge Park, view of Bridge Plaza in winter, Brooklyn, NY, 2003–08. Digital rendering. Courtesy of MVVA, Inc.

3 Wellesley College Alumnae Valley, winter view, Wellesley, MA, 2001–05. **DESIGN TEAM** Matthew Urbanski, Michael Van Valkenburgh, and Laura Solano, principals; Emily Mueller De Celis and Andrew Gutterman. **ARCHITECT** Mack Scogin Merrill Elam Architects. **CIVIL ENGINEER** Vanasse Hangen Brustlin. **GEOTECHNICAL ENGINEER** Haley & Aldrich. **SOIL SCIENTISTS** Pine & Swallow Associates. **ELECTRICAL ENGINEER** ARUP. **IRRIGATION** Irrigation Management & Services. **MEADOW CONSULTANT** Prairie Restorations. **BAMBOO CONSULTANT** Susanne Lucas. **GRAPHICS AND SIGNAGE CONSULTANT** H Plus. **PHOTO** Paul Vanderwarker
4 Brooklyn Bridge Park Master Plan, axonometric view, Brooklyn, NY, 2003–08. Digital rendering. Courtesy of MVVA, Inc.

4

SCOTT WILSON
CHICAGO, ILLINOIS

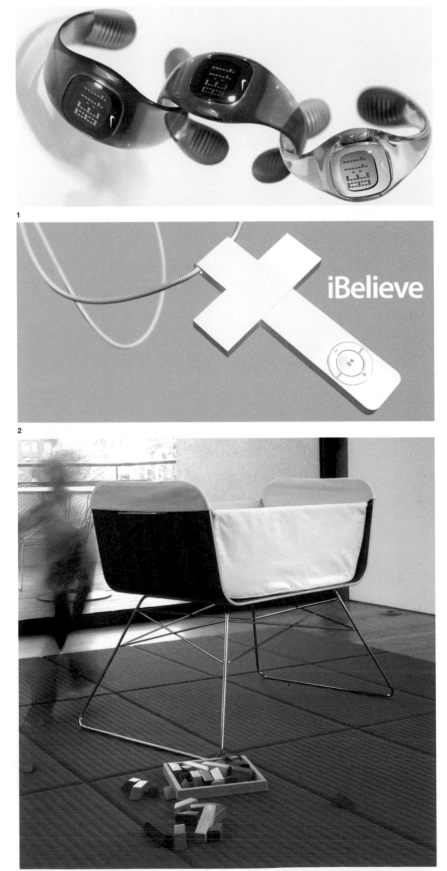

1

2

3

Scott Wilson works simultaneously for several companies and across many different brands and product types. He is former Global Creative Director for Nike Explore, a collaborative group that seeks out new partnerships, businesses, and product opportunities for one of the world's most prominent brands. As Principal of Studio MOD, a collaborative virtual-design network, Wilson serves as the creative hub, forming virtual teams tailored to specific projects. With OOBA, Wilson's newest initiative, launched in January 2006, the designer has created a brand of his own dedicated to creating modern living products and furniture for young families.

Connecting Wilson's endeavors is the intimate relationship he creates between user and product, which results in fresh and approachable designs with a streamlined contemporary sensibility. The Presto Digital Bracelet for Nike is a simple, elegant watch made of custom polymer and inspired by eyewear. Functioning as both timepiece and bracelet, it became an instant classic, selling over four million units in less than three years. Wilson's Lunaire Dinner Tray is a modern interpretation of a TV dinner tray, intended for "the bachelor" who wants to be sophisticated while expending as little effort as possible. With its integrated wells and candleholder for cheap romance, the Lunaire can easily be thrown in the dishwasher so the bachelor can focus on his real needs.

Wilson's characteristic wit is much in evidence in iBelieve. Inspired by the world's obsession with the iPod, iBelieve is a replacement cap and lanyard, or "Divine Accessory," for the iPod Shuffle. When snapped onto a Shuffle, the cruciform shape lets consumers profess their devotion in fashion. Conceived as a tongue-in-cheek commentary on consumer culture, iBelieve took advantage of viral marketing techniques. Posted to a single blog, its Web site received 255,000 hits in one day. Wilson donated sales proceeds to St. Jude's Children's Hospital.

Scott Wilson began wearing a new hat recently as a father of a young child. This led him to develop his own brand, OOBA, with several other young parents. Inspired by the streamlined simplicity of the furniture of the Eameses and other mid-century modernists, Wilson's Nest Nursery pieces for OOBA elevate baby furniture to a much higher aesthetic, bringing the baby and adult worlds closer together.

1 Presto Digital Bracelet, 2003. **DESIGNER** Scott Wilson for Nike, Inc.
MANUFACTURER Nike, China. Nylon, polyurethane. **PHOTO** Mark Cooper
2 iBelieve replacement cap and lanyard for iPod, 2005. **MANUFACTURER** Scott
Wilson, China. ABS, nylon, metal. **RENDERING** Scott Wilson
3 OOBA Nest Bassinette, 2005. **DESIGNER** Scott Wilson for OOBA. **MANUFACTURER**
OOBA. Bent plywood, lacquer, polyurethane, cotton textiles, and stainless steel.
PHOTO François Robert
4 OOBA Nest Rocker and Ottoman, 2005. **DESIGNER** Scott Wilson for OOBA.
MANUFACTURER OOBA. Bent plywood, polyurethane foam, cotton and wool
textiles, and stainless steel. **PHOTO** François Robert
5 Lunaire Dinner Tray, 2004. Corian. **RENDERING** Scott Wilson

4

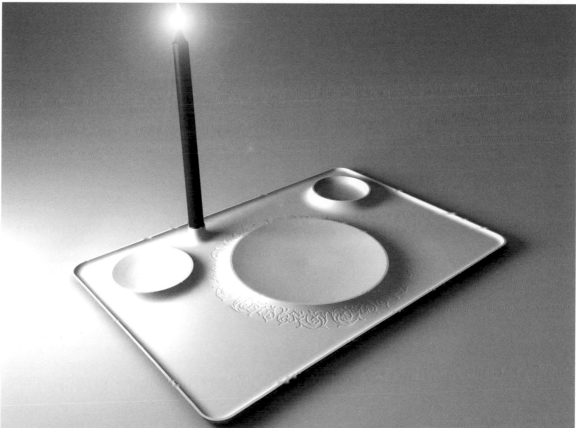

5

DAVID WISEMAN
LOS ANGELES, CALIFORNIA

1

2

3

David Wiseman brings nature indoors. In Los Angeles, a city better known for cars and concrete, Wiseman draws inspiration from its parks and gardens, an essential, yet underrated, part of the landscape. Growing up in Pasadena, California, Wiseman spent a lot of time "staring at nature," and his observations from his youth are a critical element of his work.

As a sophomore at the Rhode Island School of Design, Wiseman began selling some of his early ceramic designs, including deer hat hangers that riffed on the taxidermied trophy animal heads found in many a stuffy establishment. After graduating from RISD in 2003, Wiseman moved back home to Pasadena and bought a kiln, and began developing a series of pieces that reveal his respect for the subtleties of nature. For instance, his Wall Forests are water-based resin castings made from a collection of fallen tree branches. Wiseman attaches the pale, textured branches to a wall in loose, sculptural groupings that at once meld seamlessly with the surface and appear to be pushing through it from behind. Both a memory of something that has lived out its natural cycle and a reminder that nature is never far away, Wiseman's Wall Forests possess a quiet and powerful beauty. He also makes vases in porcelain and bronze, their asymmetrical faceted forms inspired by an imagined world of crystalline mountains.

This year, in Wiseman's most ambitious project to date, spring came early to a home in Los Angeles's Hancock Park neighborhood. In a place where the sun almost always shines and seasons can slip by unnoticed, flowering trees signal the advent of a new season. Cherry blossoms grow from intertwined branches in an exquisite, almost rococo ceiling relief Wiseman created for his client's dining room. Preferring to work alone, he spent the better part of a year casting more than 500 porcelain blossoms and nearly 100 plaster branches in his studio, then climbing up and down a ladder to attach them to the ceiling. The sinuous path of the branches across the ceiling's surface was not predetermined and, as a result, is as organic as it would be in nature.

For the *Triennial*, Wiseman will bring spring to the Carnegie Mansion in December with an explosion of cherry blossoms so lush and dense that, he predicts, "its beauty will hurt your eyes."

1 Facet vase, 2004. Porcelain. **PHOTO** Mark Hanauer
2 Bronze Facet vase, 2005. Bronze. **PHOTO** Mark Hanauer
3 Moss vase, 2004. Porcelain. **PHOTO** Mark Hanauer
4 Cherry Blossom Canopy installation, 2005. Commissioned by Rodman Primack, interior designer, for clients Anne Crawford and Dudley De Zonia. Porcelain, plaster, fiberglass, steel. **PHOTO** David Wiseman
5 Wall Forest installation, 2004. Castings of fallen trees, water-based resin, gypsum. **PHOTO** Mark Hanauer

4

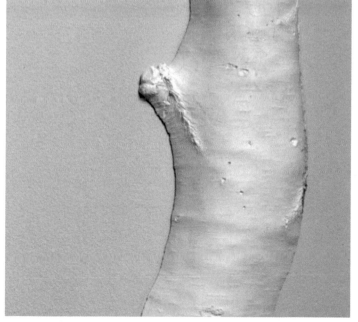

5

TOBIAS WONG
BROOKLYN, NEW YORK

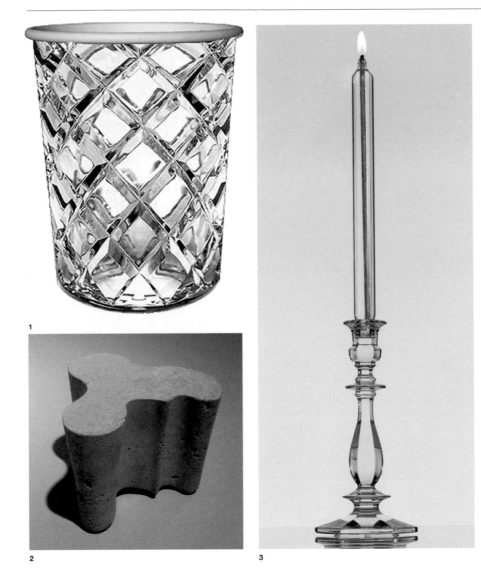

1

2

3

Tobias Wong is a provocateur who creates the unexpected from the everyday and the everyday from the unexpected. Wong's approach to his work situates him somewhere in between the worlds of art and design. He is interested in this somewhat murky threshold, and his work challenges our assumptions that design objects should perform a function while art objects transcend function.

Wong's pieces contain healthy doses of humor, beauty, irony, and craft. He treats design as a medium, rather than a discipline, to show how it can embrace an aesthetic sensibility traditionally relegated to the fine arts. His interest in the conundrum of practicing simultaneously in both the design and art worlds is such that he coined the term "paraconceptual" to describe his method of dismantling the hierarchies between the two. He often appropriates classic design objects and refashions them into something new that, in many cases, is a denial of the object's original function. He calls these pieces "readydesigneds," in a play on Marcel Duchamp's ready-mades. For example, he made a doorstop cast inside the iconic Savoy vase by Alvar Aalto, which had to be smashed to reveal the new object. A duvet cover is crafted in the traditional whole cloth quilting technique, but the fabric is black bulletproof nylon. Casper is a candlestick that has the form of a traditional base and candle, but is in fact a single piece made entirely of crystal, with the "candle" filled with paraffin oil, meaning that it will never have to be replaced. His crystal chandelier for Swarovski is almost hidden by the black shade wrapped around it; the Knoll table designed by Eero Saarinen, which sits below it, is an essential element of Wong's design. The Disposable Crystal Cup, a sixteen-ounce paper cup printed with a trompe l'oeil crystal pattern, shows how Wong can take the most mundane product and infuse it with both humor and beauty, brilliantly confounding our notions of luxury. With his paraconceptual work, Wong has succeeded in reconciling cultural commentary with aesthetics. We can enjoy his objects even without understanding their conceptual underpinnings.

1 Disposable "Crystal" cup, 2005. Paper cup with photographic image. **RENDERING** Tobias Wong
2 Aalto doorstop, 2003. Cast concrete. **PHOTO** Tobias Wong
3 Casper candle, 2003. Crystal, crystalline, fiberglass wick, paraffin. **PHOTO** James Wade
4 Bullet-proof duvet cover, 2004. Hand-quilted of 800 denier bullet-proof nylon. **PHOTO** Tobias Wong

WOWWEE LTD.
NEW YORK, NEW YORK

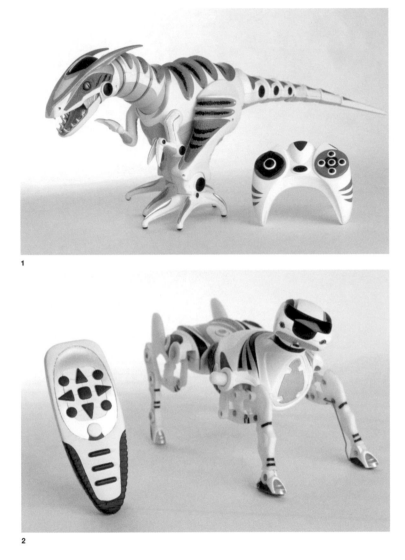

1

2

Wowwee Ltd. is the leading producer of consumer-entertainment robotics. Many of Wowwee's robots are based upon physicist Mark Tilden's pioneering work in applied resonant biomorphic principles and in analog robotics (called BEAM robotics). This differs from computer-driven digital mechanics in its use of simple electronics parts and imitation of the natural physics of nature. Tilden formerly worked at Los Alamos National Labs and has also consulted for NASA.

Tilden grew up building all of his own robot toys, drawing inspiration from comic books, television, and movies. Unlike other highly complex and expensive competitors, his Robosapien robot for Wowwee is designed for simplicity and adaptability. A single screwdriver takes it apart, and all of the parts are color-coded for convenience. These robots support third-party additions and modifications, and Wowwee provides information and support for this on its Web site. Tilden states, "I wanted a toy I would have killed for as a kid. Open him up and the possibilities skyrocket. Easy to hack, tons of extra space, power to spare, modular sealed gearboxes, gold-plated solder pads, etc."

The original Robosapien, designed in 2004, has sixty-seven preprogrammed functions, including the ability to pick up objects, throw, kick, sweep, dance, belch, rap, and imitate martial-arts manuevers. The current Robosapien V2 features more fluid motions and gestures, programmable "reflexes" to touch, pick up, or make sounds, "fluent international caveman" speech, and runs on regular batteries for up to six hours. All of these functions are handled by an ergonomic remote control that includes up to eighty-four program steps, with four program modes for advanced operations. It also has twenty-eight hidden functions that do not appear in the manual but are intended to be "discovered" over time.

Robosapien V2, introduced during Christmas 2005, is a highly evolved fusion of technology and a multi-sensory, interactive humanoid personality. Standing twenty-four inches tall and capable of autonomous behavior, his features include multiple levels of environmental interaction with humans and objects as well as sight, sound, and touch senses. He can lie down and get back up on his own. He responds verbally to environmental stimuli as well as controller commands, and can recognize colors and skin tone through his animated LED eyes.

Robosapien V2 can interact with and control other Robonetics products, including the Roboraptor and the Robopet. The Roborapter and Robopet both have mood-dependent behavior: aggressive/hunting mood, nervous/cautious mood, and friendly/playful mood; and the Robopet is trainable, actually responding to the owner's positive and negative reinforcement.

3

WILL WRIGHT
REDWOOD CITY, CALIFORNIA

When Will Wright introduced *SimCity* in 1989, the game was a surprise hit. This open-ended, non-violent game, which models the evolution of virtual towns, gave the mass market its first real taste of a simulation game—and players were hooked. Wright's company, Maxis, followed up on the success of *SimCity* with a string of popular simulation games throughout the 1990s. No one was prepared, however, for the enormous appeal of *The Sims*, introduced in 2000. *The Sims* allows players to create and control the daily lives of "Sims" (simulated people), whose behavior is dictated by artificial intelligence. The sequel, *The Sims 2*, released in 2004, adds digital DNA to the game, allowing users to track their Sims across a lifetime and over generations, as they pass genetic information onto their offspring.

Instead of putting players inside the scene—behind the wheel of a car, or in the sights of a rifle—*The Sims* games (known as "God games") place them above it, allowing players to observe a life that they have constructed but do not fully control. Much of the fun lies in designing environments—building rooms, adding walls, placing furniture—working in the 3-D isometric view of an architect. Committed players have a strong sense of ownership over their own renditions of the game; a movie-making feature allows users to record the game via a digital "camera" that can change angles and zoom in on the action.

Spore, Wright's latest development project, takes the design of life to a vast new scale, exploring everything from the struggle to survive in the primordial soup to intergalactic conquest. The game allows players to evolve from a primitive microorganism into an intelligent, tool-using creature with the power to explore and colonize the universe. Tasked with designing a creature, a player can choose to add three mouths, a spiked tail, or an extra-long backbone; the software interprets the design on the fly, determining how such a creature would walk, hunt, and interact. Slight changes in the creature's design, such as lengthening or shortening the neck, yield markedly different results.

Further reflecting Wright's revolutionary new approach to game design, all the creatures a player encounters will be designed by other players. Anyone who plays *Spore* can share content by uploading it onto a shared database. Since gamers are actually playing with their content, and not against another person, they are free to design the universe they choose using these common resources.

As Wright explains, "The players in some sense become part of the design team."[1] *Spore* is a game—and a world—built by its users, one creature at a time.

1 Quote from Wired News, interview with Daniel Terdiman, 2005-05-20. http://www.wired.com/news/e3/0,67581-1.html?tw=wn_story_page_next1 (January 22, 2006).

211

J. MEEJIN YOON

MY STUDIO/HÖWELER + YOON ARCHITECTURE
BOSTON, MASSACHUSETTS, AND NEW YORK, NEW YORK

The nature of J. Meejin Yoon's work and of her practice resists easy definition or classification. She simultaneously works as an architect, professor, artist, and occasional book and dress designer. Her professional practice consists of two entities—MY Studio in Boston, where she does solo conceptual work; and Húweler + Yoon Architecture, a multidisciplinary firm in New York she runs in partnership with Eric Húweler—that function independently and in collaboration with each other. The conceptual foundation of her work weaves all these threads together into a new kind of hybrid practice.

A passion for engaging the public and a belief in media as material are what drive Yoon's work. *Media Spill: Cast and Broadcast*, her entry in a 2003 competition for the Nam June Paik Museum in Yong-In, South Korea, proposed a synthesis of the material and the immaterial. By working with the natural topography of the site and preserving the forest, the project used the required program as a catalyst to cast the residual space of the landscape. The resulting building featured a performative roof with a liquid-like surface which converts light into electricity and displays electronic images, as well as drive- and walk-through galleries where new forms of media art can be viewed. In Yoon's vision, the museum itself became a field that is both receptacle and transmitter.

For *White Noise White Light*, an interactive installation created for the 2004 Athens Olympics, MY Studio's luminous grid of flexible fiberoptic stalks inserted in a public plaza at the base of the Acropolis created a field in flux. The field responded to human presence and natural forces, creating a beautiful and evocative new landscape of light and sound choreographed by the cumulative interaction of the public.

Yoon's fascination with the ways human presence can activate public space continues with *Low Rez HI FI*, the studio's most recent public project, in downtown Washington, D.C. LEDs and interactive pin lights are installed on both vertical and horizontal planes to register movement through light and sound and to transmit information, engaging passersby in a dynamic sensory and spatial experience. By pushing the limits of conventional practice, Yoon makes sure that her own connection with the public is always in play.

1 *Media Spill*, Nam June Paik Museum Competition, Seoul, Korea, 2003. **PROJECT TEAM** J. Meejin Yoon, Franco Vairani, Tim Morshead, Rori Dajad. **RENDERING** Franco Vairani. **PHOTO** J. Meejin Yoon

2 *White Noise White Light*, Athens, Greece, 2004. **PROJECT TEAM** J. Meejin Yoon, Eric Höweler, Marlene Kuhn, Kyle Steinfeld, Lisa Smith, Naomi Munro, and Matt Reynolds, electronics engineer. **PHOTO** J. Meejin Yoon

3 *Low Rez HI FI: Sound Grove Light Stream*, Washington, DC, 2005–06. **PROJECT TEAM** J. Meejin Yoon, Eric Höweler. **SOUND GROVE FABRICATOR** Steve Gray, Tiny Gray Matter. **LIGHT STREAM FABRICATOR** Will Pickering, Parallel Development. **SOUND COMPOSER** Erik Carlson, Area C. Aluminum, steel, LEDs, custom electronics. Courtesy of J. Meejin Yoon

1

1

INDEX

Aalto, Alvar, 82, 206
Acconci Studio, 40–41
Acconci, Vito Hannibal. See Acconci Studio
Adler, Deborah, 25, 42–43
Alessi, 132
Alfred A. Knopf, 118
Alison Berger Glassworks, 50–51
Apple Computer, Inc., 34, 44–45, 138
Architecture for Humanity, 46–47
Ayers, Joseph, 11–12, 48–49

Berger, Alison, 37–38. See also Alison Berger Glassworks
Berger, Shoshana. See Readymade magazine
Bernard Tschumi Architects, 38, 194–195
Bezalel Academy of Art and Design, 92
Bird, Brad, 12. See also Pixar
Blatter, Cornelia. See COMA
Blechman, Nicholas, 26, 31, 52–53
blik, LLC, 27, 54–55
Blu Dot, 128
Boeing Company, The, 56–57, 148
Bonsen, Joost. See Howtoons
Bourlier, Emmanuelle. See Panelite
Broom, Murray. See Clear Blue Hawaii
Browne, Thom, 19, 58–59
Buchbinder, Gregory and Jay. See Emeco
Budnitz, Paul. See Kidrobot

Calatrava, Santiago, 37, 60–61
Cao|Perrot Studio, 62–63
Cao, Andy, 11. See also Cao|Perrot Studio
Carpenter, James, 37. See also James Carpenter Design Associates
Catmull, Ed. See Pixar
Chado Ralph Rucci. See Rucci, Ralph
Chamberlain, John, 10
Clarke, Arthur C., 34
Clear Blue Hawaii, 11, 66–67
Cohen, Preston Scott, 68–69
COMA, 24, 70–71
Cook, Lia, 35, 72–73
Cornejo, Maria, 74–75

Davis, Joshua, 13, 29, 76–77
Descottes, Hervé, 38, 78–79
Designfenzider. See Gilad, Ron
Dick, Philip K., 16. See also Hanson Robotics, Inc.
Diffrient, Niels, 36, 80–81
Diller Scofidio + Renfro, 88
DJ Spooky, a.k.a. Paul Miller, 70
Domestic Element. See Smith, Jessica
Dougherty, Dale. See Make magazine
Douglas, Christopher, 37, 82–83
Dragotta, Nick. See Howtoons
Dreyfuss, Henry, 80
Dwell magazine, 122

Eames, Charles and Ray, 82
Electroland, 31, 84–85
Emeco, 86–87

Field Operations, 11, 22, 88–89
Flora, Scott. See blik, LLC
Floyd, Gwendolyn. See Ransmeier & Floyd
Foster, Norman, 86
Fry, Benjamin, 29. See also Processing
Full, Robert, 12
Fuller, R. Buckminster, 10, 122

Gehry, Frank, 50, 78, 86
Geib, Judy, 19. See also Judy Geib plus alpha
Gilad, Ron, 27, 92–93
Gilliland, Nicholas. See Architecture for Humanity
Ginsberg, Marsha, 30–31, 94–95
Glaser, Milton, 42
Gomez-Palacio, Bryony. See Speak Up
Google, 29–30, 96–97
Greg Lynn FORM, 132–33
Griffith, Saul. See Howtoons
Gyokuran, 126

Han Feng, 98–99
Hanson, David, 16. See also Hanson Robotics, Inc.
Hanson Robotics, Inc., 100–101
Haramaty, Lior. See Gilad, Ron
Hatfield, Tobie. See Nike, Inc.
Hawkes, Graham, 12, 102–3
Hawthorne, Grace. See Readymade magazine
Herman Miller, Inc., 31, 104–5
Hermans, Marcel. See COMA
Hoberman Associates, Inc., 106–7
Hoberman, Chuck, 35. See also Hoberman Associates, Inc.
Hoffman, Hunter, 108–9
Holden, Kimberly J. See SHoP
Holl, Steven, 78
Höweler + Yoon Architecture, 26. See Yoon, J. Meejin
Howtoons, 22, 28, 110–11
Humanscale Corporation. See Diffrient, Niels
Hurricane Katrina, 46

ICT Leaders Project, 16, 112–13
IDEO, 154
Institute for Creative Technologies, University of Southern California. See ICT Leaders Project
International Contemporary Furniture Fair, 142
iRobot, 14, 114–15

James Carpenter Design Associates, 64–65
Jeremijenko, Natalie, 28, 116–17
Jobs, Steve. See Pixar
Johnson Outdoors, 106
Jongerius, Hella, 24, 70–71
Judy Geib plus alpha, 90–91

Katsushika, Hokusai, 62
Ken Smith Landscape Architect, 186–187
Kidd, Chip, 36, 50, 118–19
Kidrobot, 120–21
Konyk, 122–23
Konyk, Craig, 21, 27. See also Konyk
Koolhaas, Rem. See Office for Metropolitan Architecture (OMA)
Koons, Jeff, 140

Ladd Brothers, 19, 124–25
Ladd, Steven, 27. See also Ladd brothers
Ladd, William, 27. See also Ladd brothers
Lath, Abhinand, 36, 126–27
Lazor, Charlie, 21, 27, 82. See also Lazor Office
Lazor Office, 21, 128–29
Leader, Tom. See Tom Leader Studio
Le Corbusier (Charles-Edouard Jeanneret), 136
Levin, Golan, 29
LeWitt, Sol, 54
Light Projects, Ltd., 38. See also Schwendinger, Leni
Lynn, Greg, 13, 23. See also Greg Lynn FORM
Lytle, Dana. See Planet Propaganda

Make magazine, 21, 28, 29, 134–35
Metropolis magazine, 142
Maurer, Ingo, 92
McNall, Cameron. See Electroland
Meredith, Michael, 37, 136–37
Meyerhoffer, Thomas, 138–39
Michael Van Valkenburgh Associates, 200–201
Mies van der Rohe, Ludwig, 160, 174
Miller, Jason, 11, 27, 140–41
MIT Media Lab, 29, 166
Mitman, Christian. See Panelite
Moorhead & Moorhead, 37, 142–43
Moorhead, Granger. See Moorhead & Moorhead
Moorhead, Robert. See Moorhead & Moorhead
Mori, Masahiro, 16
Mori, Toshiko, 37. See also Toshiko Mori Architect

Mouille, Serge, 92
Museum of Modern Art, The, 186
MY Studio, 26. See also Yoon, J. Meejin

NASA's Hyper-X Research Program, 146–47
NASA's Jet Propulsion Laboratory, 15, 34, 148–49
Neils, Jerinne. See blik, LLC
New York Times, The, 52
Niemann, Christoph. See Blechman, Nicholas
Nike, Inc., 11, 36, 150–51, 202
Noguchi, Isamu, 82
Northeastern University. See Ayers, Joseph

Observatoire International, L', 38. See Descottes, Hervé
Office for Metropolitan Architecture (OMA), 22, 152–53, 156
Office of Naval Research, 48
OOBA. See Wilson, Scott
O'Reilly, Tim. See Make magazine
Organ Recovery Systems, 154–55

Panelite, 36, 156–57
Pasquarelli, Gregg A. See SHoP
Pentagram, 188
Perrot, Xavier. See Cao|Perrot Studio
Pita, Orlando, 158–59
Pixar, 12, 160–61
Planet Propaganda, 30, 162–63
Ponti, Gio, 86
Predock Frane Architects, 38, 164–65
Processing, 166–67
Prouvé, Jean, 82
PSYOP, 30, 168–169

Ransmeier & Floyd, 27, 170–71
Ransmeier, Leon. See Ransmeier & Floyd
Rashid, Karim, 140
Readymade magazine, 21–22, 27, 28, 29, 172–73
Reas, C. (Casey) E. B., 29. See also Processing
Rodriguez, Narciso, 174–175
Rosburg, Klaus. See Adler, Deborah
Rucci, Ralph, 18–19, 176–177

Schwendinger, Leni, 38, 178–179
Scott, Tom, 18, 180–181
Seeley, Damon. See Electroland
SensiTile, 36. See also Lath, Abhinand
Sharples, Christopher R. See SHoP
Sharples, Coren D. See SHoP
Sharples, William W. See SHoP
SHoP (Sharples Holden Pasquarelli), 26, 31, 35, 182–183
Sinclair, Cameron. See Architecture for Humanity
Smith, Jessica, 184–185
Smith, Ken, 11, 38. See also Ken Smith Landscape Architect
Sonic Design Solutions. See Adler, Deborah
Speak Up, 25, 188–189
Starck, Philippe, 86
Stohr, Kate. See Architecture for Humanity
Studio MOD. See Wilson, Scott
Suzanne Tick, Inc., 190–191

Target Corporation, 25, 42–43, 84–85, 162
Thirst, 26. See also Valicenti, Rick
Tick, Suzanne, 38. See also Suzanne Tick, Inc.
Tilden, Mark, 15. See also Wowwee Ltd.
Toffler, Alvin, 13
Tolila, Gaston. See Architecture for Humanity
Tom Leader Studio, 130–131
Toshiko Mori Architect, 144–145
Trollbäck & Company, 27, 36, 192–193
Trollbäck, Jakob, 27. See Trollbäck & Company
Tsang Seymour Design, 178

Tschumi, Bernard. See Bernard Tschumi Architects

Ujiie, Hitoshi, 11, 35, 196–197
University of Washington. See Hoffman, Hunter

Valicenti, Rick, 10, 26, 198–199
Van Hooydonk, Adrian, 86
Van Valkenburgh, Michael, 22. See also Michael Van Valkenburgh Associates
Vit, Armin, 25. See also SpeakUp

Wade, Kevin. See Planet Propaganda
Wikipedia, 28
Wilson, Scott, 22–23, 202–3
Wiseman, David, 11, 19–20, 27, 204–5
Wong, Tobias, 23, 34, 206–7
Wowwee Ltd., 15, 208–9
Wright, Will, 13, 24, 210–11

X Design Lab. See Jeremijenko, Natalie

Yoon, J. Meejin, 23, 212–213

Zero Maria Cornejo. See Cornejo, Maria

ACKNOWLEDGMENTS

Barbara Bloemink, Brooke Hodge, Ellen Lupton, Matilda McQuaid, and Cooper-Hewitt would like to express their thanks to all of the eighty-seven designers who participated in *Design Life Now*.

The following organizations and individuals, listed in no particular order, provided invaluable help and cooperation during the preparation of this exhibition and book.

At Cooper-Hewitt: Shamus Adams, Debbie Ahn, Tom Andersen, Trevel Balser, Bill Berry, Sherine Brown, Perry C. Choe, Lucy Commoner, Jocelyn Crapo, Julie Desarbo, Melanie Fox, Diane Galt, Lauren Gray, Chris Jeannopoulos, Gregory Krum and The Shop staff, Mei Mah, Laurie Olivieri, Robert Paasch, Andrea Quintero, Wendy Rogers, Anne Shisler-Hughes, Larry Silver, Cynthia Smith, Joni Todd, Stacey Traunfeld, Katie Vagnino. Interns: Carla Cesare, Michelle Everidge, Caroline Krause
Formerly of Cooper-Hewitt: Karl Ljungquist
The Museum of Contemporary Art, Los Angeles: Theeng Kok, Cynthia Pearson
Target: Denise Garcia, Gaye Melton, Glyn Northington, Laysha Ward, Heidi Weaver
Maharam: Genevieve Fry, Annette Schaich, Allen Bianchi of A4
Tsang Seymour Design: Catarina Tsang, Patrick Seymour, Laura Howell, Thomas Ryun, Susan Brzozowski, Michael Brenner
Oceanic Graphic Printing: David Li, Barbara Zee, Meg Lindsay
Kúrner Union: Tarik Haywar
Apple: Jonathan Ive, Misty Stam, Todd Wilder
Thom Browne: Mari Fujiuchi and Miki Higasa of Kaleidoscope Consulting
Santiago Calatrava: Robertina Calatrava, Tracy Levy, Claire Whittaker
Cao | Perrot Studio: Stephen Jerrom
James Carpenter Design Associates: Richard Kress, Stephanie Hui, MW2MW, LED Effects, Depp Glass, Skidmore Owings and Merrill LLP (for Structure)
Field Operations: Sierra Bainbridge
Google: Devin Ivester
Hoberman Associates, Inc.: Johnson Outdoors, Inc.
Herman Miller, Inc.: Barb Herman, Carolyn Maalouf
Konyk: The Vinyl Institute, which has underwritten Konyk's installation in the *Triennial*; Oldcastle Glass, Kalwall Corporation, FrameRite/Marino-Ware Industries, UNICO, Metecno-Benchmark Architectural Systems, SGF Associates Special Lighting
Lazor Office: Empyrean International, InterfaceFLOR, KitchenAid
Toshiko Mori Architect: Jolie Kerns, Cara Rachele
NASA's Jet Propulsion Laboratory: Corinne Karpinsky, Stephanie Lear, Alice Wessen
Nike, Inc.: Ilana Finley, Ed Thomas
Planet Propaganda: Rob Sax
PSYOP: Sandy Selinger
Narciso Rodriguez: Casey Cadwallader
Ralph Rucci: Vivian Van Natta
Ken Smith Landscape Architects: Silverstein Properties, Goldman Sachs, Colbond, Inc., Propex, Inc.
Suzanne Tick, Inc.: Lucesco Lighting
Trollbèck & Company: Derekh Froude
Hitoshi Ujiie: Mimaki Industry, Ciba Specialty Chemical, Rohm and Haas, ErgoSoft, DyStar
Rick Valicenti: Barb Valicenti
Michael Van Valkenburgh Associates, Inc.: Rachel Gleeson
Will Wright: Tiffany Spencer of Electronic Arts
David Wiseman: Jef Bratspis, Mary Hagentorn, Jamie Tisch
Tobias Wong: Tim Cassidy

BIOGRAPHIES

Barbara Bloemink, Ph.D., Curatorial Director of Cooper-Hewitt, National Design Museum, has curated more than eighty museum exhibitions, including *Design ≠ Art: Functional Objects from Donald Judd to Rachel Whiteread*; *Fashion in Colors*; *The Egyptian Movement in American Decorative Arts*; *Re-Righting History: Contemporary African-American Art*; *Constructing Reality*; *Contemporary Photography*; and *Florine Stettheimer: Manhattan Fantastica*. She is the author of six books and more than twenty-five articles and essays for anthologies. She has previously served as Director and Chief Curator of six art museums, including the Guggenheim Las Vegas and Guggenheim Hermitage Museums, the Contemporary Art Center of Virginia, the Hudson River Museum, and the Kemper Museum of Contemporary Art and Design.

Brooke Hodge is Curator of Architecture and Design at The Museum of Contemporary Art, Los Angeles. From 1991 to 2000, she was Director of Exhibitions and Publications at the Harvard University Graduate School of Design, where she also held the positions of Adjunct Curator of Architecture at the Fogg Art Museum and Assistant Dean of Arts Programs at the Graduate School of Design. She has organized exhibitions of the work of architects Frank Gehry, Gio Ponti, Peter Eisenman, Zaha Hadid, and Norman Foster; theater designer and artist Robert Wilson; and fashion designer Rei Kawakubo/Comme des Garêons, among others. She has just completed work on a major exhibition, *Skin + Bones: Parallel Practices in Fashion and Architecture*, which opened at The Museum of Contemporary Art, Los Angeles, in November 2006.

Ellen Lupton has been Curator of Contemporary Design at Cooper-Hewitt, National Design Museum since 1992, where she has helped organize numerous exhibitions, including all three installations of the *National Design Triennial* series; *Feeding Desire: Design and the Tools of the Table, 1500–2005*; *Solos: New Design from Israel*; *Skin: Surface, Substance + Design*; *Graphic Design in the Mechanical Age*; *Mixing Messages: Graphic Design in Contemporary Culture*; and *Mechanical Brides: Women and Machines from Home to Office*. She has authored numerous books, including *D.I.Y.: Design It Yourself*, *Thinking with Type*, and *Design Writing Research*, coauthored with Abbott Miller. She is director of the MFA program in graphic design at Maryland Institute College of Art in Baltimore. She writes for *Print*, *AIGA Voice*, *Eye*, and other design publications.

Matilda McQuaid is Deputy Curatorial Director at Cooper-Hewitt, National Design Museum, where she also oversees a textile collection that includes more than 30,000 textiles produced over twenty-three centuries. She came to Cooper-Hewitt after a fifteen-year tenure at The Museum of Modern Art in New York. She has curated more than thirty exhibitions, including *Extreme Textiles: Designing for High Performance*; *Josef and Anni Albers: Designs for Living*; *Shigeru Ban: A Paper Arch*; *Structure and Surface: Contemporary Japanese Textiles*; and *Lilly Reich: Designer and Architect*. McQuaid is also an author and editor of art, architecture, and design, with many books and articles to her credit, including *Shigeru Ban: Structure of Materials*, *Envisioning Architecture: Drawings from the Museum of Modern Art*, *Structure and Surface: Contemporary Japanese Textiles*, and *Architecture: A Place for Women*.

The following Designer Profiles were written by:
Susan Brown: Lia Cook, Hitoshi Ujiie
Wava Carpenter: Deborah Adler for Target ClearRx, Jason Miller
Elizabeth Chase: Joseph Ayers, iRobot, Thomas Meyerhoffer, Wowwee Ltd.